◆ HOUGHTON MIFFLIN ◆

Mathematics

Coordinating Author
Ernest R. Duncan

Authors

| Lelon R. Capps | W.G. Quast | Mary Ann Haubner |
| William L. Cole | Leland Webb | Charles E. Allen |

Contributing Author
Harry J. Bohan

◆

Houghton Mifflin Company BOSTON

Atlanta   Dallas   Geneva, Illinois   Palo Alto   Princeton   Toronto

CONTENTS

7 MONEY 167

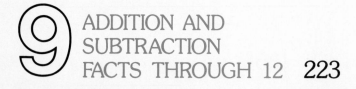

8 TIME 195

9 ADDITION AND SUBTRACTION FACTS THROUGH 12 223

10 MEASUREMENT 249

11 ADDITION AND SUBTRACTION TWO DIGIT NUMBERS 279

12 GEOMETRY AND FRACTIONS 309

13 ADDITION AND SUBTRACTION FACTS THROUGH 18 337

PROBLEM SOLVING

Ring the 🚗 nearest the 🛑.

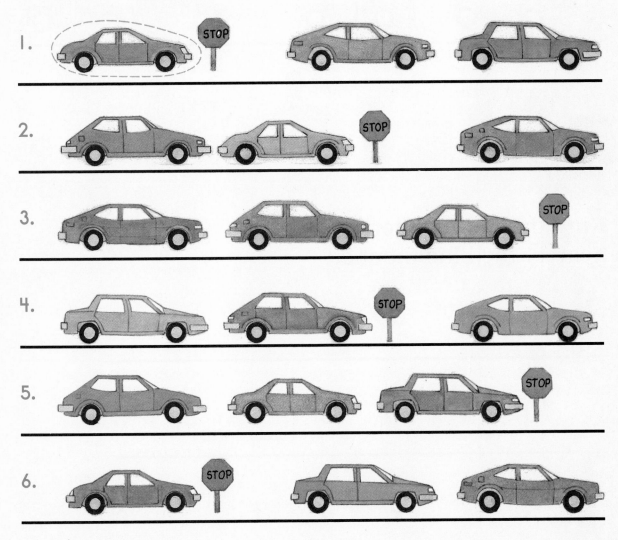

1.

2.

3.

4.

5.

6.

Ring the  nearest the .

7.

8.

9.

☆ Ring the red number
nearest the blue number.

10.   0   1   2   ③   4   5   6

11.   0   1   2   3   4   5   6

12.   0   1   2   3   4   5   6

Problem Solving

ZERO

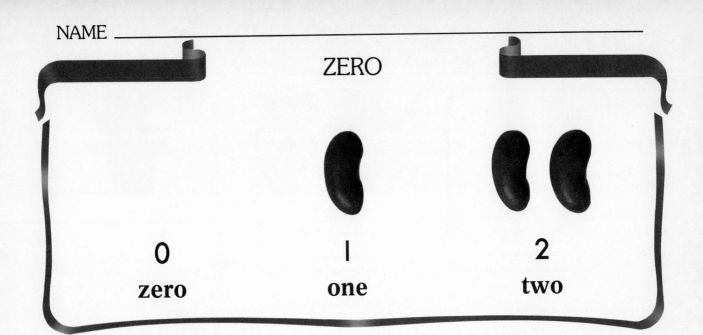

0	1	2
zero	**one**	**two**

Ring the number.

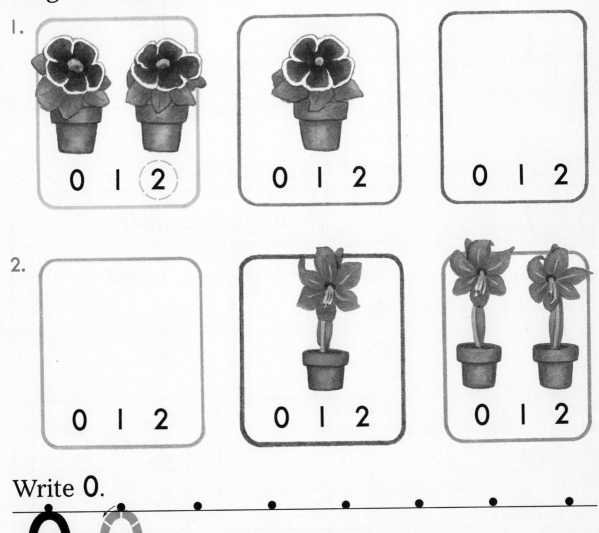

1.

0 1 (2)

0 1 2

0 1 2

2.

0 1 2

0 1 2

0 1 2

Write 0.

0

Write the number.

3.

4.

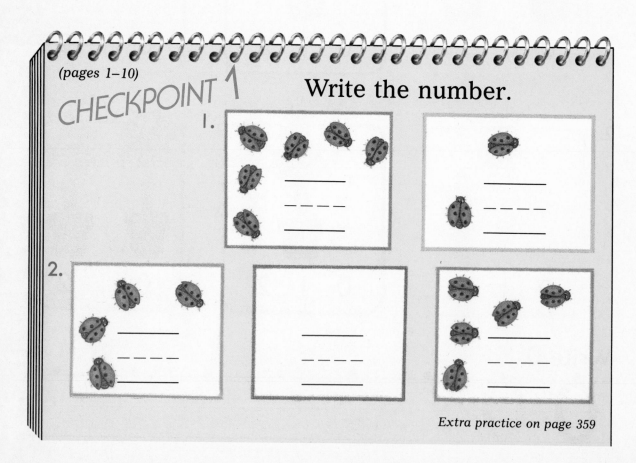

Extra practice on page 359

Writing 0

SEVEN AND EIGHT

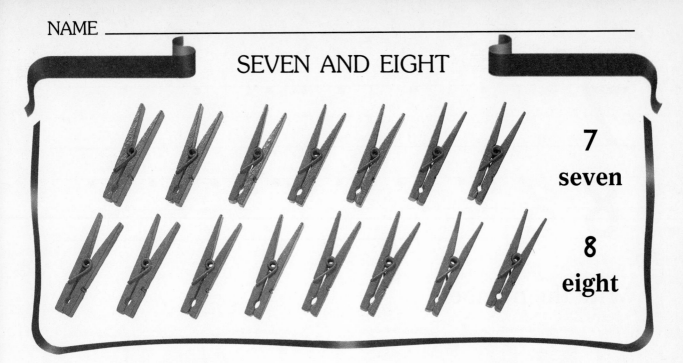

7
seven

8
eight

Ring the number.

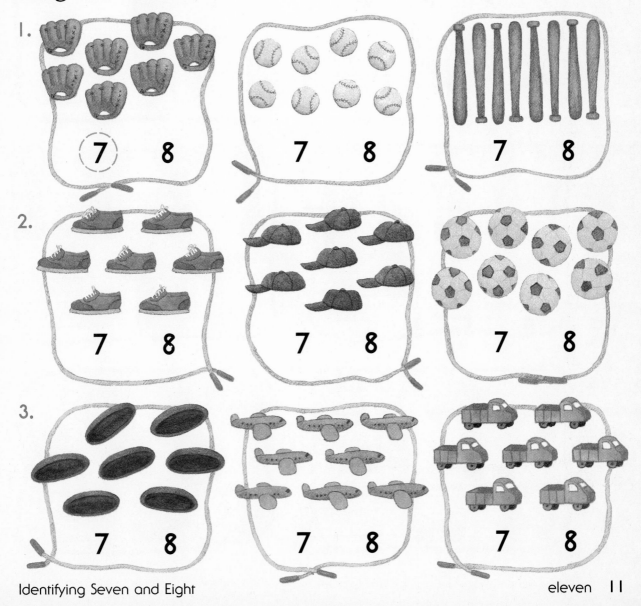

1.

7   8

7   8

7   8

2.

7   8

7   8

7   8

3.

7   8

7   8

7   8

Identifying Seven and Eight

Write **7** and **8**.

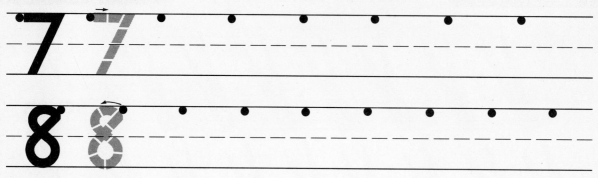

Write the number.

4.

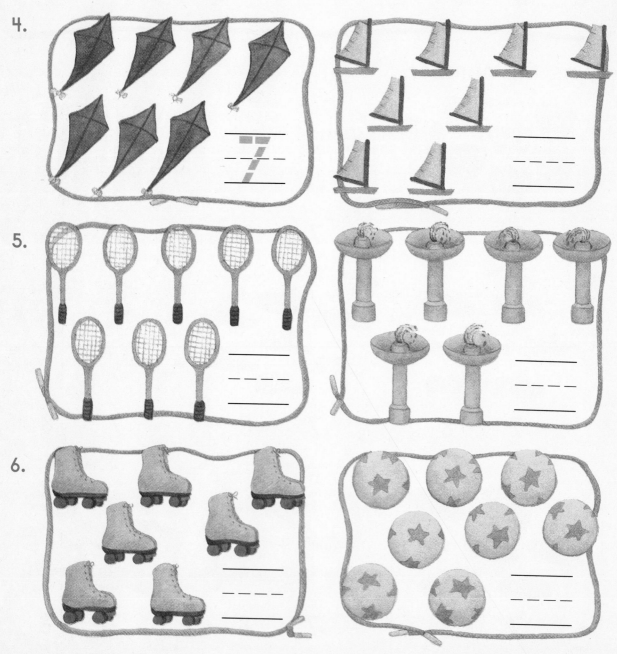

5.

6.

NINE AND TEN

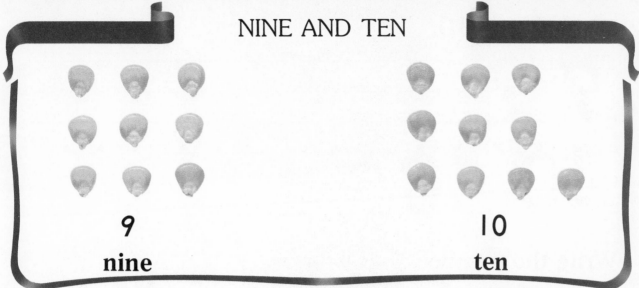

9

nine

10

ten

Ring the number.

1.

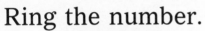

(9) 10   9 10   9 10

2.

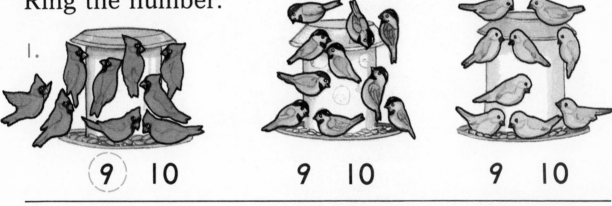

9 10   9 10   9 10

3.

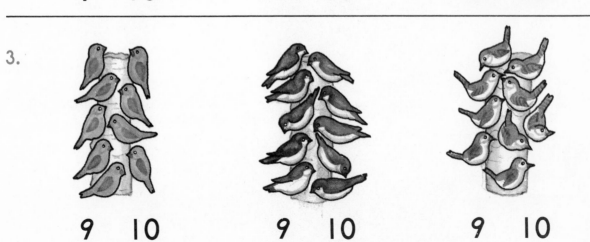

9 10   9 10   9 10

Write 9 and 10.

9 9 • • • • • •

10 10 • • • • • •

Write the number.

4.

5.

6.

TRY THIS: Use counters to show amounts.

PENNIES

1¢
penny

Write how much.

1.   __2__ ¢

2.   _____ ¢

3.   _____ ¢

4.   _____ ¢

How many pennies?

5. **4**¢ _____ pennies

6. **9**¢ _____ pennies

Ring enough pennies.

7.

8.

9.

10.

11. Use play money. Show how many pennies.

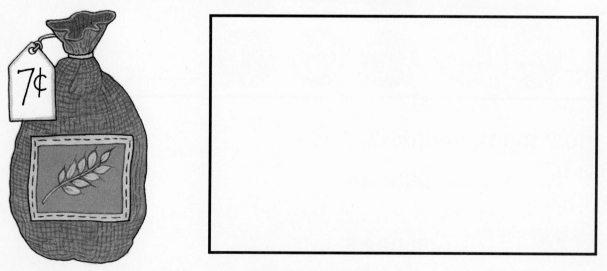

PARTNERS: Tell a story.

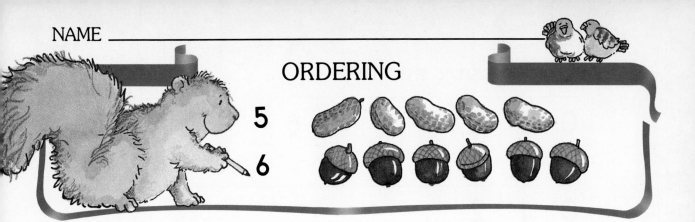

ORDERING

5

6

Write the number.

1. __0__

2. _____

3. _____

4. _____

5. _____

6. _____

7. _____

8. _____

9. _____

10. _____

11. _____

Write the missing numbers.

12.

0	1	2	3			6			9	

13.

0	1	2							10

14.

0	1	2					8		

15. Write the numbers in order.

16. Join the dots in order.

Writing Numbers in Order, 0–10

Enrichment

If **all** are , color them red.

If **some** are ⬤, color the ◯ blue.

1.

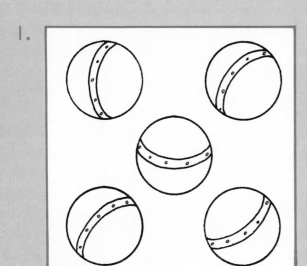

2.

3.

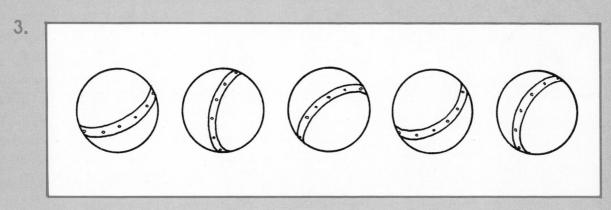

4.

5.

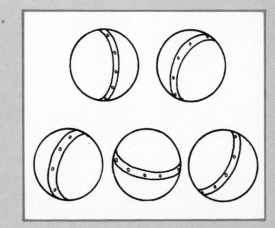

If **some** are dogs, color the dogs brown.
If **none** are dogs, do not color any.

6.

7.

8.

9.

10.

Enrichment: Logical Thinking

2

Read with the children:

Some people are
walking in the rain.
How many are children?
How many are adults?
How many are there in
all?

ADDITION
FACTS THROUGH 7

BEGINNING ADDITION

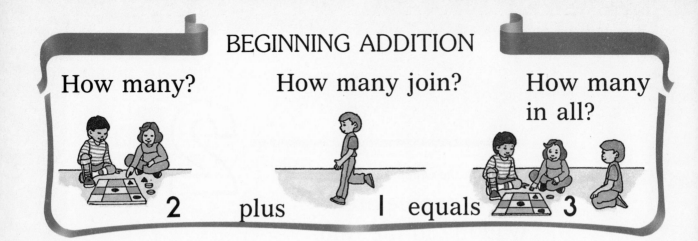

How many?   **How many join?**   **How many in all?**

2   plus   1   equals   3

How many?
Write the number.

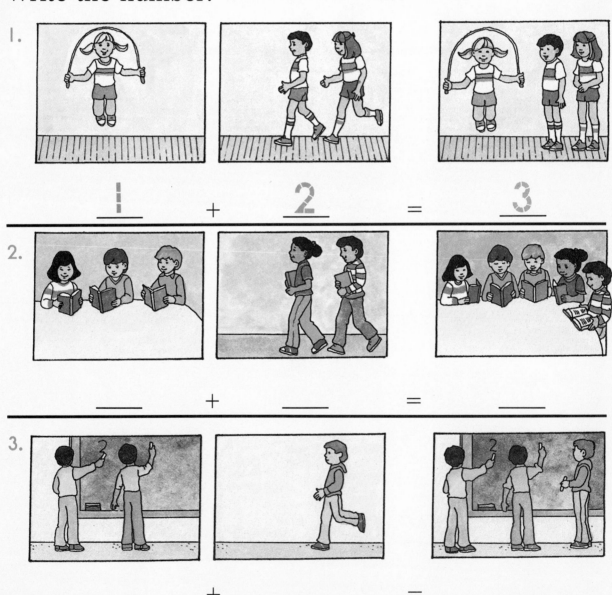

1.   1   +   2   =   3

2.   ___   +   ___   =   ___

3.   ___   +   ___   =   ___

ADDING 1 OR 2

$$3 + 2 = \underline{5}$$

$$2 + 2 = \underline{4}$$

How many?

1.

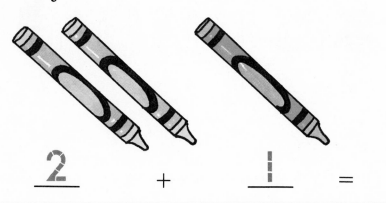

$$\underline{2} \quad + \quad \underline{1} \quad = \quad \underline{}$$

2.

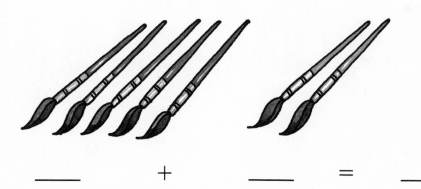

$$\underline{} \quad + \quad \underline{} \quad = \quad \underline{}$$

3.

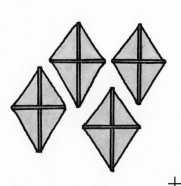

$$\underline{} \quad + \quad \underline{} \quad = \quad \underline{}$$

Add.

4.

$1 + 2 = \underline{}$

5.

$5 + 2 = \underline{}$

6.

$4 + 2 = \underline{}$

7.

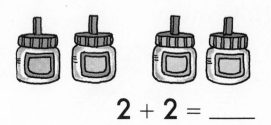

$2 + 2 = \underline{}$

Tell the story. Then add.

8.

$3 + 2 = \underline{}$

9.

$4 + 1 = \underline{}$

10.

$6 + 1 = \underline{}$

11.

$3 + 1 = \underline{}$

Adding 1 or 2

ADDING 1, 2, OR 3

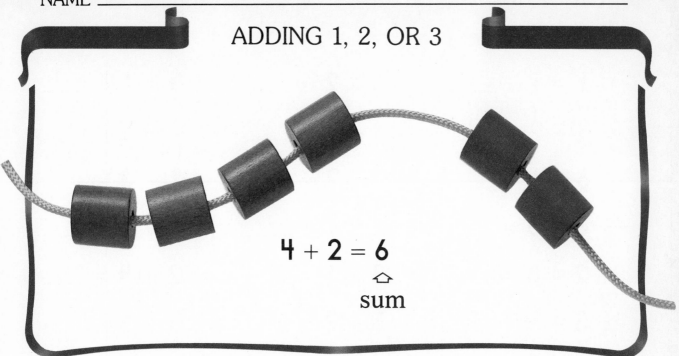

$$4 + 2 = 6$$

⇧
sum

Write the numbers. Ring the sum.

1.
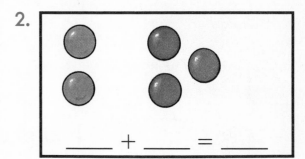

3 + 1 = 4

2.

___ + ___ = ___

3.

___ + ___ = ___

4.
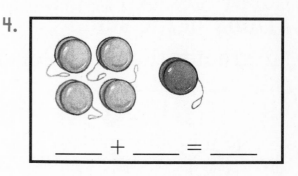

___ + ___ = ___

5.
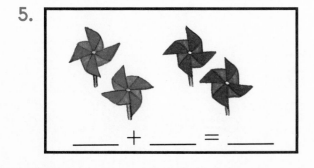

___ + ___ = ___

6.
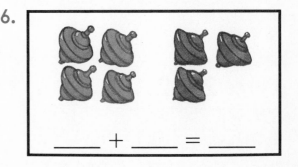

___ + ___ = ___

Write the sum.

7. $1 + 1 =$ _____ $3 + 2 =$ _____ $4 + 1 =$ _____

8. $4 + 2 =$ _____ $3 + 3 =$ _____ $1 + 2 =$ _____

9. $6 + 1 =$ _____ $2 + 2 =$ _____ $1 + 3 =$ _____

10. $3 + 3 =$ _____ $2 + 1 =$ _____ $5 + 1 =$ _____

11. $2 + 3 =$ _____ $3 + 1 =$ _____ $2 + 4 =$ _____

12. $3 + 4 =$ _____ $5 + 2 =$ _____ $4 + 3 =$ _____

$5 + 1$ is **greater than 5**.

Think of the sum.
If greater than **5**, color blue.

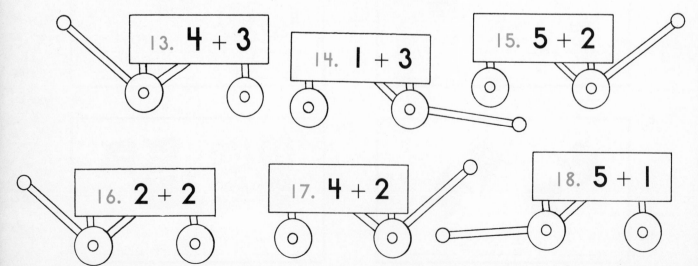

13. $4 + 3$

14. $1 + 3$

15. $5 + 2$

16. $2 + 2$

17. $4 + 2$

18. $5 + 1$

ADDING WITH ZERO

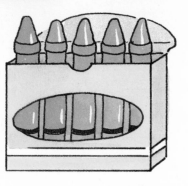 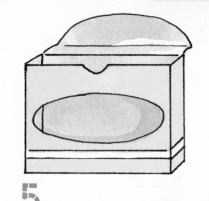

$$5 + 0 = \underline{5}$$

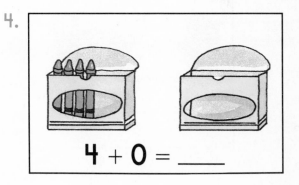

Add.

1.

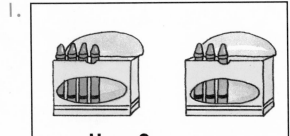

$$4 + 3 = \underline{}$$

2.

$$4 + 2 = \underline{}$$

3.

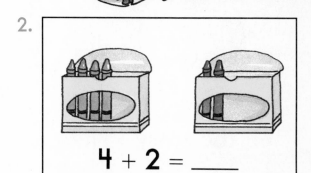

$$4 + 1 = \underline{}$$

4.

$$4 + 0 = \underline{}$$

5.

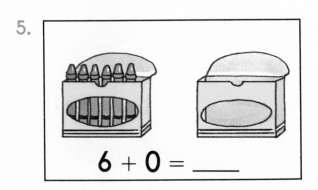

$$6 + 0 = \underline{}$$

6.

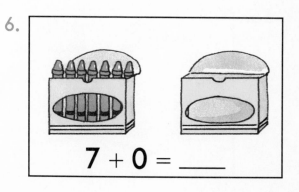

$$7 + 0 = \underline{}$$

Add.

7. $3 + 1 =$ _____ $2 + 0 =$ _____ $4 + 1 =$ _____

8. $5 + 0 =$ _____ $6 + 0 =$ _____ $3 + 0 =$ _____

9. $1 + 3 =$ _____ $2 + 2 =$ _____ $6 + 1 =$ _____

10. $5 + 1 =$ _____ $3 + 2 =$ _____ $1 + 0 =$ _____

11. $3 + 4 =$ _____ $4 + 0 =$ _____ $7 + 0 =$ _____

12. $2 + 3 =$ _____ $5 + 2 =$ _____ $4 + 0 =$ _____

13. $2 + 0 =$ _____ $4 + 2 =$ _____ $3 + 3 =$ _____

14. $6 + 0 =$ _____ $3 + 2 =$ _____ $4 + 3 =$ _____

Tell the story. Then add.

15.

$3 + 2 =$ _____

16.

$2 + 2 =$ _____

PARTNERS: Make up problems and solve together.

ADDING IN ANY ORDER

If you know	Then you know

3 + 2 = _5_   **2 + 3 =** _5_

Write the numbers. Then add.

1.

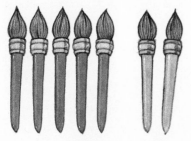 

_5_ + _2_ = _7_   _2_ + _5_ = _7_

2.

___ + ___ = ___   ___ + ___ = ___

3.

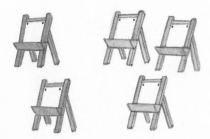 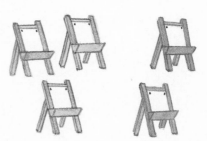

___ + ___ = ___   ___ + ___ = ___

Add.

4. 1 + 4 = ___   5. 4 + 3 = ___   6. 4 + 0 = ___

4 + 1 = ___   3 + 4 = ___   0 + 4 = ___

7. 6 + 1 = ___   8. 4 + 2 = ___   9. 2 + 3 = ___

1 + 6 = ___   2 + 4 = ___   3 + 2 = ___

10. 5 + 2 = ___   11. 6 + 0 = ___   12. 2 + 1 = ___

2 + 5 = ___   0 + 6 = ___   1 + 2 = ___

2 + 1 is **less than 5**.

Think of the sum.
If less than **5**, color  blue .

13. 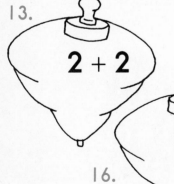 2 + 2

14. 3 + 4

15.  3 + 1

16. 5 + 2

17. 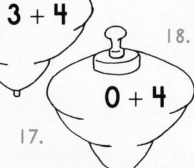 0 + 4

18. 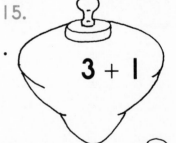 1 + 2

Order Property

NAME _____

ADDING ANOTHER WAY

$$\begin{array}{r} 5 \\ +2 \\ \hline 7 \end{array}$$

$5 + 2 =$ __7__

Add.

1.
$$\begin{array}{r} 3 \\ +1 \\ \hline \end{array}$$

2.
$$\begin{array}{r} 3 \\ +2 \\ \hline \end{array}$$

3.
$$\begin{array}{r} 2 \\ +1 \\ \hline \end{array}$$

4.
$$\begin{array}{r} 1 \\ +4 \\ \hline \end{array}$$

5.
$$\begin{array}{r} 2 \\ +2 \\ \hline \end{array}$$

6.
$$\begin{array}{r} 4 \\ +2 \\ \hline \end{array}$$

7.
$$\begin{array}{r} 4 \\ +2 \\ \hline \end{array}$$

8.
$$\begin{array}{r} 5 \\ +0 \\ \hline \end{array}$$

9.
$$\begin{array}{r} 2 \\ +3 \\ \hline \end{array}$$

Addition, Vertical Form

forty-one **41**

Add.

10.
$$\begin{array}{r} 2 \\ +0 \\ \hline \end{array}$$
$$\begin{array}{r} 1 \\ +4 \\ \hline \end{array}$$
$$\begin{array}{r} 0 \\ +3 \\ \hline \end{array}$$
$$\begin{array}{r} 4 \\ +2 \\ \hline \end{array}$$
$$\begin{array}{r} 1 \\ +5 \\ \hline \end{array}$$
$$\begin{array}{r} 4 \\ +3 \\ \hline \end{array}$$

11.
$$\begin{array}{r} 2 \\ +2 \\ \hline \end{array}$$
$$\begin{array}{r} 5 \\ +0 \\ \hline \end{array}$$
$$\begin{array}{r} 2 \\ +4 \\ \hline \end{array}$$
$$\begin{array}{r} 1 \\ +1 \\ \hline \end{array}$$
$$\begin{array}{r} 4 \\ +1 \\ \hline \end{array}$$
$$\begin{array}{r} 3 \\ +3 \\ \hline \end{array}$$

12.
$$\begin{array}{r} 1 \\ +1 \\ \hline \end{array}$$
$$\begin{array}{r} 4 \\ +1 \\ \hline \end{array}$$
$$\begin{array}{r} 3 \\ +3 \\ \hline \end{array}$$
$$\begin{array}{r} 6 \\ +0 \\ \hline \end{array}$$
$$\begin{array}{r} 5 \\ +1 \\ \hline \end{array}$$
$$\begin{array}{r} 2 \\ +5 \\ \hline \end{array}$$

13.
$$\begin{array}{r} 1 \\ +2 \\ \hline \end{array}$$
$$\begin{array}{r} 0 \\ +3 \\ \hline \end{array}$$
$$\begin{array}{r} 4 \\ +0 \\ \hline \end{array}$$
$$\begin{array}{r} 3 \\ +1 \\ \hline \end{array}$$
$$\begin{array}{r} 3 \\ +2 \\ \hline \end{array}$$
$$\begin{array}{r} 5 \\ +1 \\ \hline \end{array}$$

Tell the story. Then add.

14.
$$\begin{array}{r} 2 \\ +2 \\ \hline \end{array}$$

15.
$$\begin{array}{r} 4 \\ +1 \\ \hline \end{array}$$

DISCUSS: The different ways to make 5.

ADDING THROUGH 7

2 yellow 5 green

3 brown 6 red

4 orange 7 blue

1. Add. Then color.

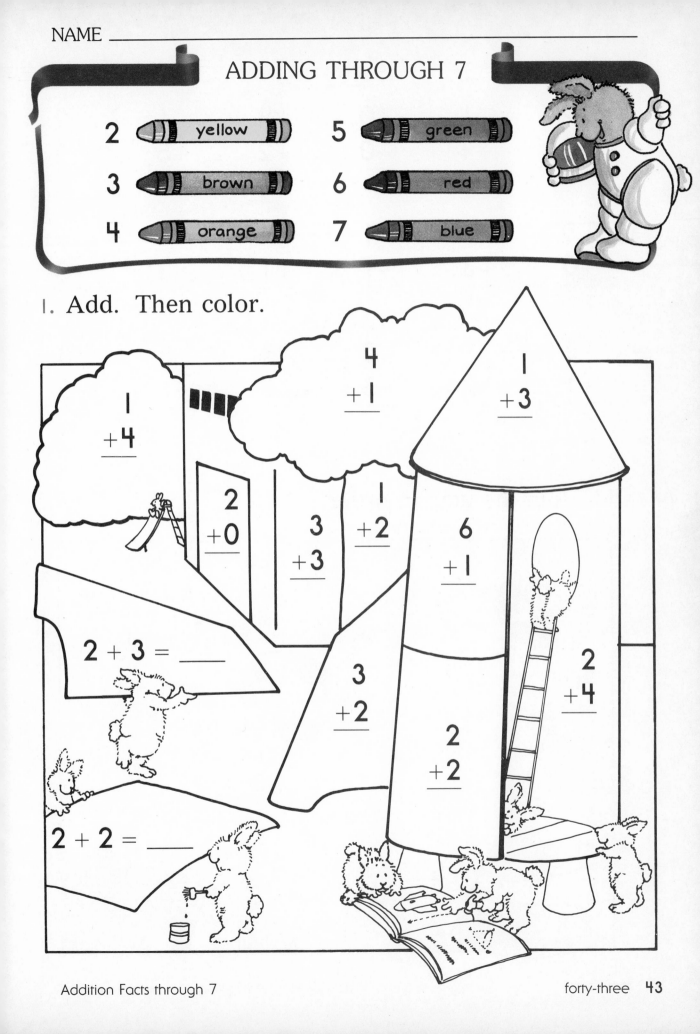

$1 + 4$

$4 + 1$

$1 + 3$

$2 + 0$

$3 + 3$

$1 + 2$

$6 + 1$

$2 + 3 =$ ___

$3 + 2$

$2 + 4$

$2 + 2$

$2 + 2 =$ ___

Add.

2.
$$2 \atop +0$$
$$1 \atop +4$$
$$0 \atop +0$$
$$4 \atop +2$$
$$1 \atop +5$$
$$2 \atop +2$$

3.
$$5 \atop +0$$
$$2 \atop +3$$
$$1 \atop +1$$
$$4 \atop +1$$
$$3 \atop +3$$
$$6 \atop +0$$

4.
$$5 \atop +1$$
$$1 \atop +2$$
$$0 \atop +3$$
$$4 \atop +0$$
$$3 \atop +1$$
$$3 \atop +2$$

☆ Add. Join the dots in order.

5.

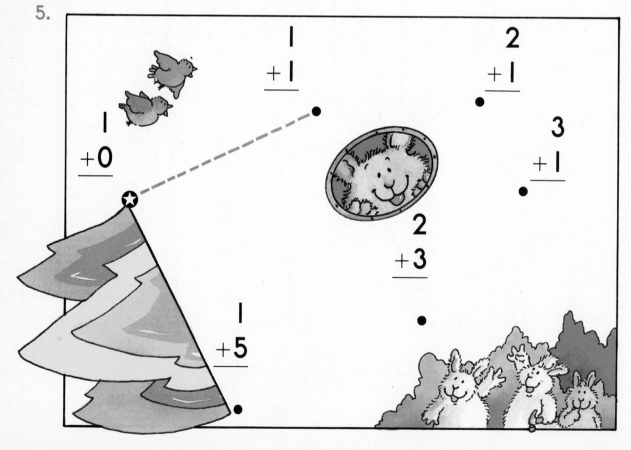

TRY THIS: Problem Solving Activities, page 394.

NAME ______________________________

PROBLEM SOLVING

Complete the number sentence.

1. 3  + 2  = 5 in all

2. ___  + ___  = ___ in all

3. ___ 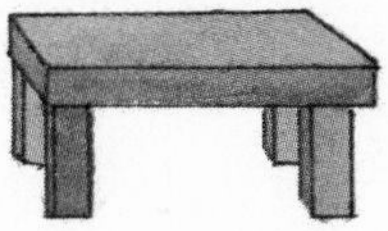 + ___ 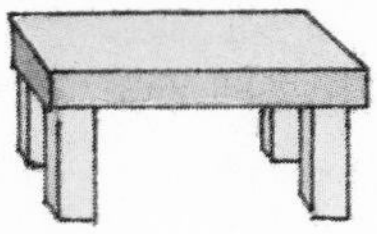 = ___ in all

4. ___  + ___  = ___ in all

Complete the number sentence.

5. ___  + ___ 🍎 = ___ in all

6. ___ 🍇 + ___ 🍇 = ___ in all

7. ___  + ___ = ___ in all

(pages 35–46)

CHECKPOINT 2   Add.

1. **5 + 0 =** ☐   **0 + 6 =** ☐   **3 + 4 =** ☐

Complete the number sentence.

2.

☐ 🐹 + ☐ 🐹 = ☐ in all

Extra practice on page 361

Problem Solving

CHAPTER 2 TEST

Add.

1.
$$5 \atop +1$$ $$3 \atop +3$$ $$4 \atop +2$$ $$2 \atop +3$$ $$6 \atop +1$$ $$3 \atop +1$$

2. $3 + 4 =$ ___ $1 + 2 =$ ___ $5 + 2 =$ ___

Color the number of each object you see.

3.

4.

Add.

5.
$$4 \atop +0$$ $$7 \atop +0$$ $$0 \atop +3$$ $$5 \atop +0$$ $$1 \atop +0$$ $$0 \atop +6$$

Complete the number sentence.

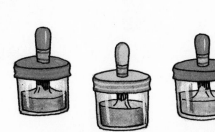    

6. ___  + ___ = ___ in all

Extra practice on page 362

MATHEMATICS and READING

Two went to the circus.

They saw three .

Each held two .

There were five .

Each had a .

Two were dancing.

Write the number.

1. How many in all? ____

2. How many in all? ____

3. How many and in all? ____

Enrichment

1. Color sums **less** than 5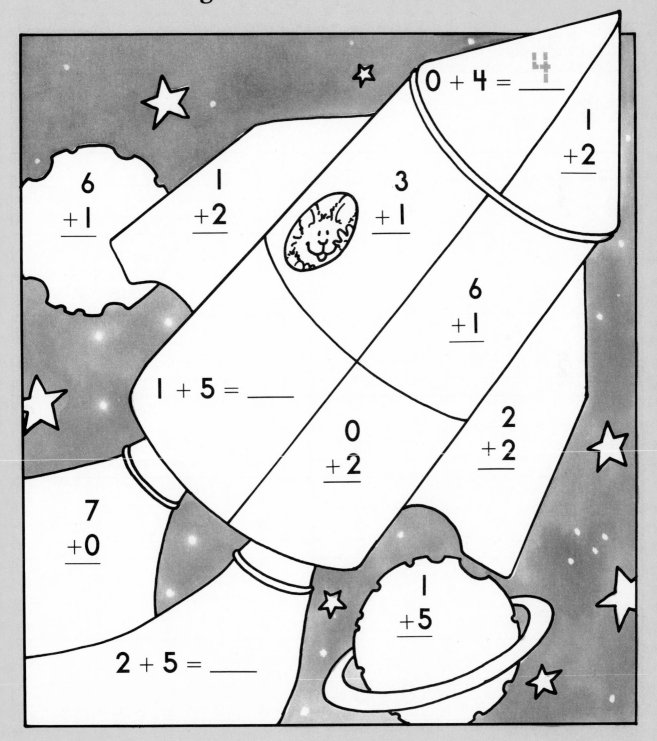

Color sums **greater** than 5

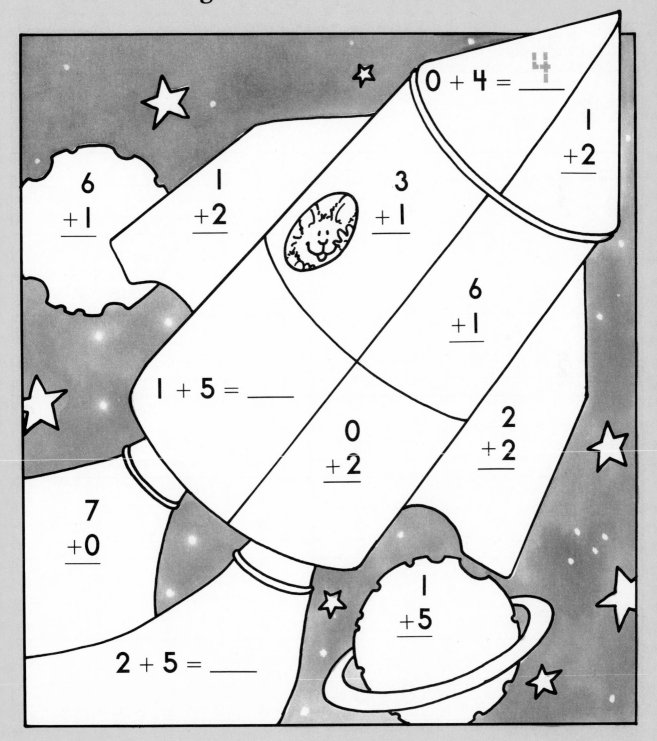

$0 + 4 =$ ___ 4

$\begin{array}{r} 1 \\ +2 \\ \hline \end{array}$

$\begin{array}{r} 6 \\ +1 \\ \hline \end{array}$

$\begin{array}{r} 1 \\ +2 \\ \hline \end{array}$

$\begin{array}{r} 3 \\ +1 \\ \hline \end{array}$

$\begin{array}{r} 6 \\ +1 \\ \hline \end{array}$

$1 + 5 =$ ___

$\begin{array}{r} 0 \\ +2 \\ \hline \end{array}$

$\begin{array}{r} 2 \\ +2 \\ \hline \end{array}$

$\begin{array}{r} 7 \\ +0 \\ \hline \end{array}$

$\begin{array}{r} 1 \\ +5 \\ \hline \end{array}$

$2 + 5 =$ ___

Add.		Which number is between the sums?
2. $2 + 3 = \underline{5}$	$4 + 3 = \underline{7}$	$\underline{6}$
3. $2 + 1 = \underline{}$	$0 + 1 = \underline{}$	$\underline{}$
4. $2 + 2 = \underline{}$	$4 + 2 = \underline{}$	$\underline{}$
5. $1 + 4 = \underline{}$	$3 + 0 = \underline{}$	$\underline{}$
6. $7 + 0 = \underline{}$	$3 + 2 = \underline{}$	$\underline{}$
7. $4 + 2 = \underline{}$	$1 + 3 = \underline{}$	$\underline{}$
8. $1 + 2 = \underline{}$	$0 + 5 = \underline{}$	$\underline{}$

Enrichment: Logical Thinking

CUMULATIVE REVIEW

Fill in the ⬭ for the correct answer.

How much?

1.

8¢ 9¢ 10¢

Ⓐ Ⓑ Ⓒ

2.

6¢ 4¢ 5¢

Ⓐ Ⓑ Ⓒ

What number is missing?

3.   1 3   4   5

      1   2   6

    Ⓐ   Ⓑ   Ⓒ

4.   7 _?_ 9   10

      6   5   8

    Ⓐ   Ⓑ   Ⓒ

Add.

5.   3
     +2
     ‾‾‾

  6   4   5

  Ⓐ   Ⓑ   Ⓒ

6.   4 + 2

  5   6   3

  Ⓐ   Ⓑ   Ⓒ

7.   3 + 3

  4   7   6

  Ⓐ   Ⓑ   Ⓒ

Add.

8. $7 + 0$	9. $3 + 0$	10. $4 + 0$
0 7 6	3 0 4	1 4 5
Ⓐ Ⓑ Ⓒ	Ⓐ Ⓑ Ⓒ	Ⓐ Ⓑ Ⓒ

How many 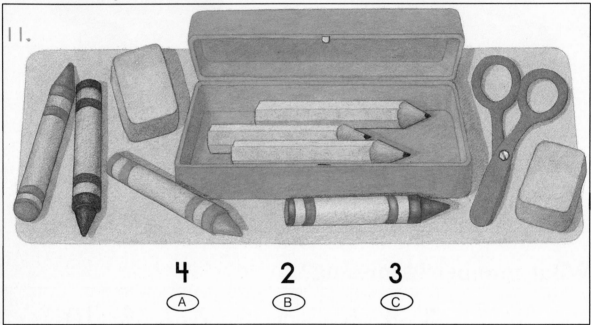 ?

11.

4	2	3
Ⓐ	Ⓑ	Ⓒ

LANGUAGE and VOCABULARY REVIEW

Match the number to the word.

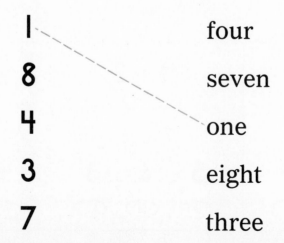

1	four
8	seven
4	one
3	eight
7	three

3

Read with the children:

How many puffins are
on top of the rock?
How many are below?
How many puffins in all?

ADDITION
FACTS THROUGH 10

REVIEWING ADDITION

$5 + 2 = \underline{7}$

Add.

1. $2 + 3 = \underline{}$ $2 + 4 = \underline{}$ $2 + 5 = \underline{}$

2. $1 + 6 = \underline{}$ $1 + 5 = \underline{}$ $1 + 4 = \underline{}$

3. $3 + 3 = \underline{}$ $5 + 2 = \underline{}$ $4 + 3 = \underline{}$

4.
$$\begin{array}{r} 3 \\ +3 \\ \hline \end{array} \qquad \begin{array}{r} 0 \\ +7 \\ \hline \end{array} \qquad \begin{array}{r} 2 \\ +3 \\ \hline \end{array}$$

5.
$$\begin{array}{r} 6 \\ +1 \\ \hline \end{array} \qquad \begin{array}{r} 7 \\ +0 \\ \hline \end{array} \qquad \begin{array}{r} 2 \\ +4 \\ \hline \end{array}$$

6.
$$\begin{array}{r} 2 \\ +1 \\ \hline \end{array} \qquad \begin{array}{r} 1 \\ +4 \\ \hline \end{array} \qquad \begin{array}{r} 0 \\ +6 \\ \hline \end{array}$$

7.
$$\begin{array}{r} 3 \\ +4 \\ \hline \end{array} \qquad \begin{array}{r} 1 \\ +3 \\ \hline \end{array} \qquad \begin{array}{r} 5 \\ +2 \\ \hline \end{array}$$

$$\begin{array}{r} 4 \\ +2 \\ \hline 6 \end{array}$$

ADDING THROUGH 8

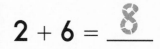

$2 + 6 =$ ___

Add.

1.

$5 + 3 =$ ___

2.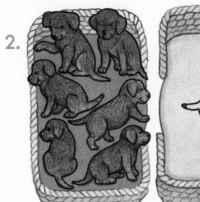

$6 + 1 =$ ___

3.

$1 + 7 =$ ___

4.

$4 + 4 =$ ___

5. $2 + 4 =$ ___ $2 + 5 =$ ___ $2 + 6 =$ ___

6. $3 + 2 =$ ___ $3 + 3 =$ ___ $3 + 4 =$ ___

7. $1 + 7 =$ ___ $1 + 6 =$ ___ $1 + 5 =$ ___

Add.

8. $6 + 0 =$ _____ $7 + 0 =$ _____ $8 + 0 =$ _____

9. $2 + 4 =$ _____ $3 + 4 =$ _____ $4 + 4 =$ _____

10. $3 + 5 =$ _____ $1 + 6 =$ _____ $0 + 8 =$ _____

11. $2 + 6 =$ _____ $1 + 7 =$ _____ $2 + 5 =$ _____

12. $5 + 3 =$ _____ $7 + 0 =$ _____ $6 + 2 =$ _____

13. $0 + 8 =$ _____ $5 + 2 =$ _____ $7 + 1 =$ _____

14. $1 + 5 =$ _____ $3 + 5 =$ _____ $4 + 0 =$ _____

15. $3 + 2 =$ _____ $4 + 2 =$ _____ $1 + 5 =$ _____

Tell the story. Then add.

16.

5 children + **3** children = _____ children

17.

4 children + **3** children = _____ children

DISCUSS: The different ways to make 8.

ADDING THROUGH 8

$$\begin{array}{r} 4 \\ +4 \\ \hline 8 \end{array}$$

$$\begin{array}{r} 5 \\ +3 \\ \hline 8 \end{array}$$

Add.

1.
$$\begin{array}{r} 1 \\ +7 \\ \hline \end{array}$$

2.
$$\begin{array}{r} 6 \\ +2 \\ \hline \end{array}$$

3.
$$\begin{array}{r} 5 \\ +2 \\ \hline \end{array}$$

4.
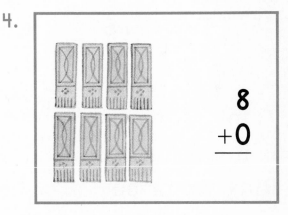
$$\begin{array}{r} 8 \\ +0 \\ \hline \end{array}$$

5.
$$\begin{array}{r} 3 \\ +3 \\ \hline \end{array} \qquad \begin{array}{r} 3 \\ +4 \\ \hline \end{array} \qquad \begin{array}{r} 3 \\ +5 \\ \hline \end{array} \qquad \begin{array}{r} 1 \\ +5 \\ \hline \end{array} \qquad \begin{array}{r} 1 \\ +4 \\ \hline \end{array} \qquad \begin{array}{r} 1 \\ +3 \\ \hline \end{array}$$

6.
$$\begin{array}{r} 5 \\ +1 \\ \hline \end{array} \qquad \begin{array}{r} 5 \\ +2 \\ \hline \end{array} \qquad \begin{array}{r} 5 \\ +3 \\ \hline \end{array} \qquad \begin{array}{r} 4 \\ +4 \\ \hline \end{array} \qquad \begin{array}{r} 3 \\ +4 \\ \hline \end{array} \qquad \begin{array}{r} 2 \\ +4 \\ \hline \end{array}$$

Add.

7.
$$8 \atop +0$$

$$5 \atop +2$$

$$6 \atop +2$$

$$3 \atop +5$$

$$4 \atop +2$$

$$4 \atop +4$$

8.
$$1 \atop +7$$

$$3 \atop +5$$

$$5 \atop +1$$

$$6 \atop +1$$

$$2 \atop +3$$

$$5 \atop +1$$

9.
$$6 \atop +2$$

$$4 \atop +1$$

$$0 \atop +0$$

$$1 \atop +7$$

$$2 \atop +5$$

$$8 \atop +0$$

10.
$$4 \atop +4$$

$$1 \atop +6$$

$$0 \atop +6$$

$$5 \atop +3$$

$$3 \atop +4$$

$$7 \atop +0$$

Think of the sum.
Is it greater than 7?
Ring yes or no.

11. $2 + 4$

   yes (no)

  $3 + 2$

   yes no

  $9 + 0$

   yes no

12. $3 + 3$

   yes no

  $8 + 0$

   yes no

  $6 + 2$

   yes no

ADDING THROUGH 9

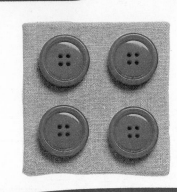 

$4 + 5 = \underline{9}$

Add.

1.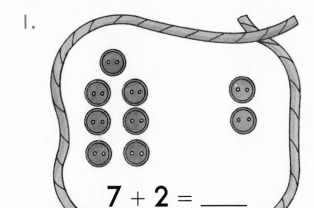

$7 + 2 = \underline{}$

2.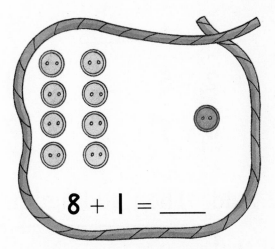

$8 + 1 = \underline{}$

3.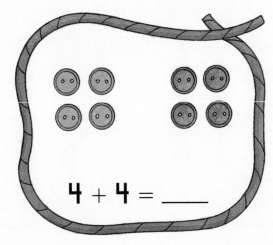

$4 + 4 = \underline{}$

4.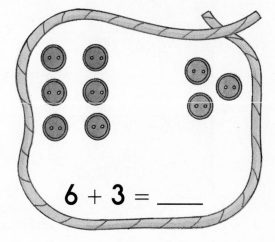

$6 + 3 = \underline{}$

5. $4 + 3 = \underline{}$ $4 + 4 = \underline{}$ $4 + 5 = \underline{}$

6. $3 + 6 = \underline{}$ $3 + 5 = \underline{}$ $3 + 4 = \underline{}$

7. $6 + 1 = \underline{}$ $6 + 2 = \underline{}$ $6 + 3 = \underline{}$

Add.

8. $3 + 4 =$ _____ $4 + 4 =$ _____ $5 + 4 =$ _____

9. $1 + 6 =$ _____ $1 + 7 =$ _____ $1 + 8 =$ _____

10. $3 + 5 =$ _____ $4 + 5 =$ _____ $2 + 7 =$ _____

11. $9 + 0 =$ _____ $2 + 6 =$ _____ $3 + 6 =$ _____

12. $7 + 1 =$ _____ $6 + 2 =$ _____ $5 + 3 =$ _____

13. $8 + 1 =$ _____ $7 + 2 =$ _____ $6 + 3 =$ _____

14. $2 + 5 =$ _____ $4 + 3 =$ _____ $4 + 4 =$ _____

15. $0 + 9 =$ _____ $7 + 0 =$ _____ $0 + 3 =$ _____

☆ Add. Then add again.

16.

17.

18.

TRY THIS: Problem Solving Activities, page 395.

ADDING THROUGH 9

$$\begin{array}{r} 4 \\ +5 \\ \hline 9 \end{array}$$

Add.

1.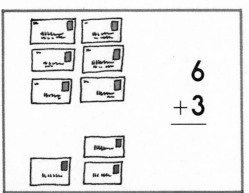

$$\begin{array}{r} 6 \\ +3 \\ \hline \end{array}$$

2.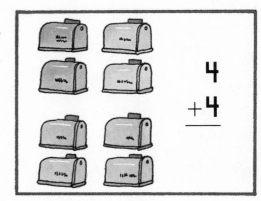

$$\begin{array}{r} 4 \\ +4 \\ \hline \end{array}$$

3.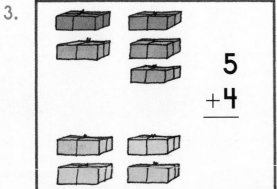

$$\begin{array}{r} 5 \\ +4 \\ \hline \end{array}$$

4.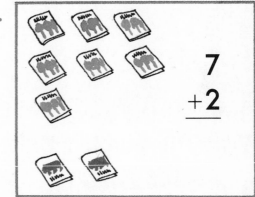

$$\begin{array}{r} 7 \\ +2 \\ \hline \end{array}$$

5.
$$\begin{array}{r} 1 \\ +6 \\ \hline \end{array}$$
$$\begin{array}{r} 1 \\ +7 \\ \hline \end{array}$$
$$\begin{array}{r} 1 \\ +8 \\ \hline \end{array}$$
$$\begin{array}{r} 3 \\ +4 \\ \hline \end{array}$$
$$\begin{array}{r} 3 \\ +5 \\ \hline \end{array}$$
$$\begin{array}{r} 3 \\ +6 \\ \hline \end{array}$$

6.
$$\begin{array}{r} 3 \\ +3 \\ \hline \end{array}$$
$$\begin{array}{r} 4 \\ +3 \\ \hline \end{array}$$
$$\begin{array}{r} 5 \\ +3 \\ \hline \end{array}$$
$$\begin{array}{r} 4 \\ +5 \\ \hline \end{array}$$
$$\begin{array}{r} 2 \\ +6 \\ \hline \end{array}$$
$$\begin{array}{r} 2 \\ +5 \\ \hline \end{array}$$

Add.

7.
$$\begin{array}{r} 6 \\ +1 \\ \hline \end{array}$$
$$\begin{array}{r} 2 \\ +7 \\ \hline \end{array}$$
$$\begin{array}{r} 6 \\ +2 \\ \hline \end{array}$$
$$\begin{array}{r} 5 \\ +2 \\ \hline \end{array}$$
$$\begin{array}{r} 5 \\ +4 \\ \hline \end{array}$$
$$\begin{array}{r} 0 \\ +9 \\ \hline \end{array}$$

8.
$$\begin{array}{r} 5 \\ +3 \\ \hline \end{array}$$
$$\begin{array}{r} 4 \\ +4 \\ \hline \end{array}$$
$$\begin{array}{r} 4 \\ +5 \\ \hline \end{array}$$
$$\begin{array}{r} 0 \\ +5 \\ \hline \end{array}$$
$$\begin{array}{r} 3 \\ +6 \\ \hline \end{array}$$
$$\begin{array}{r} 1 \\ +8 \\ \hline \end{array}$$

9.
$$\begin{array}{r} 1 \\ +7 \\ \hline \end{array}$$
$$\begin{array}{r} 7 \\ +2 \\ \hline \end{array}$$
$$\begin{array}{r} 6 \\ +3 \\ \hline \end{array}$$
$$\begin{array}{r} 5 \\ +4 \\ \hline \end{array}$$
$$\begin{array}{r} 8 \\ +1 \\ \hline \end{array}$$
$$\begin{array}{r} 3 \\ +4 \\ \hline \end{array}$$

10.
$$\begin{array}{r} 2 \\ +6 \\ \hline \end{array}$$
$$\begin{array}{r} 6 \\ +3 \\ \hline \end{array}$$
$$\begin{array}{r} 8 \\ +0 \\ \hline \end{array}$$
$$\begin{array}{r} 3 \\ +5 \\ \hline \end{array}$$
$$\begin{array}{r} 2 \\ +7 \\ \hline \end{array}$$
$$\begin{array}{r} 9 \\ +0 \\ \hline \end{array}$$

Think of the sum.
Write the number that comes just after the sum.

11.

$5 + 2 = ?$

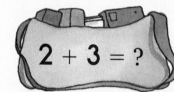
$2 + 3 = ?$

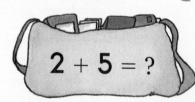
$2 + 5 = ?$

____

12.

$5 + 0 = ?$

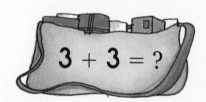
$4 + 3 = ?$

$3 + 3 = ?$

____   ____

Addition Facts through 9

ADDING IN ANY ORDER

If you know

$5 + 4 = \underline{9}$

Then you know

$4 + 5 = \underline{9}$

Add.

1. $9 + 0 = \underline{\hspace{1cm}}$

$0 + 9 = \underline{\hspace{1cm}}$

2. $3 + 5 = \underline{\hspace{1cm}}$

$5 + 3 = \underline{\hspace{1cm}}$

3. $2 + 7 = \underline{\hspace{1cm}}$

$7 + 2 = \underline{\hspace{1cm}}$

4. $1 + 8 = \underline{\hspace{1cm}}$

$8 + 1 = \underline{\hspace{1cm}}$

5. $3 + 6 = \underline{\hspace{1cm}}$

$6 + 3 = \underline{\hspace{1cm}}$

6. $2 + 6 = \underline{\hspace{1cm}}$

$6 + 2 = \underline{\hspace{1cm}}$

7. $4 + 3 = \underline{\hspace{1cm}}$

$3 + 4 = \underline{\hspace{1cm}}$

8. $5 + 4 = \underline{\hspace{1cm}}$

$4 + 5 = \underline{\hspace{1cm}}$

Add.

9. $\begin{array}{r} 1 \\ +8 \\ \hline \end{array}$ $\begin{array}{r} 8 \\ +1 \\ \hline \end{array}$ 10. $\begin{array}{r} 3 \\ +5 \\ \hline \end{array}$ $\begin{array}{r} 5 \\ +3 \\ \hline \end{array}$ 11. $\begin{array}{r} 1 \\ +7 \\ \hline \end{array}$ $\begin{array}{r} 7 \\ +1 \\ \hline \end{array}$

12. $\begin{array}{r} 6 \\ +3 \\ \hline \end{array}$ $\begin{array}{r} 3 \\ +6 \\ \hline \end{array}$ 13. $\begin{array}{r} 4 \\ +3 \\ \hline \end{array}$ $\begin{array}{r} 3 \\ +4 \\ \hline \end{array}$ 14. $\begin{array}{r} 6 \\ +1 \\ \hline \end{array}$ $\begin{array}{r} 1 \\ +6 \\ \hline \end{array}$

15. $\begin{array}{r} 2 \\ +5 \\ \hline \end{array}$ $\begin{array}{r} 5 \\ +2 \\ \hline \end{array}$ 16. $\begin{array}{r} 4 \\ +5 \\ \hline \end{array}$ $\begin{array}{r} 5 \\ +4 \\ \hline \end{array}$ 17. $\begin{array}{r} 0 \\ +8 \\ \hline \end{array}$ $\begin{array}{r} 8 \\ +0 \\ \hline \end{array}$

18. $\begin{array}{r} 2 \\ +4 \\ \hline \end{array}$ $\begin{array}{r} 4 \\ +2 \\ \hline \end{array}$ 19. $\begin{array}{r} 6 \\ +2 \\ \hline \end{array}$ $\begin{array}{r} 2 \\ +6 \\ \hline \end{array}$ 20. $\begin{array}{r} 2 \\ +7 \\ \hline \end{array}$ $\begin{array}{r} 7 \\ +2 \\ \hline \end{array}$

(pages 53–64)

CHECKPOINT 1   Add.

1. $7 + 1 = \boxed{}$ $5 + 4 = \boxed{}$ $4 + 3 = \boxed{}$

2. $\begin{array}{r} 2 \\ +6 \\ \hline \end{array}$ $\begin{array}{r} 3 \\ +5 \\ \hline \end{array}$ $\begin{array}{r} 3 \\ +6 \\ \hline \end{array}$ $\begin{array}{r} 9 \\ +0 \\ \hline \end{array}$ $\begin{array}{r} 5 \\ +2 \\ \hline \end{array}$ $\begin{array}{r} 0 \\ +8 \\ \hline \end{array}$

Extra practice on page 363

Order Property

PROBLEM SOLVING

How much in all?

1. $\underline{3}$¢ + $\underline{2}$¢ = $\underline{5}$¢

2. ___¢ + ___¢ = ___¢

3. ___¢ + ___¢ = ___¢

4. ___¢ + ___¢ = ___¢

5. ___¢ + ___¢ = ___¢

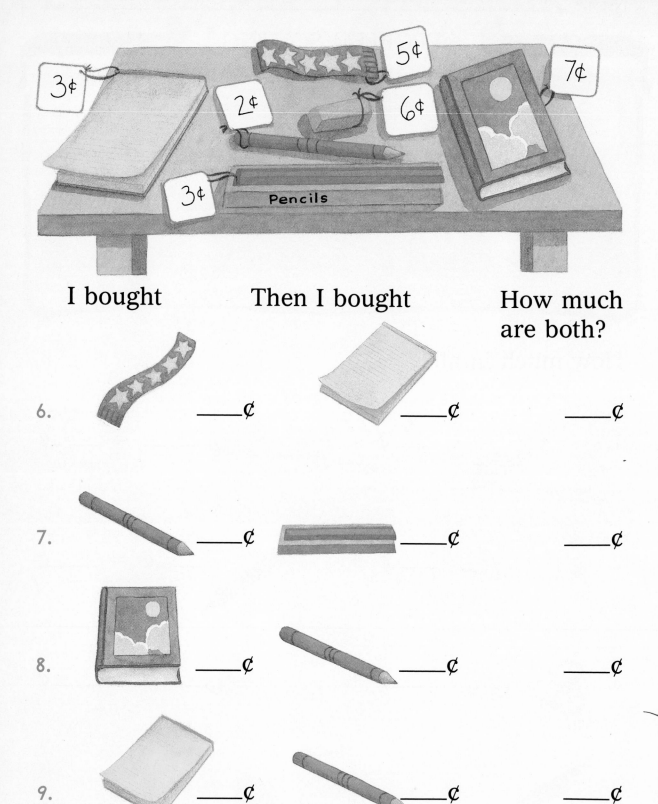

I bought Then I bought How much are both?

6. ____¢ ____¢ ____¢

7. ____¢ ____¢ ____¢

8. ____¢ ____¢ ____¢

9. ____¢ ____¢ ____¢

10. ____¢ ____¢ ____¢

TRY THIS: Use play money to show amounts.

ADDING THROUGH 10

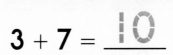

$$3 + 7 = \underline{10}$$

Add.

1. $1 + 9 = \underline{}$

   $9 + 1 = \underline{}$

2. $2 + 8 = \underline{}$

   $8 + 2 = \underline{}$

3. $3 + 7 = \underline{}$

   $7 + 3 = \underline{}$

4. $5 + 3 = \underline{}$ $5 + 4 = \underline{}$ $5 + 5 = \underline{}$

5. $10 + 0 = \underline{}$ $9 + 0 = \underline{}$ $8 + 0 = \underline{}$

Add.

6. $9 + 1 =$ _____ $4 + 6 =$ _____ $5 + 5 =$ _____

7. $8 + 2 =$ _____ $3 + 6 =$ _____ $2 + 8 =$ _____

8. $7 + 3 =$ _____ $2 + 7 =$ _____ $1 + 9 =$ _____

9. $6 + 4 =$ _____ $6 + 3 =$ _____ $7 + 2 =$ _____

10. $3 + 5 =$ _____ $3 + 7 =$ _____ $4 + 6 =$ _____

11. $9 + 1 =$ _____ $2 + 8 =$ _____ $1 + 6 =$ _____

12. $4 + 4 =$ _____ $3 + 6 =$ _____ $9 + 0 =$ _____

13. $4 + 2 =$ _____ $4 + 5 =$ _____ $6 + 2 =$ _____

Tell the story.
Write the numbers.
Then add.

14.   _____ children

     +_____ children
     _____

      _____ children

PARTNERS: Use punchouts to show different
ways to make 10.

ADDING FACTS THROUGH 10

$$\begin{array}{r} 4 \\ +6 \\ \hline 10 \end{array}$$

Add.

1.
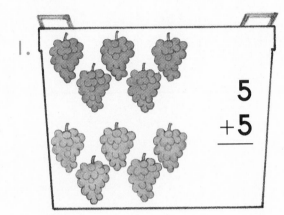
$$\begin{array}{r} 5 \\ +5 \\ \hline \end{array}$$

2.
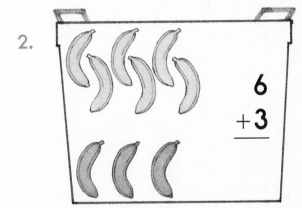
$$\begin{array}{r} 6 \\ +3 \\ \hline \end{array}$$

3.
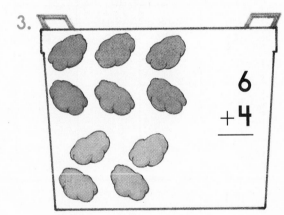
$$\begin{array}{r} 6 \\ +4 \\ \hline \end{array}$$

4.
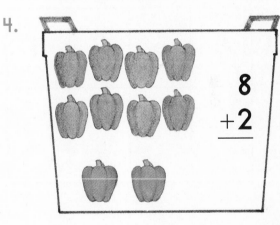
$$\begin{array}{r} 8 \\ +2 \\ \hline \end{array}$$

5.
$$\begin{array}{r} 7 \\ +1 \\ \hline \end{array} \qquad \begin{array}{r} 8 \\ +1 \\ \hline \end{array} \qquad \begin{array}{r} 9 \\ +1 \\ \hline \end{array} \qquad \begin{array}{r} 7 \\ +3 \\ \hline \end{array} \qquad \begin{array}{r} 7 \\ +2 \\ \hline \end{array} \qquad \begin{array}{r} 7 \\ +1 \\ \hline \end{array}$$

6.
$$\begin{array}{r} 3 \\ +3 \\ \hline \end{array} \qquad \begin{array}{r} 3 \\ +4 \\ \hline \end{array} \qquad \begin{array}{r} 3 \\ +5 \\ \hline \end{array} \qquad \begin{array}{r} 5 \\ +5 \\ \hline \end{array} \qquad \begin{array}{r} 4 \\ +5 \\ \hline \end{array} \qquad \begin{array}{r} 3 \\ +5 \\ \hline \end{array}$$

Complete the tables.

7.

Add 2			
8	3	6	5
10	5		

8.

Add 3			
7	3	5	6

9.

Add 4			
5	6	2	4

10.

Add 5			
4	2	3	5

Think of the sum.
Then write the number that
comes just before the sum.

11.

$6 + 3 = ?$

8
_____

$5 + 2 = ?$

_____

$3 + 7 = ?$

_____

Addition Facts through 10

PROBLEM SOLVING

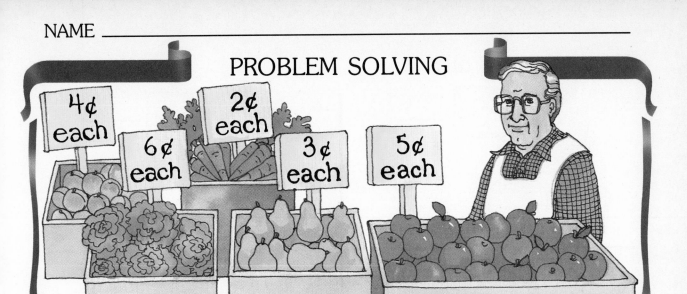

How much in all? Write the numbers. Use ¢.

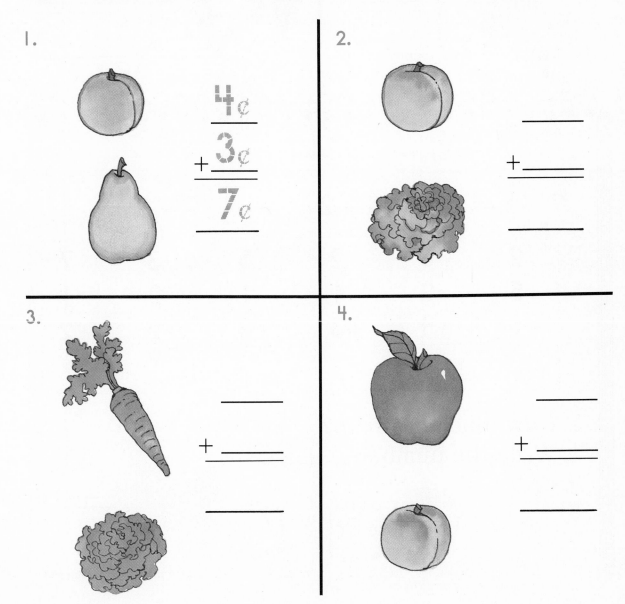

1.

$$\begin{array}{r} 4\text{¢} \\ +\ 3\text{¢} \\ \hline 7\text{¢} \end{array}$$

2.

$$\begin{array}{r} \underline{\quad} \\ +\ \underline{\quad} \\ \hline \underline{\quad} \end{array}$$

3.

$$\begin{array}{r} \underline{\quad} \\ +\ \underline{\quad} \\ \hline \underline{\quad} \end{array}$$

4.

$$\begin{array}{r} \underline{\quad} \\ +\ \underline{\quad} \\ \hline \underline{\quad} \end{array}$$

How much in all?

5.  5¢ ____

3¢ + ____

____

6.  7¢ ____

3¢ + ____

____

7.  3¢ ____

5¢ + ____

____

8. 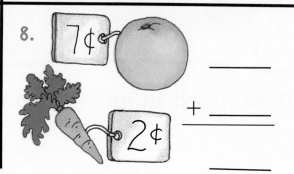 7¢ ____

2¢ + ____

____

(pages 65–74)

CHECKPOINT 2   Add.

1. $9 + 1 =$ ☐ $8 + 2 =$ ☐ $7 + 2 =$ ☐

2.

2	3	2	5	3	7
5	2	1	1	2	1
+1	+4	+3	+2	+2	+2

3. How much are both?
Write the numbers. Use ¢.

 5¢    4¢

____

+ ____

Extra practice on page 363

Problem Solving

CHAPTER 3 TEST

Add.

1.
2	3	0	8	6	4
+7	+5	+9	+0	+2	+4

Add.

2.
4	3	3	6	7	9
+6	+7	+6	+4	+2	+1

Add.

3.
4	7	2	5	1	3
1	1	3	2	4	5
+3	+2	+2	+3	+4	+1

How much in all?
Write the numbers. Use ¢.

4.

___
+ ___
___

5.

___
+ ___
___

Extra practice on page 364

MATHEMATICS and SOCIAL STUDIES

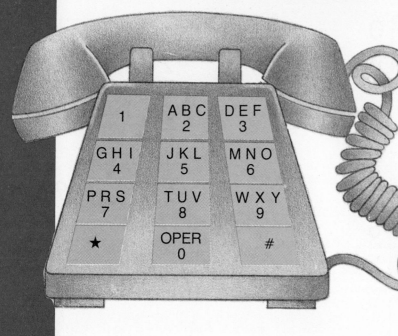

Write the phone number for the business.

1. P E T   S H O P

___ ___ ___ - ___ ___ ___ ___

2. A L ' S   C A F E

___ ___ ___ - ___ ___ ___ ___

3. T O Y   S H O P

___ ___ ___ - ___ ___ ___ ___

4. C A B   R I D E

___ ___ ___ - ___ ___ ___ ___

5. What is your phone number?

___ ___ ___ - ___ ___ ___ ___

Mathematics and Social Studies

Enrichment

How many animals?
Write the numbers.

1. Table A   _____

   Table B   +_____

   in all   _____

2. Table B   _____

   Table C   +_____

   in all   _____

3. Table A   _____

   Table C   +_____

   in all   _____

4. How many foxes at all the tables? 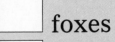 foxes

5. How many bears at all the tables? bears

6. How many animals in all? 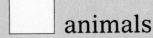 animals

Interpreting a Picture

A

B

C

How many animals? Write the numbers.

7. Table A   ____

    Table B   +____

    in all   ____

8. Table B   ____

    Table C   +____

    in all   ____

9. Table A   ____

    Table C   +____

    in all   ____

10. How many animals at Table A?   ☐ animals

11. How many animals at Table A and Table B?   ☐ animals

12. How many animals are making birdhouses?   ☐ animals

Enrichment: Interpreting a Picture

NAME _____

CUMULATIVE REVIEW

Fill in the ◯ for the correct answer.

How much?

1.	2.

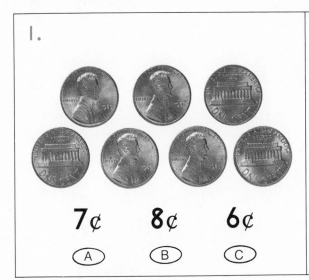

7¢   8¢   6¢

Ⓐ   Ⓑ   Ⓒ

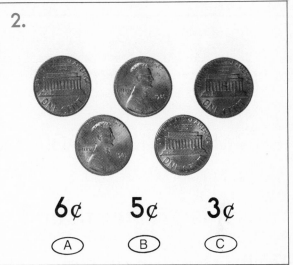

6¢   5¢   3¢

Ⓐ   Ⓑ   Ⓒ

What number is missing?

3.   3,   4,   __?__

     6   7   5

     Ⓐ   Ⓑ   Ⓒ

4.   7,   __?__ ,   9

     6   8   7

     Ⓐ   Ⓑ   Ⓒ

Add.

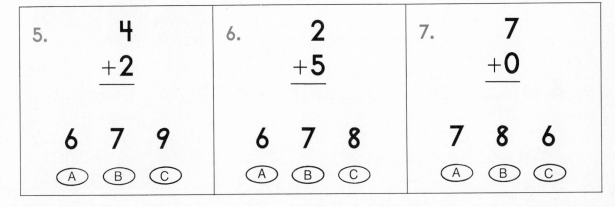

5.
$$\begin{array}{r} 4 \\ +2 \\ \hline \end{array}$$

6   7   9

Ⓐ   Ⓑ   Ⓒ

6.
$$\begin{array}{r} 2 \\ +5 \\ \hline \end{array}$$

6   7   8

Ⓐ   Ⓑ   Ⓒ

7.
$$\begin{array}{r} 7 \\ +0 \\ \hline \end{array}$$

7   8   6

Ⓐ   Ⓑ   Ⓒ

Fill in the ◯ for the correct answer.

8.

Ⓐ 2 + 2

Ⓑ 3 + 2

Ⓒ 2 + 3

LANGUAGE and VOCABULARY REVIEW

7 is *greater* than **3**.   **4** is *less* than **9**.

Write greater or less.

1. **9** is ___greater___ than **7**.

2. **3** is _____ than **4**.

3. **7** is _____ than **10**.

4. **8** is _____ than **6**.

5. **5** is _____ than **3**.

Language and Vocabulary Review

Read with the children:

How many bags of fruit are there?
How many bags of oranges?
How many bags of grapefruit?
If 4 bags are sold, how many are left?

4

SUBTRACTION FACTS THROUGH 7

BEGINNING SUBTRACTION

How many?   How many go?   How many are left?

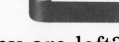

__3__ minus __1__ equals __2__

How many?

Write the numbers.

1.

_____ − _____ = _____

2.

_____ − _____ = _____

3.

_____ − _____ = _____

Beginning Subtraction

SUBTRACTING 1, 2, OR 3

$$4 - 1 = \underline{3}$$

$$5 - 2 = \underline{3}$$

How many?

1.

____ – ____ = ____

2.

____ – ____ = ____

3.

____ – ____ = ____

Subtract.

4.

$6 - 1 = \underline{}$

5.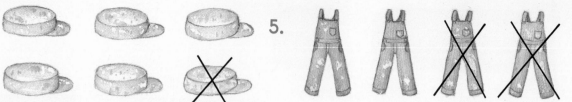

$4 - 2 = \underline{}$

6.

$6 - 3 = \underline{}$

7.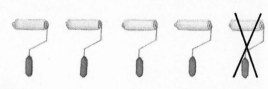

$5 - 1 = \underline{}$

Tell the story. Then subtract.

8.

$6 - 2 = \underline{}$

9.

$3 - 2 = \underline{}$

10.

$5 - 3 = \underline{}$

11.

$7 - 2 = \underline{}$

Subtracting 1, 2, or 3

SUBTRACTING 1 TO 6

$$5 - 4 = 1$$

⇧ difference

Write the numbers. Ring the difference.

1.
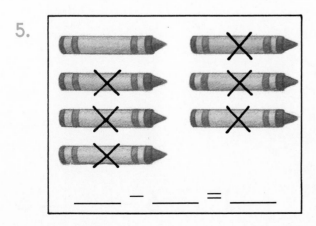

$$6 - 4 = (2)$$

2.
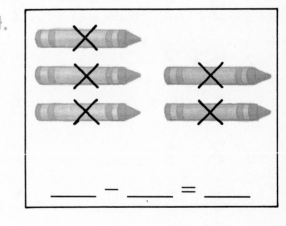

___ − ___ = ___

3.
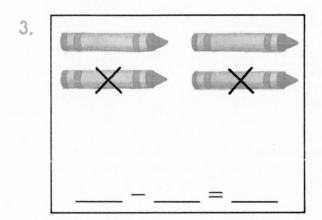

___ − ___ = ___

4.
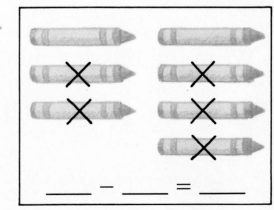

___ − ___ = ___

5.

___ − ___ = ___

6.

___ − ___ = ___

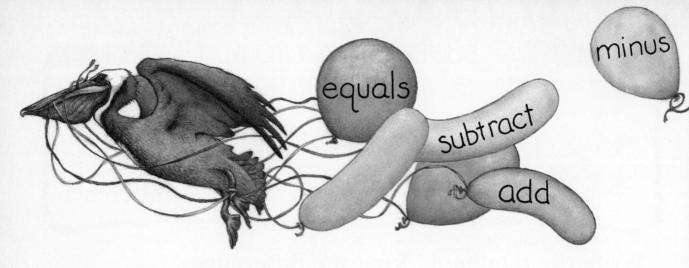

Write the difference.

7. $4 - 1 = \underline{\hspace{1.2em}}$ $5 - 2 = \underline{\hspace{1.2em}}$ $5 - 4 = \underline{\hspace{1.2em}}$

8. $6 - 5 = \underline{\hspace{1.2em}}$ $2 - 2 = \underline{\hspace{1.2em}}$ $7 - 5 = \underline{\hspace{1.2em}}$

9. $5 - 1 = \underline{\hspace{1.2em}}$ $6 - 4 = \underline{\hspace{1.2em}}$ $4 - 3 = \underline{\hspace{1.2em}}$

10. $7 - 6 = \underline{\hspace{1.2em}}$ $7 - 3 = \underline{\hspace{1.2em}}$ $6 - 1 = \underline{\hspace{1.2em}}$

11. $5 - 3 = \underline{\hspace{1.2em}}$ $2 - 1 = \underline{\hspace{1.2em}}$ $4 - 4 = \underline{\hspace{1.2em}}$

12. $4 - 2 = \underline{\hspace{1.2em}}$ $6 - 6 = \underline{\hspace{1.2em}}$ $7 - 2 = \underline{\hspace{1.2em}}$

13. $5 - 5 = \underline{\hspace{1.2em}}$ $6 - 2 = \underline{\hspace{1.2em}}$ $6 - 3 = \underline{\hspace{1.2em}}$

14. $7 - 1 = \underline{\hspace{1.2em}}$ $7 - 4 = \underline{\hspace{1.2em}}$ $3 - 2 = \underline{\hspace{1.2em}}$

15. $6 - 5 = \underline{\hspace{1.2em}}$ $3 - 3 = \underline{\hspace{1.2em}}$ $6 - 4 = \underline{\hspace{1.2em}}$

☆ Write the missing number.

16. $4 - \boxed{1} = 3$ $4 - \boxed{} = 1$ $5 - \boxed{} = 1$

17. $5 - \boxed{} = 4$ $6 - \boxed{} = 1$ $6 - \boxed{} = 5$

TRY THIS: Use counters to show differences.

RELATED FACTS

If you know   5 – 2 = _3_

Then you know   5 – 3 = _2_

Subtract.

1.

$$5 - 1 = \_\_\_$$

$$5 - 4 = \_\_\_$$

2.

$$6 - 1 = \_\_\_$$

$$6 - 5 = \_\_\_$$

3.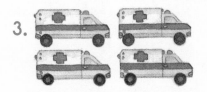

$$6 - 2 = \_\_\_$$

$$6 - 4 = \_\_\_$$

4.

$$3 - 1 = \_\_\_$$

$$3 - 2 = \_\_\_$$

5.

$$4 - 1 = \_\_\_$$

$$4 - 3 = \_\_\_$$

6.

$$7 - 5 = \_\_\_$$

$$7 - 2 = \_\_\_$$

 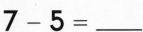

Subtract.

7. $3 - 1 =$ _____   8. $6 - 1 =$ _____   9. $7 - 1 =$ _____

$3 - 2 =$ _____ $6 - 5 =$ _____ $7 - 6 =$ _____

10. $5 - 4 =$ _____   11. $7 - 2 =$ _____   12. $6 - 2 =$ _____

$5 - 1 =$ _____ $7 - 5 =$ _____ $6 - 4 =$ _____

13. $7 - 3 =$ _____   14. $5 - 2 =$ _____   15. $4 - 1 =$ _____

$7 - 4 =$ _____ $5 - 3 =$ _____ $4 - 3 =$ _____

Use 7 cubes. Tell a story.
Then subtract.

16. $7 - 1 =$ _____   17. $7 - 2 =$ _____   18. $7 - 4 =$ _____

$7 - 6 =$ _____ $7 - 5 =$ _____ $7 - 3 =$ _____

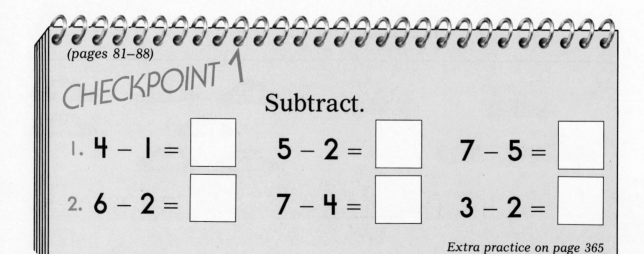

(pages 81–88)

CHECKPOINT 1

Subtract.

1. $4 - 1 = \boxed{}$ $5 - 2 = \boxed{}$ $7 - 5 = \boxed{}$

2. $6 - 2 = \boxed{}$ $7 - 4 = \boxed{}$ $3 - 2 = \boxed{}$

Extra practice on page 365

Related Subtraction Facts

PROBLEM SOLVING

How many in all?

4 ⊞ 1 = __5__

Write + or − in the ☐.
Add or subtract.

1.

How many are left?

4 ☐ 1 = ___

2.

How many in all?

4 ☐ 2 = ___

3.

How many are left?

4 ☐ 2 = ___

4.

How many are left?

4 ☐ 3 = ___

Write + or − in the ☐.
Add or subtract.

5.    How many are left?

$5 \boxed{} 4 = \rule{1cm}{0.4pt}$

6.    How many in all?

$3 \boxed{} 2 = \rule{1cm}{0.4pt}$

7.    How many in all?

$3 \boxed{} 3 = \rule{1cm}{0.4pt}$

8.    How many are left?

$6 \boxed{} 3 = \rule{1cm}{0.4pt}$

9.    How many in all?

$2 \boxed{} 2 = \rule{1cm}{0.4pt}$

PARTNERS: Tell a story.

SUBTRACTION ANOTHER WAY

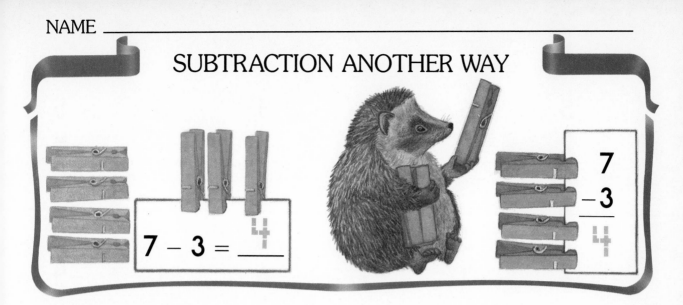

$7 - 3 = \underline{4}$

$$\begin{array}{r} 7 \\ -3 \\ \hline 4 \end{array}$$

Subtract.

1.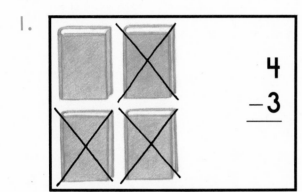

$$\begin{array}{r} 4 \\ -3 \\ \hline \end{array}$$

2.
$$\begin{array}{r} 5 \\ -4 \\ \hline \end{array}$$

3.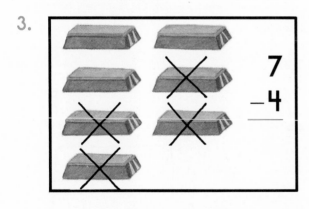

$$\begin{array}{r} 7 \\ -4 \\ \hline \end{array}$$

4.
$$\begin{array}{r} 5 \\ -3 \\ \hline \end{array}$$

5.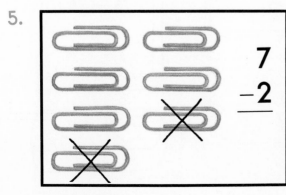

$$\begin{array}{r} 7 \\ -2 \\ \hline \end{array}$$

6.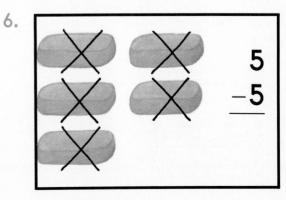

$$\begin{array}{r} 5 \\ -5 \\ \hline \end{array}$$

Subtraction, Vertical Form

Subtract.

7.
$$\begin{array}{r} 5 \\ -2 \\ \hline \end{array}$$
$$\begin{array}{r} 6 \\ -1 \\ \hline \end{array}$$
$$\begin{array}{r} 2 \\ -1 \\ \hline \end{array}$$
$$\begin{array}{r} 4 \\ -3 \\ \hline \end{array}$$
$$\begin{array}{r} 3 \\ -1 \\ \hline \end{array}$$
$$\begin{array}{r} 5 \\ -4 \\ \hline \end{array}$$

8.
$$\begin{array}{r} 7 \\ -2 \\ \hline \end{array}$$
$$\begin{array}{r} 6 \\ -4 \\ \hline \end{array}$$
$$\begin{array}{r} 3 \\ -1 \\ \hline \end{array}$$
$$\begin{array}{r} 6 \\ -6 \\ \hline \end{array}$$
$$\begin{array}{r} 5 \\ -1 \\ \hline \end{array}$$
$$\begin{array}{r} 7 \\ -4 \\ \hline \end{array}$$

9.
$$\begin{array}{r} 4 \\ -1 \\ \hline \end{array}$$
$$\begin{array}{r} 3 \\ -2 \\ \hline \end{array}$$
$$\begin{array}{r} 4 \\ -4 \\ \hline \end{array}$$
$$\begin{array}{r} 7 \\ -3 \\ \hline \end{array}$$
$$\begin{array}{r} 4 \\ -2 \\ \hline \end{array}$$
$$\begin{array}{r} 1 \\ -1 \\ \hline \end{array}$$

10.
$$\begin{array}{r} 7 \\ -5 \\ \hline \end{array}$$
$$\begin{array}{r} 7 \\ -6 \\ \hline \end{array}$$
$$\begin{array}{r} 5 \\ -3 \\ \hline \end{array}$$
$$\begin{array}{r} 7 \\ -7 \\ \hline \end{array}$$
$$\begin{array}{r} 6 \\ -2 \\ \hline \end{array}$$
$$\begin{array}{r} 5 \\ -5 \\ \hline \end{array}$$

Think of the difference.
If greater than **3**, color 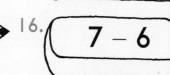 red .

11.
$7 - 3$

12.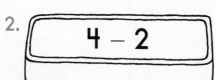
$4 - 2$

13.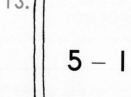
$5 - 1$

14.
$3 - 2$

15.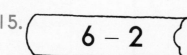
$6 - 2$

16.
$7 - 6$

Subtraction, Vertical Form

SUBTRACTING FROM 7

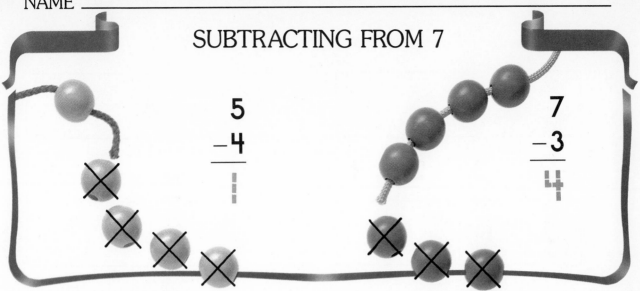

$$\begin{array}{r} 5 \\ -4 \\ \hline 1 \end{array}$$

$$\begin{array}{r} 7 \\ -3 \\ \hline 4 \end{array}$$

Subtract.

1.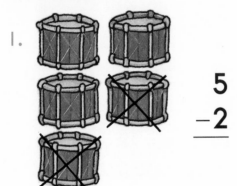

$$\begin{array}{r} 5 \\ -2 \\ \hline \end{array}$$

2.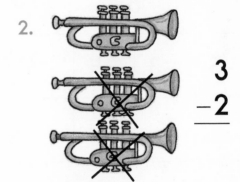

$$\begin{array}{r} 3 \\ -2 \\ \hline \end{array}$$

3.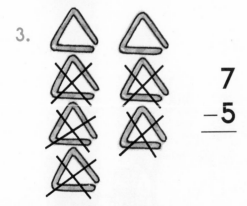

$$\begin{array}{r} 7 \\ -5 \\ \hline \end{array}$$

4.

$$\begin{array}{r} 4 \\ -2 \\ \hline \end{array}$$

5.

$$\begin{array}{r} 6 \\ -2 \\ \hline \end{array}$$

6.

$$\begin{array}{r} 5 \\ -3 \\ \hline \end{array}$$

Subtract.

7.

4			
−1	−3	−2	−4
3	1		

8.

5			
−1	−3	−2	−4

9.

6			
−5	−3	−4	−6

10.

7			
−1	−5	−6	−4

Tell the story. Then add or subtract.

11.

$$4 + 2 = \underline{\quad}$$

12.

$$7 - 3 = \underline{\quad}$$

DISCUSS: The kinds of instruments the children know.

SUBTRACTING WITH ZERO

$$3 - 0 = \underline{\;3\;}$$

Subtract.

1.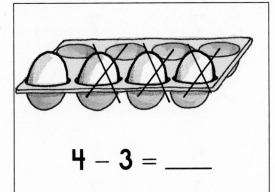

$$4 - 3 = \underline{}$$

2.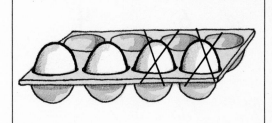

$$4 - 2 = \underline{}$$

3.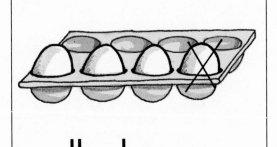

$$4 - 1 = \underline{}$$

4.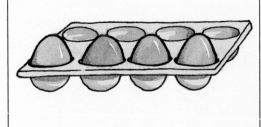

$$4 - 0 = \underline{}$$

5.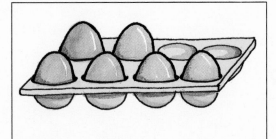

$$6 - 0 = \underline{}$$

6.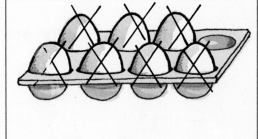

$$7 - 7 = \underline{}$$

Subtract.

7. $5 - 0 =$ _____ $2 - 1 =$ _____

8. $7 - 6 =$ _____ $4 - 0 =$ _____

9. $1 - 0 =$ _____ $3 - 3 =$ _____

10. $6 - 3 =$ _____ $4 - 3 =$ _____

11. $3 - 0 =$ _____ $4 - 1 =$ _____

12.
$$\begin{array}{cccccc} 6 & 4 & 2 & 7 & 7 & 6 \\ -0 & -2 & -2 & -0 & -5 & -6 \\ \hline \end{array}$$

13.
$$\begin{array}{cccccc} 4 & 1 & 6 & 5 & 7 & 5 \\ -3 & -0 & -4 & -3 & -7 & -0 \\ \hline \end{array}$$

14.
$$\begin{array}{cccccc} 7 & 1 & 5 & 6 & 2 & 4 \\ -2 & -1 & -4 & -5 & -0 & -1 \\ \hline \end{array}$$

☆ Write the missing number.

15.
$$\begin{array}{cccccc} 5 & 3 & 7 & 4 & 2 & 6 \\ -\boxed{3} & -\boxed{} & -\boxed{} & -\boxed{} & -\boxed{} & -\boxed{} \\ \hline 2 & 3 & 4 & 0 & 2 & 2 \end{array}$$

TRY THIS: Problem Solving Activities, page 396.

FACT FAMILIES

If you know $2 + 4 = \underline{6}$

Then you know $6 - 4 = \underline{2}$

$4 + 2 = \underline{6}$

$6 - 2 = \underline{4}$

Add or subtract.

1.

$5 + 2 = \underline{}$

$7 - 2 = \underline{}$

$2 + 5 = \underline{}$

$7 - 5 = \underline{}$

2.

$2 + 3 = \underline{}$

$5 - 3 = \underline{}$

$3 + 2 = \underline{}$

$5 - 2 = \underline{}$

3.

$3 + 4 = \underline{}$

$7 - 4 = \underline{}$

$4 + 3 = \underline{}$

$7 - 3 = \underline{}$

Add or subtract.

4.

1, 5, 6
1 + 5 = ___
6 − 5 = ___
5 + 1 = ___
6 − 1 = ___

5.

3, 4, 7
3 + 4 = ___
7 − 4 = ___
4 + 3 = ___
7 − 3 = ___

6.

2, 3, 5

$$2 \quad\quad 5$$
$$+3 \quad\quad -3$$

$$3 \quad\quad 5$$
$$+2 \quad\quad -2$$

7.

1, 3, 4

$$1 \quad\quad 4$$
$$+3 \quad\quad -3$$

$$3 \quad\quad 4$$
$$+1 \quad\quad -1$$

Think of the difference.
If less than 4, color 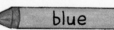 blue .

8.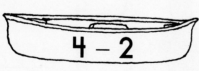
4 − 2

9.
5 − 3

10.
7 − 2

11.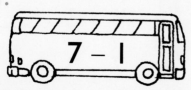
7 − 1

12.
6 − 3

13.
5 − 2

Fact Families

PROBLEM SOLVING

5

2 join.

How many in all?

$\begin{array}{r} 5 \\ +2 \\ \hline \end{array}$

$\begin{array}{r} 5 \\ -2 \\ \hline \end{array}$

Ring the correct example.

1.

7

2 go away.

How many are left?

$\begin{array}{r} 7 \\ +2 \\ \hline \end{array}$

$\begin{array}{r} 7 \\ -2 \\ \hline \end{array}$

2.

7

6 go away.

How many are left?

$\begin{array}{r} 7 \\ -6 \\ \hline \end{array}$

$\begin{array}{r} 7 \\ +6 \\ \hline \end{array}$

Ring the correct example.

3.

4

3

 join.

How many in all?

$$\begin{array}{r} 4 \\ +3 \\ \hline \end{array}$$

$$\begin{array}{r} 4 \\ -3 \\ \hline \end{array}$$

4.

5

1

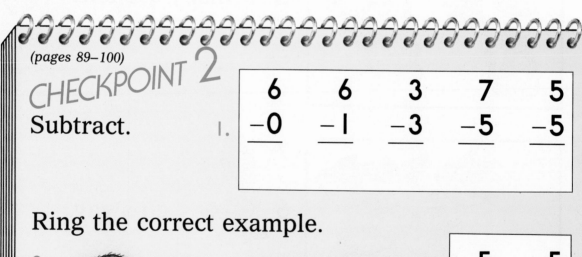 goes away.

How many are left?

$$\begin{array}{r} 5 \\ +1 \\ \hline \end{array}$$

$$\begin{array}{r} 5 \\ -1 \\ \hline \end{array}$$

(pages 89–100)

CHECKPOINT 2

Subtract.

1.

$$\begin{array}{r} 6 \\ -0 \\ \hline \end{array} \quad \begin{array}{r} 6 \\ -1 \\ \hline \end{array} \quad \begin{array}{r} 3 \\ -3 \\ \hline \end{array} \quad \begin{array}{r} 7 \\ -5 \\ \hline \end{array} \quad \begin{array}{r} 5 \\ -5 \\ \hline \end{array}$$

Ring the correct example.

2.

$$\begin{array}{r} 5 \\ +2 \\ \hline \end{array} \quad \begin{array}{r} 5 \\ -2 \\ \hline \end{array}$$

Extra practice on page 365

Problem Solving

CHAPTER 4 TEST

Subtract.

1. 4 – 2 = ____   5 – 3 = ____   6 – 4 = ____

2. 7 – 4 = ____   6 – 2 = ____   7 – 5 = ____

3.
| 4 | 7 | 3 | 6 | 7 | 5 |
| –3 | –2 | –2 | –5 | –4 | –3 |

Subtract.

4. 5 – 0 = ____   6 – 6 = ____   7 – 0 = ____

5. 7 – 3 = ____   6 – 0 = ____   4 – 4 = ____

Write + or – in the ☐.
Then add or subtract.

6.

6 ☐ 2 = ____

Extra practice on page 366

MATHEMATICS and SCIENCE

Machines can
help us count.
Trace the word.

1.

calculator

2.

computer

3.
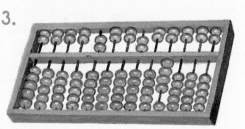

abacus

4.

clock

5.

cash register

Enrichment

Draw a picture. Write the missing number.

1.

$$5 - \underline{} = 4$$

$$6 - \underline{} = 4$$

2.

$$4 - \underline{} = 4$$

$$7 - \underline{} = 3$$

3.

$$7 - \underline{} = 2$$

$$6 - \underline{} = 3$$

Drawing a Picture

Draw a picture. Write the missing number.

4.

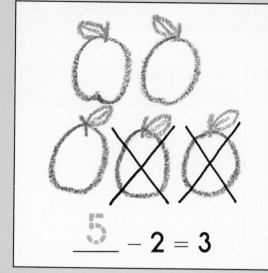

_____ − 2 = 3

_____ − 3 = 4

5.

_____ − 4 = 3

_____ − 2 = 4

6.

_____ − 1 = 5

_____ − 6 = 0

Enrichment: Drawing a Picture

CUMULATIVE REVIEW

Fill in the ◯ for the correct answer.

Add.

1. $\begin{array}{r} 5 \\ +0 \\ \hline \end{array}$	2. $\begin{array}{r} 0 \\ +7 \\ \hline \end{array}$	3. $6 + 0$
5 6 8 Ⓐ Ⓑ Ⓒ	6 8 7 Ⓐ Ⓑ Ⓒ	5 6 7 Ⓐ Ⓑ Ⓒ

Add.

4. $\begin{array}{r} 2 \\ +7 \\ \hline \end{array}$	5. $\begin{array}{r} 4 \\ +6 \\ \hline \end{array}$	6. $3 + 6$
8 9 7 Ⓐ Ⓑ Ⓒ	10 9 7 Ⓐ Ⓑ Ⓒ	9 8 10 Ⓐ Ⓑ Ⓒ

Add.

7. $\begin{array}{r} 2 \\ 4 \\ +3 \\ \hline \end{array}$	8. $\begin{array}{r} 5 \\ 1 \\ +2 \\ \hline \end{array}$	9. $\begin{array}{r} 3 \\ 4 \\ +3 \\ \hline \end{array}$
9 8 10 Ⓐ Ⓑ Ⓒ	8 9 7 Ⓐ Ⓑ Ⓒ	10 9 8 Ⓐ Ⓑ Ⓒ

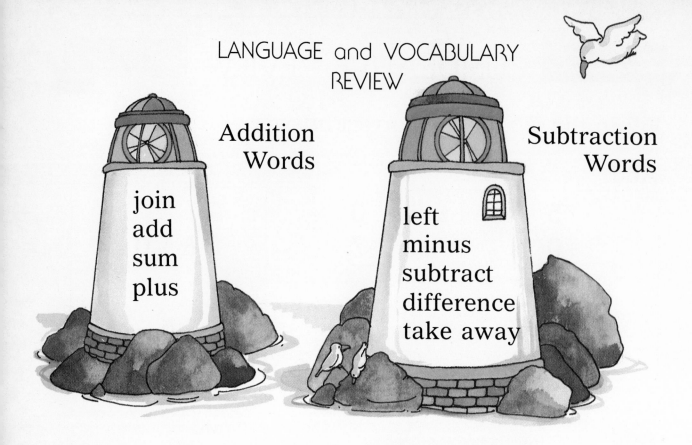

Addition Words

join
add
sum
plus

Subtraction Words

left
minus
subtract
difference
take away

Color the addition words red.

Color the subtraction words blue.

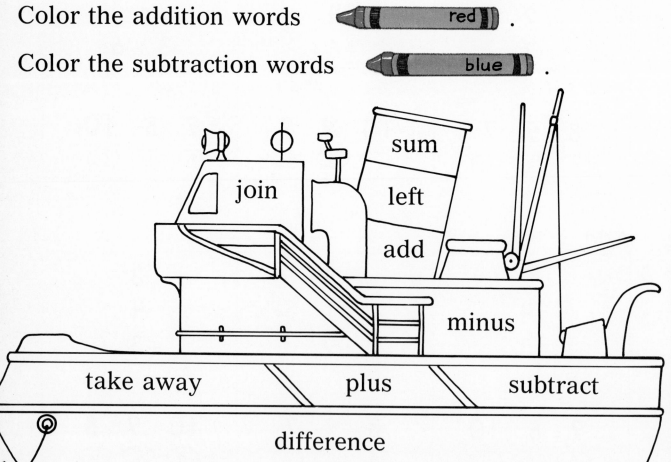

sum
join
left
add
minus
take away
plus
subtract
difference

5

Read with the children:

The farmer has 10 cows.
Some are in the field.
Some are in the barn.
How many in the field?
How many in the barn?

SUBTRACTION
FACTS THROUGH 10

REVIEWING SUBTRACTION

7 – 3 = _4_

Subtract.

1. 7 – 1 = ___   6 – 1 = ___   6 – 6 = ___

2. 5 – 4 = ___   5 – 0 = ___   6 – 5 = ___

3. 6 – 3 = ___   6 – 4 = ___   4 – 1 = ___

$$\begin{array}{r} 6 \\ -4 \\ \hline 2 \end{array}$$

4.
$$\begin{array}{r} 7 \\ -1 \\ \hline \end{array} \qquad \begin{array}{r} 7 \\ -4 \\ \hline \end{array} \qquad \begin{array}{r} 4 \\ -3 \\ \hline \end{array} \qquad \begin{array}{r} 6 \\ -3 \\ \hline \end{array} \qquad \begin{array}{r} 3 \\ -2 \\ \hline \end{array} \qquad \begin{array}{r} 4 \\ -1 \\ \hline \end{array}$$

5.
$$\begin{array}{r} 6 \\ -0 \\ \hline \end{array} \qquad \begin{array}{r} 5 \\ -4 \\ \hline \end{array} \qquad \begin{array}{r} 7 \\ -7 \\ \hline \end{array} \qquad \begin{array}{r} 7 \\ -3 \\ \hline \end{array} \qquad \begin{array}{r} 4 \\ -0 \\ \hline \end{array} \qquad \begin{array}{r} 6 \\ -3 \\ \hline \end{array}$$

Reviewing Subtraction

SUBTRACTING FROM 8

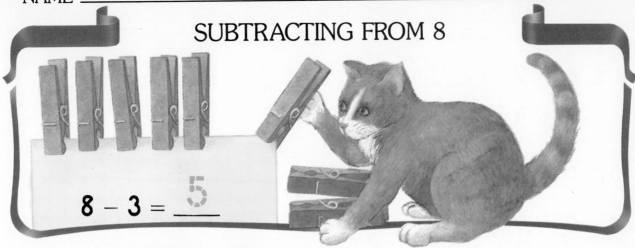

8 – 3 = __5__

Subtract.

1.

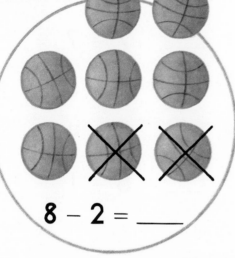

8 – 2 = ____

2.

8 – 5 = ____

3.

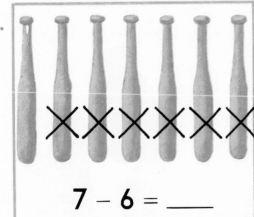

7 – 6 = ____

4.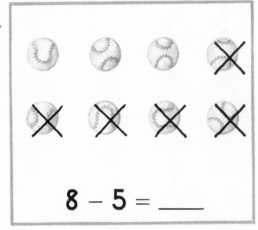

8 – 1 = ____

5. 8 – 5 = ____   8 – 4 = ____   8 – 3 = ____

6. 8 – 2 = ____   7 – 2 = ____   6 – 2 = ____

7. 8 – 6 = ____   8 – 7 = ____   8 – 8 = ____

Subtract.

8. $6 - 2 = $ _____ $7 - 2 = $ _____ $8 - 2 = $ _____

9. $6 - 3 = $ _____ $7 - 3 = $ _____ $8 - 3 = $ _____

10. $6 - 4 = $ _____ $7 - 4 = $ _____ $8 - 4 = $ _____

11. $6 - 5 = $ _____ $7 - 5 = $ _____ $8 - 5 = $ _____

12. $6 - 6 = $ _____ $7 - 6 = $ _____ $8 - 6 = $ _____

13. $5 - 4 = $ _____ $8 - 1 = $ _____ $7 - 7 = $ _____

14. $5 - 2 = $ _____ $6 - 0 = $ _____ $5 - 3 = $ _____

15. $8 - 0 = $ _____ $8 - 7 = $ _____ $5 - 4 = $ _____

16. $6 - 6 = $ _____ $8 - 8 = $ _____ $5 - 1 = $ _____

Tell the story. Then add or subtract.

17.

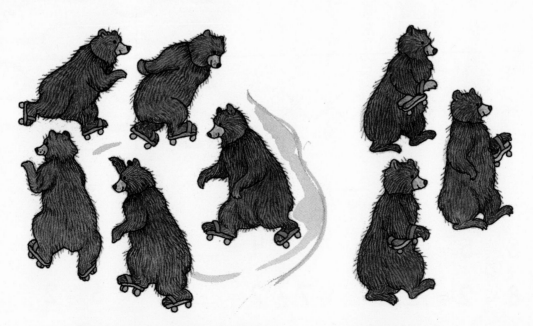

8 bears − **3** bears = _____ bears

TRY THIS: Use punchouts to show differences.

SUBTRACTING FROM 8

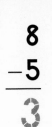

$$\begin{array}{r} 8 \\ -5 \\ \hline 3 \end{array}$$

Subtract.

1.

$$\begin{array}{r} 8 \\ -6 \\ \hline \end{array}$$

2.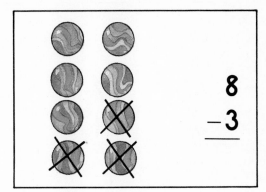

$$\begin{array}{r} 8 \\ -3 \\ \hline \end{array}$$

3.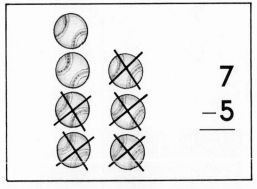

$$\begin{array}{r} 7 \\ -5 \\ \hline \end{array}$$

4.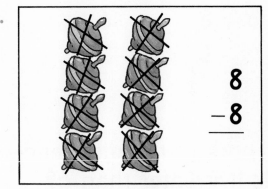

$$\begin{array}{r} 8 \\ -8 \\ \hline \end{array}$$

5.
$$\begin{array}{r} 8 \\ -0 \\ \hline \end{array} \qquad \begin{array}{r} 8 \\ -1 \\ \hline \end{array} \qquad \begin{array}{r} 8 \\ -2 \\ \hline \end{array} \qquad \begin{array}{r} 8 \\ -6 \\ \hline \end{array} \qquad \begin{array}{r} 7 \\ -6 \\ \hline \end{array} \qquad \begin{array}{r} 6 \\ -6 \\ \hline \end{array}$$

6.
$$\begin{array}{r} 8 \\ -4 \\ \hline \end{array} \qquad \begin{array}{r} 8 \\ -5 \\ \hline \end{array} \qquad \begin{array}{r} 8 \\ -6 \\ \hline \end{array} \qquad \begin{array}{r} 5 \\ -5 \\ \hline \end{array} \qquad \begin{array}{r} 5 \\ -4 \\ \hline \end{array} \qquad \begin{array}{r} 5 \\ -3 \\ \hline \end{array}$$

Subtract.

7.
$$
\begin{array}{cccccc}
8 & 7 & 6 & 8 & 6 & 8 \\
-2 & -6 & -1 & -3 & -4 & -6 \\
\end{array}
$$

8.
$$
\begin{array}{cccccc}
7 & 8 & 7 & 6 & 7 & 8 \\
-7 & -4 & -5 & -6 & -2 & -7 \\
\end{array}
$$

9.
$$
\begin{array}{cccccc}
8 & 7 & 6 & 8 & 7 & 8 \\
-3 & -4 & -3 & -5 & -3 & -0 \\
\end{array}
$$

10.
$$
\begin{array}{cccccc}
8 & 6 & 8 & 7 & 8 & 5 \\
-8 & -2 & -1 & -0 & -4 & -5 \\
\end{array}
$$

Think of the difference.
Is it **greater** than **6**?
Ring yes or no.

11.   8 – 1   8 – 4   7 – 3

   (yes)   no   yes   no   yes   no

12.   7 – 5   8 – 3   7 – 0

    yes   no   yes   no   yes   no

Subtraction Facts through 8

SUBTRACTING FROM 9

$9 - 7 = \underline{2}$

$9 - 5 = \underline{4}$

Subtract.

1.

$9 - 1 = \underline{}$

2.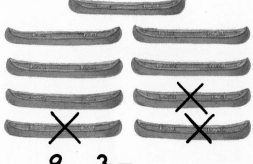

$9 - 3 = \underline{}$

3.

$8 - 4 = \underline{}$

4.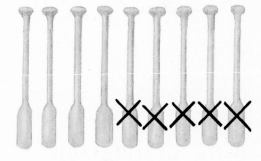

$9 - 5 = \underline{}$

5. $9 - 2 = \underline{}$ $9 - 3 = \underline{}$ $9 - 4 = \underline{}$

6. $8 - 6 = \underline{}$ $7 - 6 = \underline{}$ $6 - 6 = \underline{}$

7. $9 - 9 = \underline{}$ $9 - 8 = \underline{}$ $9 - 7 = \underline{}$

8. **Subtract.**
Color.

5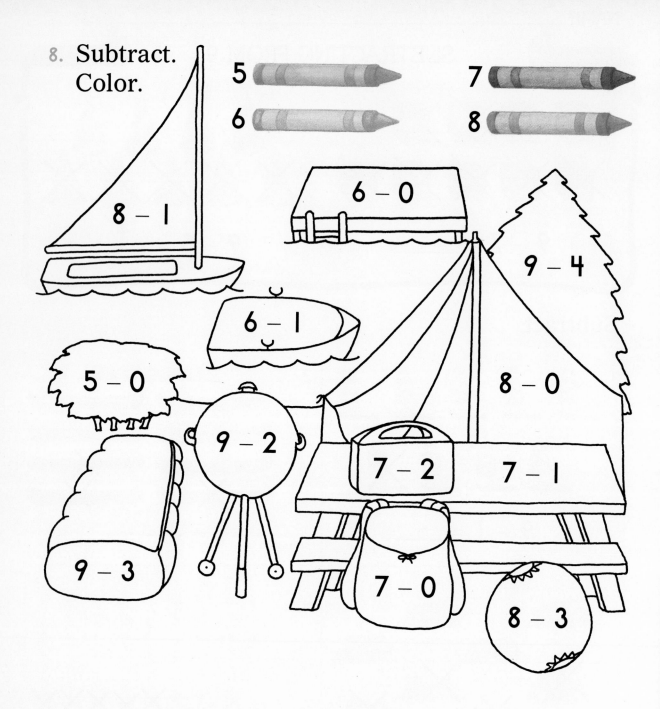
6
7
8

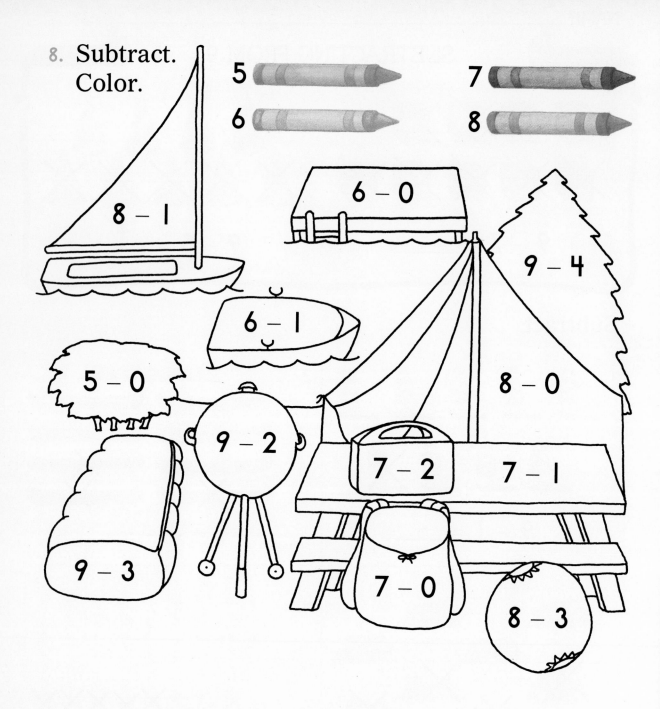

8 – 1

6 – 0

9 – 4

6 – 1

5 – 0

8 – 0

9 – 2

7 – 2

7 – 1

9 – 3

7 – 0

8 – 3

☆ **Ring all the names for the number.**

9.	6	⟨7 – 1⟩	⟨8 – 2⟩	8 – 1
10.	7	8 – 3	8 – 1	7 – 0
11.	8	9 – 1	7 – 6	8 – 0

Subtraction Facts through 9

SUBTRACTING FROM 9

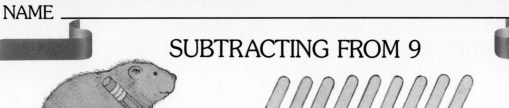

$$\begin{array}{r} 9 \\ -7 \\ \hline 2 \end{array}$$

Subtract.

1.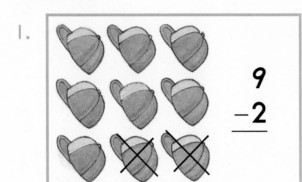

$$\begin{array}{r} 9 \\ -2 \\ \hline \end{array}$$

2.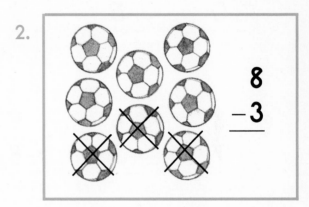

$$\begin{array}{r} 8 \\ -3 \\ \hline \end{array}$$

3.

$$\begin{array}{r} 9 \\ -0 \\ \hline \end{array}$$

4.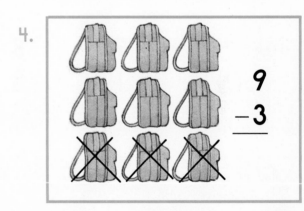

$$\begin{array}{r} 9 \\ -3 \\ \hline \end{array}$$

5.
$$\begin{array}{r} 9 \\ -1 \\ \hline \end{array}$$
$$\begin{array}{r} 9 \\ -2 \\ \hline \end{array}$$
$$\begin{array}{r} 9 \\ -3 \\ \hline \end{array}$$
$$\begin{array}{r} 9 \\ -8 \\ \hline \end{array}$$
$$\begin{array}{r} 9 \\ -7 \\ \hline \end{array}$$
$$\begin{array}{r} 9 \\ -6 \\ \hline \end{array}$$

6.
$$\begin{array}{r} 9 \\ -4 \\ \hline \end{array}$$
$$\begin{array}{r} 8 \\ -4 \\ \hline \end{array}$$
$$\begin{array}{r} 7 \\ -4 \\ \hline \end{array}$$
$$\begin{array}{r} 9 \\ -2 \\ \hline \end{array}$$
$$\begin{array}{r} 9 \\ -3 \\ \hline \end{array}$$
$$\begin{array}{r} 9 \\ -4 \\ \hline \end{array}$$

Add or subtract.

7.
$$\begin{array}{r} 9 \\ -7 \\ \hline \end{array}$$
$$\begin{array}{r} 9 \\ -5 \\ \hline \end{array}$$
$$\begin{array}{r} 8 \\ +1 \\ \hline \end{array}$$
$$\begin{array}{r} 9 \\ -6 \\ \hline \end{array}$$
$$\begin{array}{r} 7 \\ -4 \\ \hline \end{array}$$
$$\begin{array}{r} 6 \\ +2 \\ \hline \end{array}$$

8.
$$\begin{array}{r} 9 \\ +0 \\ \hline \end{array}$$
$$\begin{array}{r} 8 \\ -5 \\ \hline \end{array}$$
$$\begin{array}{r} 9 \\ -2 \\ \hline \end{array}$$
$$\begin{array}{r} 8 \\ -4 \\ \hline \end{array}$$
$$\begin{array}{r} 4 \\ +3 \\ \hline \end{array}$$
$$\begin{array}{r} 9 \\ -9 \\ \hline \end{array}$$

9.
$$\begin{array}{r} 8 \\ -7 \\ \hline \end{array}$$
$$\begin{array}{r} 6 \\ +3 \\ \hline \end{array}$$
$$\begin{array}{r} 9 \\ -8 \\ \hline \end{array}$$
$$\begin{array}{r} 8 \\ -1 \\ \hline \end{array}$$
$$\begin{array}{r} 5 \\ +2 \\ \hline \end{array}$$
$$\begin{array}{r} 9 \\ -1 \\ \hline \end{array}$$

10.
$$\begin{array}{r} 4 \\ +4 \\ \hline \end{array}$$
$$\begin{array}{r} 9 \\ -1 \\ \hline \end{array}$$
$$\begin{array}{r} 8 \\ -8 \\ \hline \end{array}$$
$$\begin{array}{r} 7 \\ +2 \\ \hline \end{array}$$
$$\begin{array}{r} 7 \\ -7 \\ \hline \end{array}$$
$$\begin{array}{r} 9 \\ -0 \\ \hline \end{array}$$

(pages 107–116)

CHECKPOINT 1   Subtract.

1. $9 - 6 = \boxed{}$ $8 - 3 = \boxed{}$ $8 - 6 = \boxed{}$

2.
$$\begin{array}{r} 9 \\ -3 \\ \hline \end{array}$$
$$\begin{array}{r} 7 \\ -5 \\ \hline \end{array}$$
$$\begin{array}{r} 8 \\ -7 \\ \hline \end{array}$$
$$\begin{array}{r} 9 \\ -2 \\ \hline \end{array}$$
$$\begin{array}{r} 6 \\ -4 \\ \hline \end{array}$$
$$\begin{array}{r} 8 \\ -3 \\ \hline \end{array}$$

Extra practice on page 367

PARTNERS: Draw pictures to show differences.

PROBLEM SOLVING

6 + 2

(6 − 2)

3 + 3

Tell the story. Ring the correct example.

1.

3 + 2

5 + 2

5 − 3

2.

7 − 2

7 − 5

5 + 2

3.

8 − 3

5 + 3

7 − 4

Tell the story. Ring the correct example.

4.
5 + 2
3 + 5
5 − 3

5.
4 + 3
7 + 0
4 − 3

6.
8 − 5
5 + 3
8 − 4

7.
8 − 8
8 − 0
8 + 1

☆ **8.** Draw a picture to show **7 + 2**.

SUBTRACTING FROM 10

$10 - 5 =$ __5__

$10 - 3 =$ __7__

Subtract.

1.

$10 - 7 =$ ___

2.

$10 - 6 =$ ___

3.

$10 - 6 =$ ___

4.

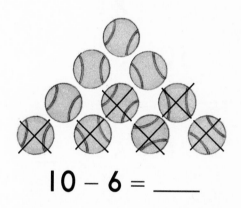

$10 - 4 =$ ___

5. $10 - 7 =$ ___ $10 - 6 =$ ___ $10 - 5 =$ ___

6. $10 - 9 =$ ___ $10 - 8 =$ ___ $10 - 7 =$ ___

7. $10 - 1 =$ ___ $9 - 1 =$ ___ $8 - 1 =$ ___

Subtract.

8. $8 - 2 =$ ___ $\qquad$ $9 - 2 =$ ___ $\qquad$ $10 - 2 =$ ___

9. $8 - 3 =$ ___ $\qquad$ $9 - 3 =$ ___ $\qquad$ $10 - 3 =$ ___

10. $8 - 4 =$ ___ $\qquad$ $9 - 4 =$ ___ $\qquad$ $10 - 4 =$ ___

11. $8 - 5 =$ ___ $\qquad$ $9 - 5 =$ ___ $\qquad$ $10 - 5 =$ ___

12. $10 - 4 =$ ___ $\qquad$ $10 - 6 =$ ___ $\qquad$ $10 - 7 =$ ___

13. $9 - 8 =$ ___ $\qquad$ $8 - 7 =$ ___ $\qquad$ $10 - 2 =$ ___

14. $10 - 3 =$ ___ $\qquad$ $9 - 5 =$ ___ $\qquad$ $10 - 1 =$ ___

15. $9 - 4 =$ ___ $\qquad$ $10 - 5 =$ ___ $\qquad$ $9 - 3 =$ ___

16. $10 - 6 =$ ___ $\qquad$ $9 - 3 =$ ___ $\qquad$ $10 - 7 =$ ___

Think of the difference.
Write the number that comes
just after the difference.

17. $10 - 2 = ?$

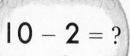

___

18. $8 - 3 = ?$

___

19. $7 - 2 = ?$

___

20. $8 - 1 = ?$

___

21. $9 - 2 = ?$

___

22. $10 - 2 = ?$

___

Subtraction Facts through 10

SUBTRACTING FROM 10

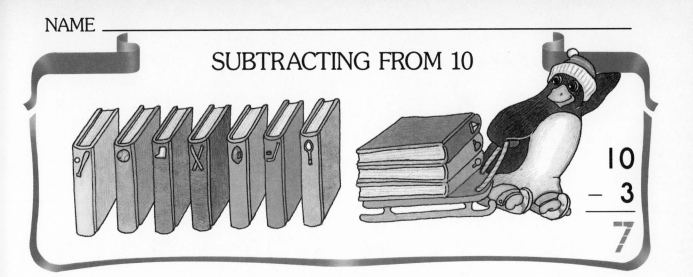

$$\begin{array}{r} 10 \\ -\ 3 \\ \hline 7 \end{array}$$

Subtract.

1.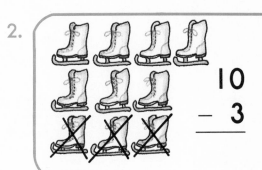
$$\begin{array}{r} 10 \\ -\ 4 \\ \hline \end{array}$$

2.
$$\begin{array}{r} 10 \\ -\ 3 \\ \hline \end{array}$$

3.
$$\begin{array}{r} 8 \\ -\ 2 \\ \hline \end{array}$$

4.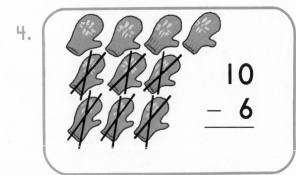
$$\begin{array}{r} 10 \\ -\ 6 \\ \hline \end{array}$$

5.
$$\begin{array}{r} 10 \\ -\ 5 \\ \hline \end{array}\qquad\begin{array}{r} 10 \\ -\ 4 \\ \hline \end{array}\qquad\begin{array}{r} 10 \\ -\ 3 \\ \hline \end{array}\qquad\begin{array}{r} 8 \\ -4 \\ \hline \end{array}\qquad\begin{array}{r} 7 \\ -4 \\ \hline \end{array}\qquad\begin{array}{r} 6 \\ -4 \\ \hline \end{array}$$

6.
$$\begin{array}{r} 10 \\ -\ 1 \\ \hline \end{array}\qquad\begin{array}{r} 10 \\ -\ 2 \\ \hline \end{array}\qquad\begin{array}{r} 10 \\ -\ 3 \\ \hline \end{array}\qquad\begin{array}{r} 10 \\ -10 \\ \hline \end{array}\qquad\begin{array}{r} 10 \\ -\ 9 \\ \hline \end{array}\qquad\begin{array}{r} 10 \\ -\ 8 \\ \hline \end{array}$$

Add or subtract.

7.
10	5	10	5	10	8
− 2	+4	− 1	+5	− 8	−3

8.
10	7	6	10	2	9
− 9	−5	+3	− 5	+8	−2

9.
10	9	10	2	10	9
− 4	+1	− 7	+6	− 3	−0

Tell a story.
Write the numbers. Write + or − in the ☐.
Then add or subtract.

10.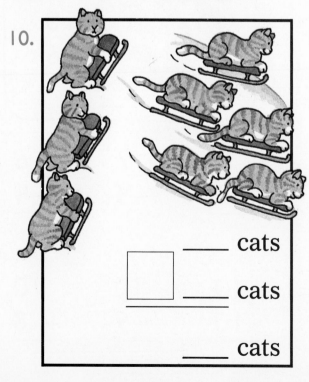

☐ ____ cats
____ cats
____ cats

11.

☐ ____ dogs
____ dogs
____ dogs

TRY THIS: Problem Solving Activities, page 397.

PROBLEM SOLVING

Bob has **7¢**.
He spends **6¢**.
How much does he have left?

```
  7¢
– 6¢
─────
  1¢
```

Write **+** or **–** in the ☐. Then add or subtract.

1. Kim has **5¢**.
   She earns **3¢**.
   How much does she have now?

```
  5¢
☐ 3¢
────
   ¢
```

2. Maria has **8¢**.
   She buys an apple for **6¢**.
   How much does she have left?

```
  8¢
☐ 6¢
────
   ¢
```

3. Jane has **4¢**.
   She saved **3¢** more.
   How much does she have in all?

```
  4¢
☐ 3¢
────
   ¢
```

Write + or − in the ☐. Then add or subtract.

4. Jessica had **5¢**.
She earned **2¢**.
How much does she have now?

$$\begin{array}{r} \boxed{}\ 5¢ \\ 2¢ \\ \hline ¢ \end{array}$$

5. Michael had **4¢**.
He gave **2¢** to Jessica.
How much does he have now?

$$\begin{array}{r} \boxed{}\ 4¢ \\ 2¢ \\ \hline ¢ \end{array}$$

6. Kathy has **7¢**.
She lost **2¢**.
How much does she have left?

$$\begin{array}{r} \boxed{}\ 7¢ \\ 2¢ \\ \hline ¢ \end{array}$$

☆ Write the numbers to show the story.

7. Roberto bought a car for **3¢**.
Then he bought a truck for **6¢**.
How much did he spend in all?

$$\begin{array}{r} \boxed{}\ \underline{}¢ \\ \underline{}¢ \\ \hline ¢ \end{array}$$

Problem Solving

FAMILY OF FACTS

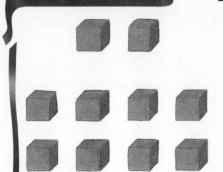

If you know $2 + 8 = \underline{10}$

Then you know $10 - 8 = \underline{2}$

$8 + 2 = \underline{10}$

$10 - 2 = \underline{8}$

2   **8**   **10**

Write the three numbers.
Then add or subtract.

1.

$4 + 5 = \underline{}$ $5 + 4 = \underline{}$

$9 - 5 = \underline{}$ $9 - 4 = \underline{}$

_____ , _____ , _____

2.

$3 + 6 = \underline{}$ $6 + 3 = \underline{}$

$9 - 6 = \underline{}$ $9 - 3 = \underline{}$

_____ , _____ , _____

3.

$1 + 9 = \underline{}$ $9 + 1 = \underline{}$

$10 - 9 = \underline{}$ $10 - 1 = \underline{}$

_____ , _____ , _____

4.

2, 7, 9
$2 + 7 =$ _____
$9 - 7 =$ _____
$7 + 2 =$ _____
$9 - 2 =$ _____

5.

3, 5, 8
$3 + 5 =$ _____
$8 - 5 =$ _____
$5 + 3 =$ _____
$8 - 3 =$ _____

6.

5, 2, 7	
5 +2 ___	7 −2 ___
2 +5 ___	7 −5 ___

7.

3, 4, 7	
3 +4 ___	7 −4 ___
4 +3 ___	7 −3 ___

(pages 117–126)

CHECKPOINT 2   Subtract.

1. $10 - 6 =$ ☐ $9 - 5 =$ ☐ $10 - 2 =$ ☐

Write + or − in the ☐.
Then add or subtract.

2. Tim had **5¢**. He saved **2¢** more.
How much does he have now?

5¢
2¢
──── ☐
☐ ¢

Extra practice on page 367

DISCUSS: The different names for 10.

CHAPTER 5 TEST

Subtract.

1. $\quad 7 \atop -2$ $\qquad 9 \atop -6$ $\qquad 8 \atop -3$ $\qquad 9 \atop -3$ $\qquad 9 \atop -4$ $\qquad 8 \atop -2$

2. $8 - 4 = \underline{\quad}$ $\qquad 9 - 8 = \underline{\quad}$ $\qquad 9 - 2 = \underline{\quad}$

Ring the correct example.

3.

3 + 5
5 − 3
5 − 2

4.

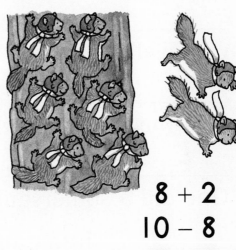

8 + 2
10 − 8
8 − 2

Subtract.

5. $\quad 10 \atop -\ 6$ $\qquad 9 \atop -9$ $\qquad 10 \atop -\ 1$ $\qquad 10 \atop -\ 3$ $\qquad 9 \atop -7$ $\qquad 10 \atop -\ 5$

6. $10 - 7 = \underline{\quad}$ $\qquad 10 - 2 = \underline{\quad}$ $\qquad 10 - 8 = \underline{\quad}$

Extra practice on page 368

MATHEMATICS and LANGUAGE

Write the word.

__Ten__ little pumpkins sitting on a line,
One went away and then there were nine.

_____ little pumpkins sitting on a gate,
One fell off and then there were eight.

_____ little pumpkins all named Kevin,
One walked away and then there were seven.

_____ little pumpkins picking up sticks,
One ran away and then there were six.

_____ little pumpkins happy to be alive,
One did a somersault and then there were five.

_____ little pumpkins and no more,
One went away and then there were four.

_____ little pumpkins as happy as could be,
One ran away and then there were three.

_____ little pumpkins with nothing to do,
One did a jump and then there were two.

_____ little pumpkins smiling at the sun,
One felt a raindrop and then there was one.

Mathematics and Language

Enrichment

Draw a picture to help.
Write the numbers.
Then add or subtract.

1.

There are **6** bugs on the 🪵 .
There are **2** bugs on the ground.
How many in all?

$$\begin{array}{r} 6 \\ +\ 2 \\ \hline 8 \end{array}$$

2.

There are **6** birds in the 🌿 .
3 birds fly away.
How many are left?

$$\begin{array}{r} \underline{} \\ -\ \underline{} \\ \hline \end{array}$$

Draw a picture to help.
Write the numbers.
Then add or subtract.

3.

There are **2** plates on the  .
5 plates are on the .
How many plates are there?

____
+ ____
____

4.

There are **6** bees on the .
Then **4** bees fly away.
How many bees are left?

____
− ____
____

Enrichment: Drawing a Picture

 CUMULATIVE REVIEW

Fill in the ◯ for the correct answer.

Choose the missing numbers.

1.	0, 1, 2, 3, 4, _?_, _?_, _?_, _?_, 9, 10

6, 5, 7, 8	5, 7, 6, 8	5, 6, 7, 8
Ⓐ	Ⓑ	Ⓒ

Add.

2.	$5 + 2$	3.	$7 + 3$	4.	$8 + 1$

3	4	7	10	8	4	7	8	9
Ⓐ	Ⓑ	Ⓒ	Ⓐ	Ⓑ	Ⓒ	Ⓐ	Ⓑ	Ⓒ

Subtract.

5.	6 -1	6.	7 -2	7.	5 -5

7	5	4	5	9	4	10	5	0
Ⓐ	Ⓑ	Ⓒ	Ⓐ	Ⓑ	Ⓒ	Ⓐ	Ⓑ	Ⓒ

8.	5 -3	9.	6 -5	10.	1 -0

4	2	1	2	3	1	0	1	2
Ⓐ	Ⓑ	Ⓒ	Ⓐ	Ⓑ	Ⓒ	Ⓐ	Ⓑ	Ⓒ

Choose the correct number sentence.

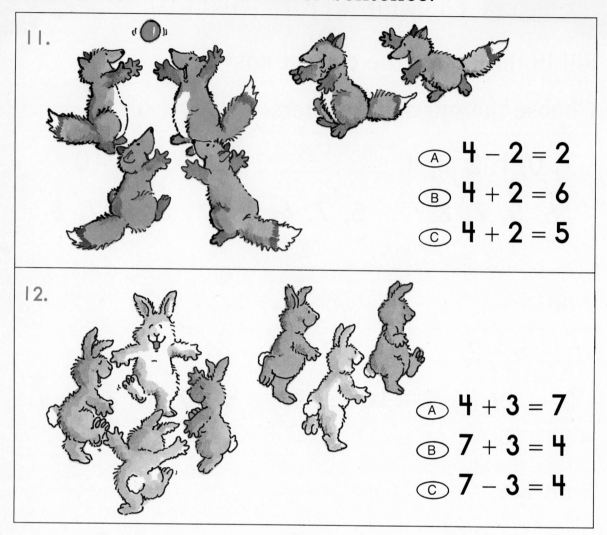

11.

- (A) $4 - 2 = 2$
- (B) $4 + 2 = 6$
- (C) $4 + 2 = 5$

12.

- (A) $4 + 3 = 7$
- (B) $7 + 3 = 4$
- (C) $7 - 3 = 4$

LANGUAGE and VOCABULARY REVIEW

Write the correct sign next to the word.

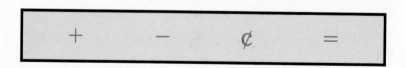

| $+$ | $-$ | ¢ | $=$ |

1. equals ____
2. subtract ____
3. cents ____
4. add ____

Ring the computer parts.

1.

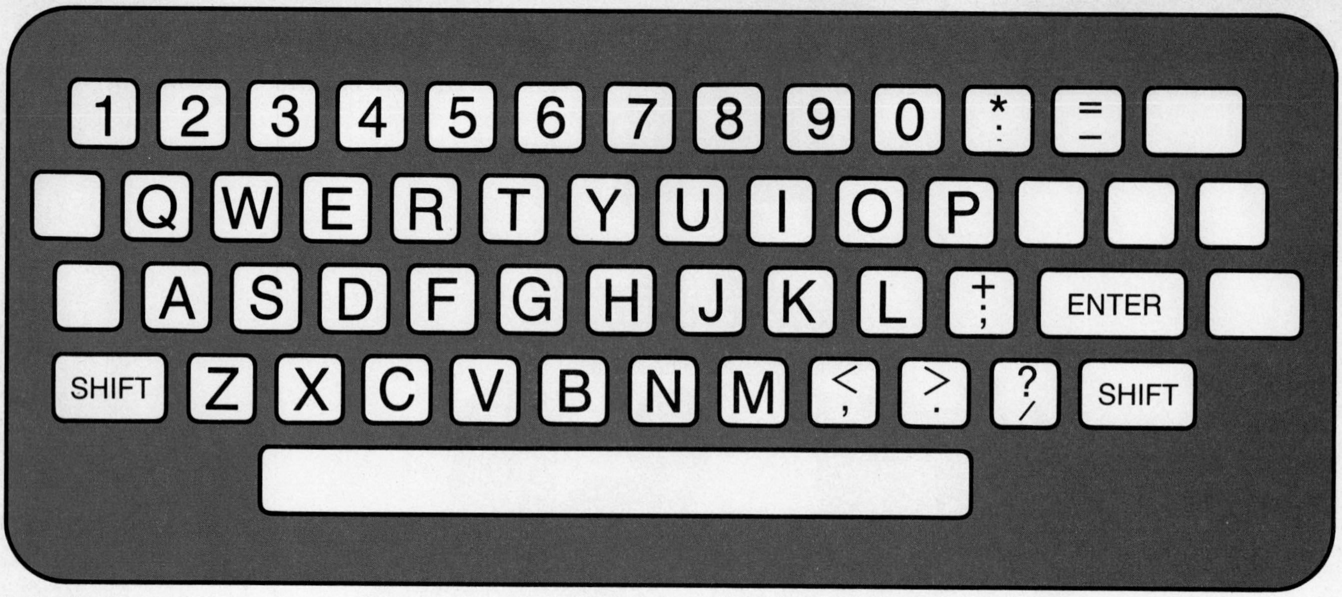

Keyboard:

```
1 2 3 4 5 6 7 8 9 0 *:  =_  □
□ Q W E R T Y U I O P  □ □ □
□ A S D F G H J K L †;  ENTER □
SHIFT Z X C V B N M <, >. ?/ SHIFT
         [space bar]
```

Write the letter.

2. Which ☐ is below Q ?

3. Which ☐ is to the left of K ?

4. Which ☐ is to the right of U ?

5. Which ☐ is below S and

 to the right of X ?

6. Which ☐ is above S and

 to the left of E ?

Answer boxes (right side): A, ☐, ☐, ☐, ☐

7. Write the number.

1 ☐ 3 ☐ ☐ ☐ ☐ ☐ ☐ 0

6

Read with the children:

Suppose you have 14 balloons. If you gave 10 balloons to a friend, how many balloons would you still have?

PLACE VALUE THROUGH 99

TENS AND ONES TO 15

10 ones   is   1 ten

Write how many tens and ones.
Then write the number.

1.

1 ten   **2** ones

12

2.

____ ten   ____ ones

____

3.

____ ten   ____ ones

____

4.

____ ten   ____ ones

____

5.

____ ten   ____ ones

____

6.

____ ten   ____ one

____

TENS AND ONES TO 19

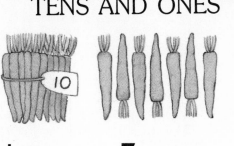

1 ten   **7** ones   is   17

Write how many tens and ones.
Then write the number.

1.
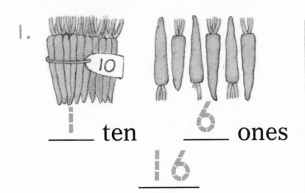

_1_ ten   _6_ ones

_16_

2.
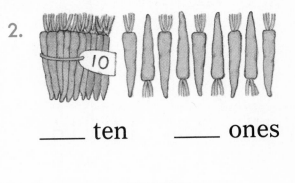

____ ten   ____ ones

____

3.
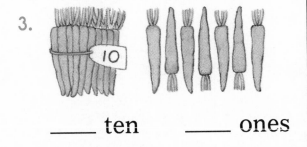

____ ten   ____ ones

____

4.
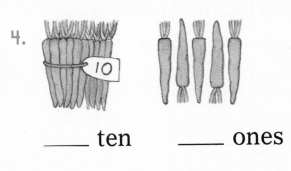

____ ten   ____ ones

____

5.
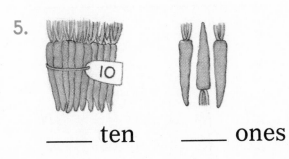

____ ten   ____ ones

____

6.
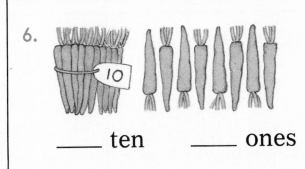

____ ten   ____ ones

____

Ring the number.

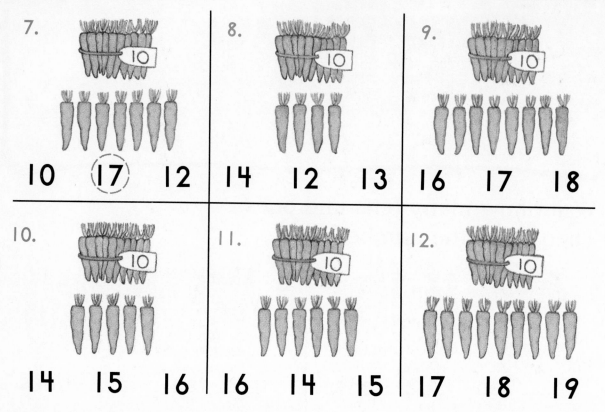

7. 10 (17) 12

8. 14 12 13

9. 16 17 18

10. 14 15 16

11. 16 14 15

12. 17 18 19

Write the number.

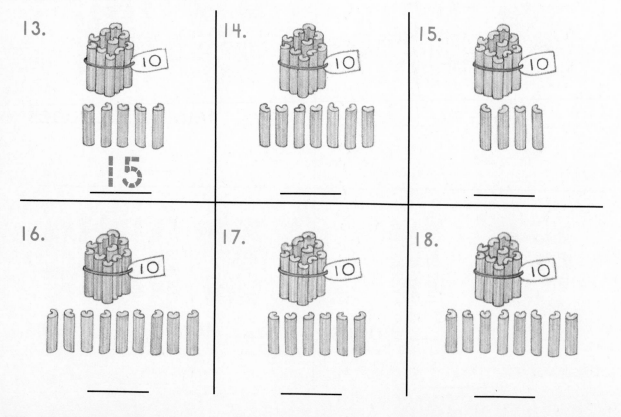

13. 15

14. _____

15. _____

16. _____

17. _____

18. _____

Identifying Tens and Ones to 19

TENS TO 90

7 tens is **7** tens **0** ones   **70**

Write how many tens and ones.
Then write the number.

1.

   __3__ tens __0__ ones

   __30__

2.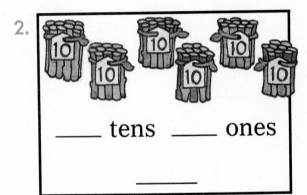

   ____ tens ____ ones

   ____

3.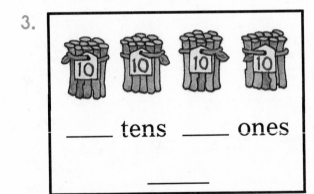

   ____ tens ____ ones

   ____

4.

   ____ tens ____ ones

   ____

5.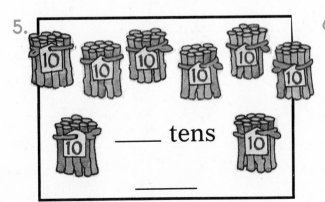

   ____ tens

   ____

6.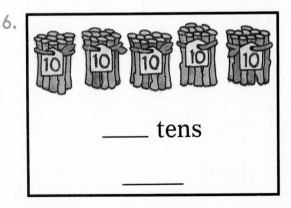

   ____ tens

   ____

Identifying Tens to 90

Write the number.

7.

_____

8.

_____

9.

_____

10. _____

Count by tens.
Write the missing numbers.

| 11. | 10 | 20 | 30 | 40 | 50 | | | | 90 |

| 12. | 10 | | | | | 60 | | | |

| 13. | | | 30 | | | | 70 | | |

| 14. | | 20 | | 40 | | | | | |

| 15. | 10 | | | | | | | | |

Identifying Tens to 90

NUMBERS TO 50

tens	ones
3	4

3 tens **4** ones

34

Write how many tens and ones.

1.

__2__ tens   __5__ ones

tens	ones
2	5

2.

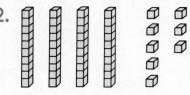

____ tens   ____ ones

tens	ones

3.

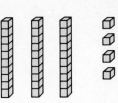

____ tens   ____ ones

tens	ones

4.

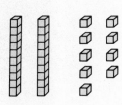

____ tens   ____ ones

tens	ones

Identifying Tens and Ones to 50

one hundred forty-one   **141**

Write how many tens and ones.
Then write the number.

5.

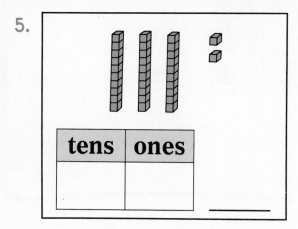

tens	ones

_____

6.

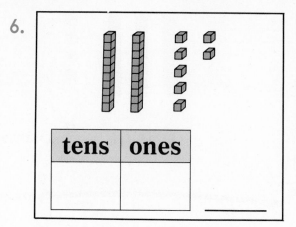

tens	ones

_____

7.

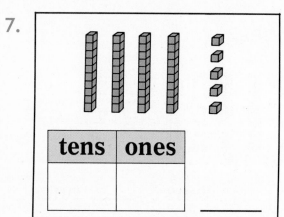

tens	ones

_____

8.

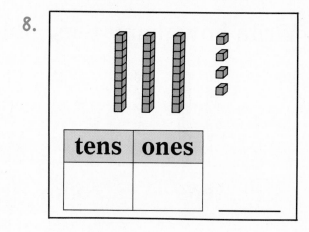

tens	ones

_____

How many in all?

9.

_____ chicks

10.

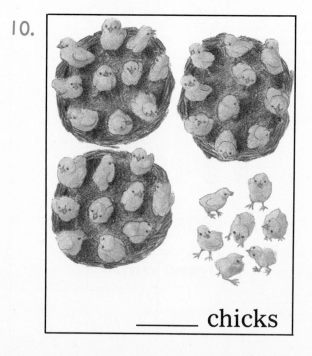

_____ chicks

Identifying Tens and Ones to 50

NUMBERS TO 80

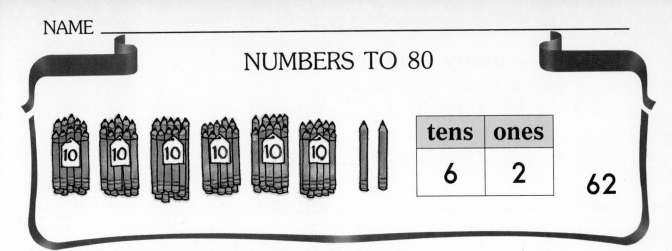

tens	ones
6	2

62

Write how many tens and ones.
Then write the number.

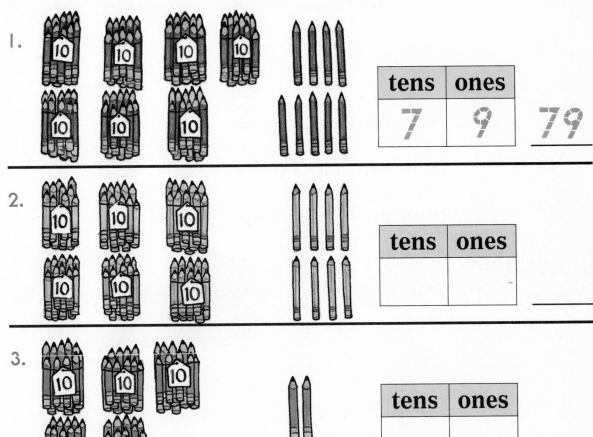

1.

tens	ones
7	9

79

2.

tens	ones

____

3.

tens	ones

____

4.

tens	ones

____

Identifying Tens and Ones to 80

Write how many tens and ones.

5. 65 = __6__ tens and __5__ ones

53 = ____ tens and ____ ones

34 = ____ tens and ____ ones

6. 48 = ____ tens and ____ ones

50 = ____ tens and ____ ones

75 = ____ tens and ____ ones

7. 56 = ____ tens and ____ ones

63 = ____ tens and ____ ones

77 = ____ tens and ____ ones

If you know **2 + 3 = 5**, then you know **2 + 4 = 6**. Add.

8.

| 4 + 1 = ____ | 3 + 3 = ____ | 5 + 2 = ____ |
| 4 + 2 = ____ | 3 + 4 = ____ | 5 + 3 = ____ |

9.

| 4 + 2 = ____ | 7 + 1 = ____ | 3 + 6 = ____ |
| 4 + 3 = ____ | 7 + 2 = ____ | 3 + 7 = ____ |

TRY THIS: Use punchouts to show tens and ones.

NUMBERS TO 99

tens	ones
9	4

94

Write how many tens and ones.
Then write the number.

1.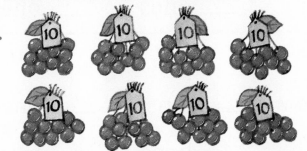

tens	ones
8	3

83 ___

2.

tens	ones

___

3.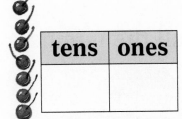

tens	ones

___

4.

tens	ones

___

Write how many tens and ones.

5.

38	64	75	19
__3__ tens	___ ones	___ ones	___ ten
__8__ ones	___ tens	___ tens	___ ones

6.

29	47	57	62
___ tens	___ ones	___ tens	___ tens
___ ones	___ tens	___ ones	___ ones

7.

73	97	86	59
___ ones	___ tens	___ tens	___ ones
___ tens	___ ones	___ ones	___ tens

☆ Color all the numbers in the **60**'s.

8.

68 62 70 65 73 32 67 69 56 65

146 one hundred forty-six

TRY THIS: Problem Solving Activities, page 398.

ORDER TO 100

1. Write the missing numbers.

1	2	3			6				10
11		13				17			20
21			24				28		
			34			37			
41							48		50
					56				
								69	
	72								
		93							100

Write the missing numbers.

2.

61		63

63		65

66		68

3.

90		92

89		91

97		99

4.

32		34

35		37

38		40

5.

61	62			66			69	

Write the next number.

6. 29 ____   59 ____   19 ____   99 ____

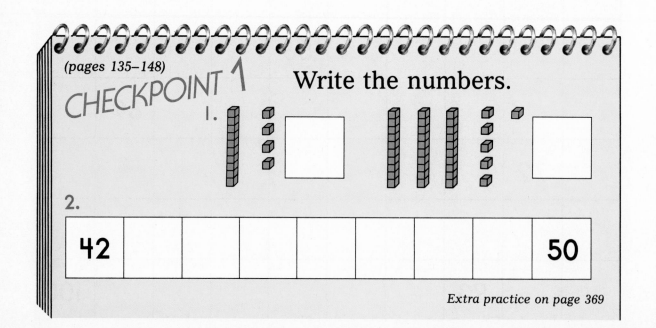

(pages 135–148)

CHECKPOINT 1

Write the numbers.

1.

2.

42								50

Extra practice on page 369

Ordering Numbers through 99

PROBLEM SOLVING

The **graph** shows how many pets.

PETS

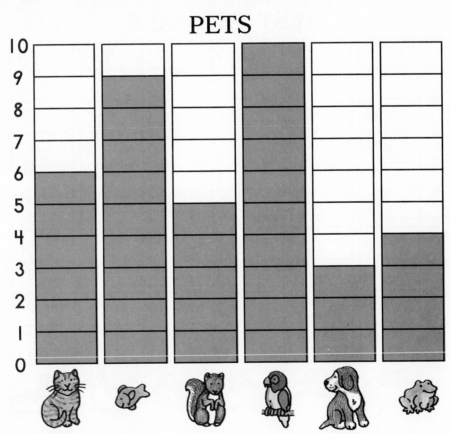

Write how many.

 1. _6_

2. _____

3. _____

4. _____

5. _____

6. _____

7. Color boxes to show how many.

FOREST ANIMALS

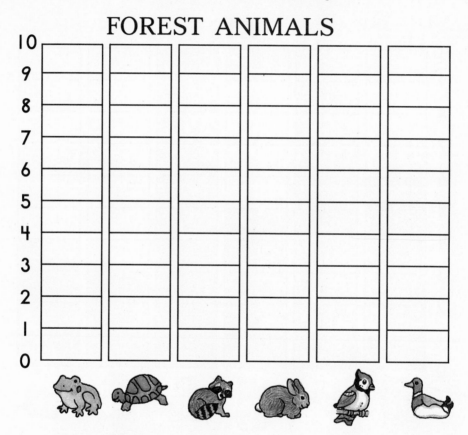

Write how many. Then add.

8. _____ + _____ = _____ in all.

9. _____ + _____ = _____ in all.

10. _____ + _____ = _____ in all.

DISCUSS: The pets the children have. Make a graph.

GREATER THAN

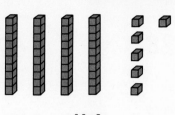

62   **46**

62 is **greater than 46**

Write the numbers.
Then ring the number that is greater.

1.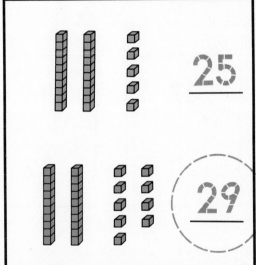

2.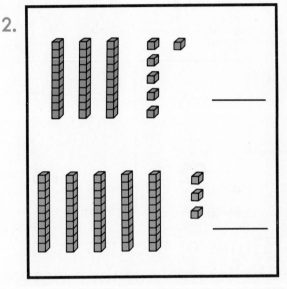

3.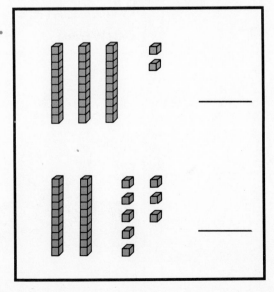

4.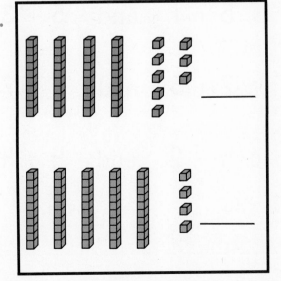

Ring the number that is greater.

5.

28	62	71	96
(37)	56	83	86

6.

37	13	25	34
53	19	26	73

7.

56	87	37	46
92	78	30	52

Think of the two sums.
Write the number between the sums.

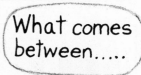

What comes between.....

8. 5 + 1   and   5 + 3   ____

9. 2 + 5   and   2 + 7   ____

10. 4 + 2   and   4 + 4   ____

LESS THAN

56   **72**

56 is **less than** 72

Write the numbers.
Then ring the number that is less.

1.
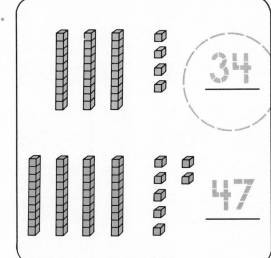
34

47

2.
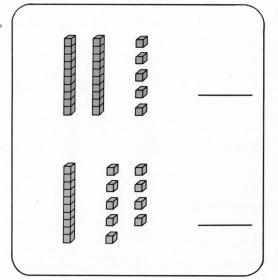
___

___

3.
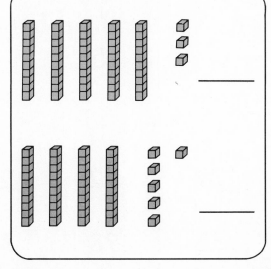
___

___

4.
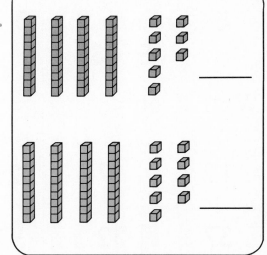
___

___

Ring the number that is less.

5. 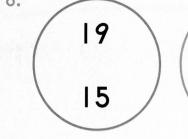 **25** **32** **39** **93** **56** **59** **38** **26**

6. **19** **15** **31** **29** **44** **45** **58** **68**

7. **66** **56** **92** **98** **78** **69** **85** **73**

5 is greater than **3**
    5 > 3

3 is less than **5**
    3 < 5

 Write > or <.

8. 12 [<] 17   25 [ ] 37   42 [ ] 26

9. 37 [ ] 32   47 [ ] 65   98 [ ] 89

ORDINALS

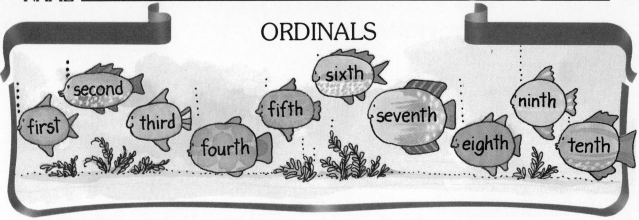

Ring the correct animal.

1.

first

2.

fourth

3.

seventh

4.

eighth

5.

tenth

Color the correct objects.

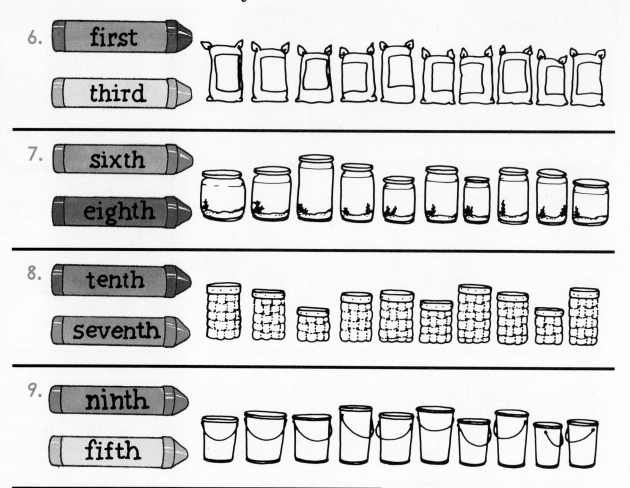

6. first
   third

7. sixth
   eighth

8. tenth
   seventh

9. ninth
   fifth

Write the number.

10. Lila has **4** boxes of berries.
    Each box holds **10** berries.
    How many berries
    does she have? ☐ berries

11. How many berries would
    fill **8** boxes? ☐ berries

PROBLEM SOLVING

Ring what comes next.

1.

2.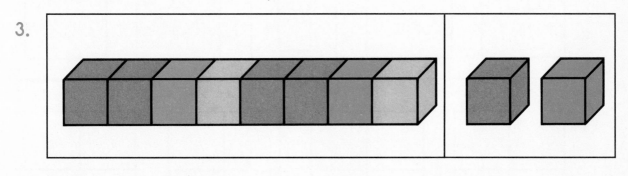

3.

4. | 10 | 20 | 30 | 40 | 50 | 60 | 80 | 70 |

Draw what comes next.

5.

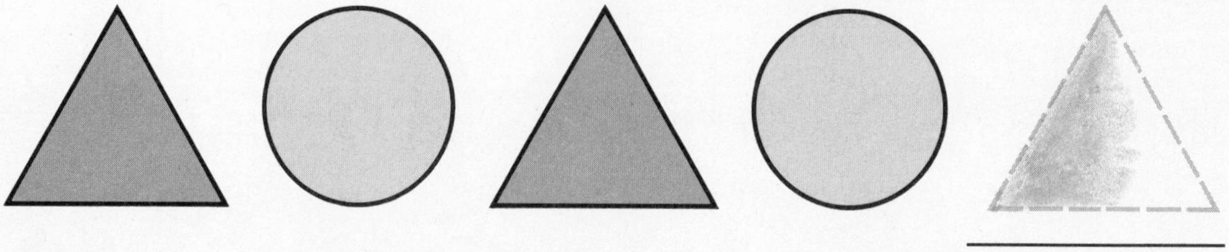

△ ○ △ ○ △

_____

6.

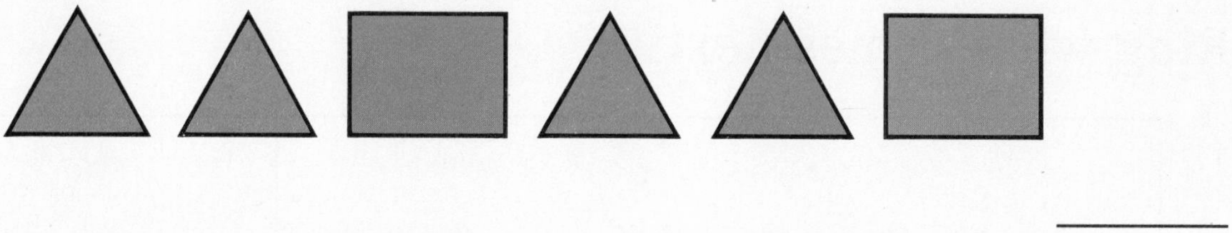

△ △ ■ △ △ ■

_____

7.

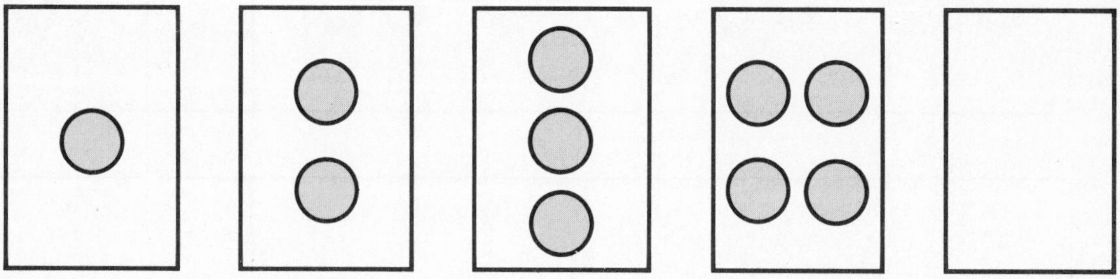

8.

9.

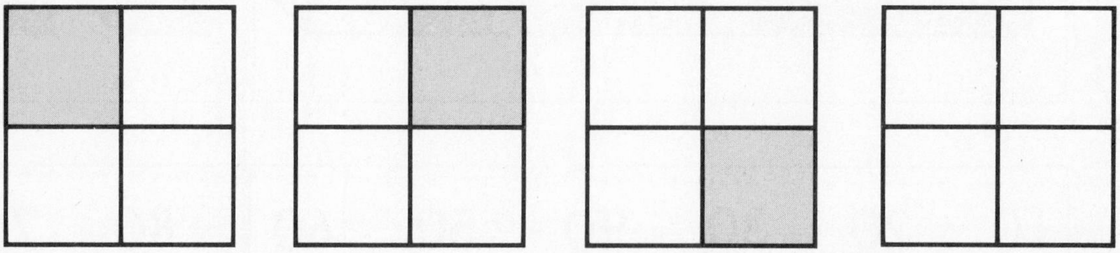

PARTNERS: Use punchouts to make patterns.

COUNTING BY TWOS

| 2 | 4 | 6 | 8 | 10 | 12 |

Count by twos. Ring the numbers.

1.

1	2	3	4	5	6	7	8	9	10
11	12	13	14	15	16	17	18	19	20
21	22	23	24	25	26	27	28	29	30
31	32	33	34	35	36	37	38	39	40

Count by twos.
Write the numbers.

2.

2, 4, _6_, _____, _____, _____, _____, _____, _____

3.

34, 36, _____, _____, _____, _____, _____, _____, _____

4.

56, 58, _____, _____, _____, _____, _____, _____, _____

5. Count by twos to connect the dots in order.

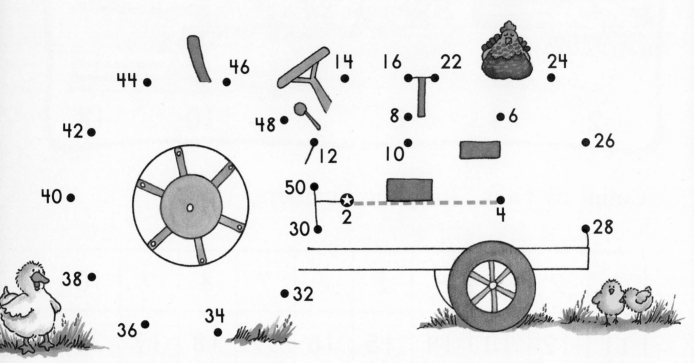

18 20
44 46 14 16 22 24
42 48 8 6
12 10 26
50 2 4
30 28
38 32
36 34

(pages 149–160)

CHECKPOINT 2

1. Ring the number that is greater.

17	23		37	29		78	68

2. Count by twos.

2				

3. Ring the third flower.

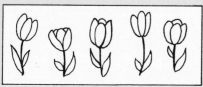

4. Draw what comes next.

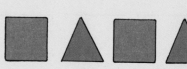

Extra practice on page 369

Counting by Twos

CHAPTER 6 TEST

Write the number.

1. 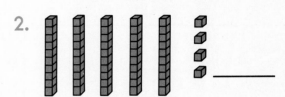 _____

2. _____

Write the missing numbers.

3. 51, 52, ____, 54, ____, ____, 57, ____, 59

4. 12, 14, ____, ____, ____, ____, ____

Ring the number that is less.

5. 23   12   31   36   46   36

Ring the third animal.

6.

Look at the graph. Write how many.

BIRDS

7. How many 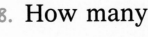 ? ____

8. How many ? ____

Extra practice on page 370

MATHEMATICS and LANGUAGE

ten	10	one	1
twenty	20	two	2
thirty	30	three	3
forty	40	four	4
fifty	50	five	5
sixty	60	six	6
seventy	70	seven	7
eighty	80	eight	8
ninety	90	nine	9

Write the number for the word.

1. sixty-nine __69__   fifty-three _____

2. forty-eight _____   thirty-six _____

3. seventy-two _____   eighty-five _____

4. sixty-seven _____   ninety-one _____

Write the word for the number.

5. 61 __sixty-one__   43 _____

6. 97 _____   82 _____

7. 56 _____   35 _____

8. 29 _____   78 _____

NAME _____

Enrichment

| 2 | 4 | 6 | 8 | 10 |

are **even** numbers.

| 1 | 3 | 5 | 7 | 9 |

are **odd** numbers.

Write the next **4** odd numbers.

1. 1   3   5   7   9 ___ ___ ___ ___

2. 21   23   25   27 ___ ___ ___ ___

3. 37   39   41   43 ___ ___ ___ ___

4. 45   47   49   51 ___ ___ ___ ___

Write the next **4** even numbers.

5. 0   2   4   6   8 ___ ___ ___ ___

6. 20   22   24   26 ___ ___ ___ ___

7. 34   36   38   40 ___ ___ ___ ___

8. 50   52   54   56 ___ ___ ___ ___

Odd and Even Numbers

9. Color the odd numbers 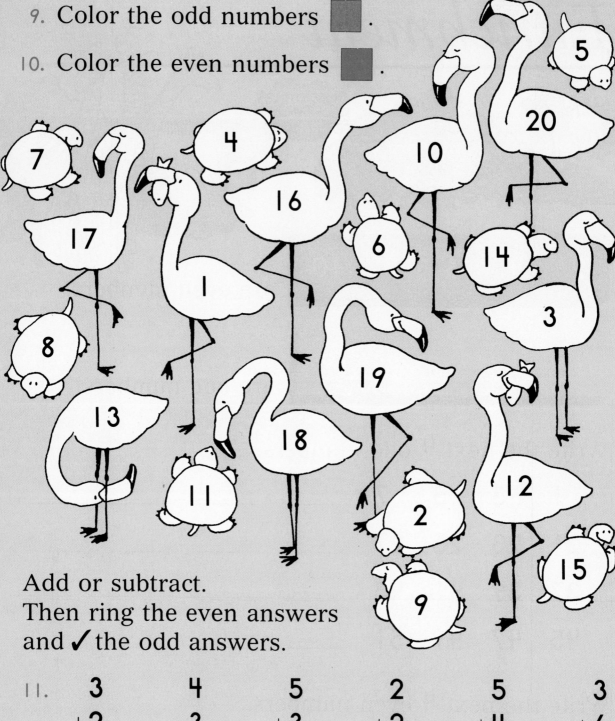.

10. Color the even numbers .

Add or subtract.
Then ring the even answers
and ✓ the odd answers.

11.

3	4	5	2	5	3
+2	−3	+3	+2	+4	+6
✓5					

12.

5	8	9	4	6	7
+4	−6	−6	+4	−6	−3

Enrichment: Odd and Even Numbers

CUMULATIVE REVIEW

Fill in the ⬭ for the correct answer.

Add.

1. $7 + 0$	2. $6 + 4$	3. $5 + 3$
0 6 7	8 10 2	2 8 5
Ⓐ Ⓑ Ⓒ	Ⓐ Ⓑ Ⓒ	Ⓐ Ⓑ Ⓒ
4. $\begin{array}{r} 8 \\ +1 \\ \hline \end{array}$	5. $\begin{array}{r} 3 \\ +7 \\ \hline \end{array}$	6. $\begin{array}{r} 6 \\ +2 \\ \hline \end{array}$
7 8 9	4 10 7	6 8 4
Ⓐ Ⓑ Ⓒ	Ⓐ Ⓑ Ⓒ	Ⓐ Ⓑ Ⓒ

How much in all?

7.

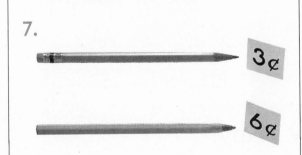

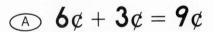

3¢

6¢

- Ⓐ $6¢ + 3¢ = 9¢$
- Ⓑ $6¢ + 3¢ = 3¢$
- Ⓒ $3¢ + 3¢ = 6¢$

8.

2¢

8¢

- Ⓐ $8¢ + 2¢ = 6¢$
- Ⓑ $2¢ + 2¢ = 4¢$
- Ⓒ $8¢ + 2¢ = 10¢$

Subtract.

9.	10.	11.
$\begin{array}{r} 9 \\ -1 \\ \hline \end{array}$	$\begin{array}{r} 8 \\ -4 \\ \hline \end{array}$	$\begin{array}{r} 10 \\ -7 \\ \hline \end{array}$
8 10 7 (A) (B) (C)	6 8 4 (A) (B) (C)	3 2 1 (A) (B) (C)
12.	13.	14.
10 − 4	7 − 5	9 − 0
6 8 4 (A) (B) (C)	1 2 5 (A) (B) (C)	0 9 10 (A) (B) (C)

LANGUAGE and VOCABULARY REVIEW

Ring the sentence if it is correct.

1. (**5** is less than **7**.)

2. **29** is greater than **63**.

3. A graph may show how many.

4. You say **1**, **2**, **3**, **4**, **5** when you count by twos.

5. **5** tens make **60**.

6. **27** is **2** tens and **7** ones.

☆ 7. **2 + 2** is one less than **2 + 3**.

Read with the children:

What is the toll?
A quarter is worth **25¢**.
If five red cars and three
blue cars each pay
the toll, how many
quarters is that?

7

MONEY

PENNY AND NICKEL

penny		nickel
1 cent		**5** cents
1¢		**5**¢

Write the amount.

1.

 _____ ¢

2.

_____ ¢

3.

_____ ¢

4.

_____ ¢

5.

_____ ¢

6.

_____ ¢

7.

_____ ¢

8.

_____ ¢

9.

_____ ¢

Penny and Nickel

COUNTING BY FIVES

(**Think**) 5¢ 10¢ 15¢ 20¢ 25¢ _30_¢

Count by fives.

1.

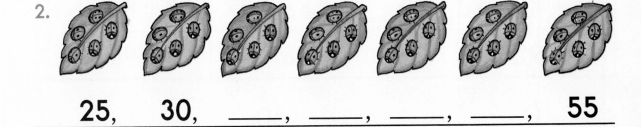

5, 10, __15__, __20__, __25__, __30__, 35

2.

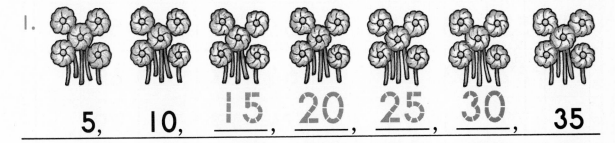

25, 30, ____, ____, ____, ____, 55

3.

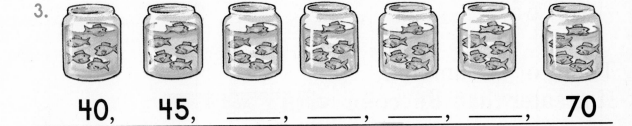

40, 45, ____, ____, ____, ____, 70

4.

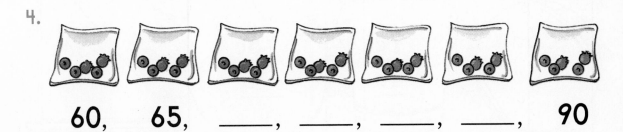

60, 65, ____, ____, ____, ____, 90

Count by fives.

5.

1	2	3	4	5	6	7	8	9	10
11	12	13	14		16	17	18	19	
21	22	23	24		26	27	28	29	
31	32	33	34		36	37	38	39	
41	42	43	44		46	47	48	49	
51	52	53	54		56	57	58	59	
61	62	63	64		66	67	68	69	
71	72	73	74		76	77	78	79	
81	82	83	84		86	87	88	89	
91	92	93	94		96	97	98	99	100

6. 5, 10, 15, ____, ____, 30, ____, ____, ____

7. 60, 65, ____, ____, ____, ____, 90, ____, ____

Think of the amount.
If greater than 8¢, color ▨ Red

8.
6¢
+3¢
‾‾‾

9.
7¢
−4¢
‾‾‾

10.
6¢
+4¢
‾‾‾

11.
5¢
+4¢
‾‾‾

170   one hundred seventy

Counting by Fives

DIME

Count by tens to find the amount.

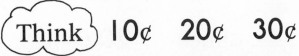

dime
10 cents
10¢

Think 10¢ 20¢ 30¢ ___40___ ¢

Write the amount.

1.

_____ ¢

2.

_____ ¢

3.

_____ ¢

4.

_____ ¢

5.

_____ ¢

6.

_____ ¢

Identifying Value of Dimes

Write the number.

7. 30¢ = <u>3</u> dimes   50¢ = ___ dimes

8. 60¢ = ___ dimes   70¢ = ___ dimes

9. 80¢ = ___ dimes   40¢ = ___ dimes

10. 90¢ = ___ dimes   20¢ = ___ dimes

11. 3 dimes = <u>30</u> ¢   6 dimes = ___ ¢

12. 7 dimes = ___ ¢   9 dimes = ___ ¢

13. 2 dimes = ___ ¢   6 dimes = ___ ¢

Ring enough dimes.

Juice 10¢ A Glass

14.

15.

16.

PARTNERS: Make up problems. Use play money to solve. Discuss your answers.

NICKEL AND DIME

Count by tens and fives to find the amount.

(Think) 10¢   20¢   25¢   30¢

Write the amount.

1.

10 ¢   20 ¢   25 ¢   30 ¢   35 ¢

2.

_____ ¢   _____ ¢   _____ ¢   _____ ¢   _____ ¢

3.

_____ ¢   _____ ¢   _____ ¢   _____ ¢   _____ ¢   _____ ¢

4.

_____ ¢   _____ ¢   _____ ¢   _____ ¢   _____ ¢   _____ ¢

Ring the coins to show the amount.

5. **30¢**

6. **40¢**

7. **30¢**

8. **40¢**

9. **20¢**

10. **50¢**

Use play money.
⭐ Write the number.

11. **1** dime = **2** nickels

12. **3** dimes = _____ nickels

13. **4** nickels = _____ dimes

Identifying Value of Nickels and Dimes

NAME _____

COUNTING MONEY

Count by tens, fives, and ones to find the amount.

(Think) 10¢   20¢   25¢   30¢   35¢   36¢   _37_ ¢

Write the amount.

1.

_10_¢   _20_¢   _25_¢   _30_¢   _35_¢

2.

____¢ ____¢ ____¢ ____¢ ____¢

3.

____¢ ____¢ ____¢ ____¢ ____¢ ____¢

4.

____¢ ____¢ ____¢ ____¢ ____¢ ____¢

Counting Pennies, Nickels, and Dimes   one hundred seventy-five   175

Write the amount.

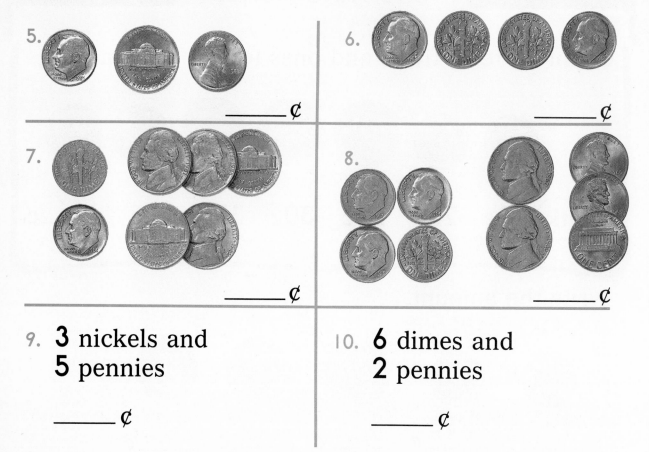

5. _____ ¢

6. _____ ¢

7. _____ ¢

8. _____ ¢

9. **3** nickels and **5** pennies

_____ ¢

10. **6** dimes and **2** pennies

_____ ¢

(pages 167–176)

CHECKPOINT 1

Write the amount.

1. _____ ¢

2. _____ ¢

3. Count by fives.

5	10				

Extra practice on page 371

Counting Pennies, Nickels, and Dimes

PROBLEM SOLVING

You have **75¢**.

You could buy  35¢ or  50¢ or 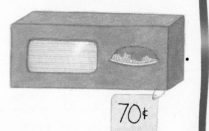 70¢ .

You could not buy  97¢ .

Ring any of the items you could buy.

1. You have **45¢**.

40¢
30¢
35¢
55¢

2. You have **70¢**.

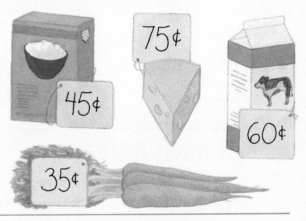

75¢
45¢
60¢
35¢

3. You have **95¢**.

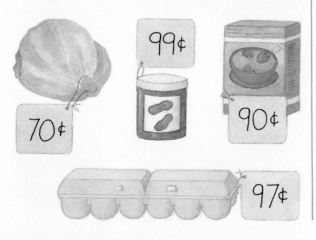

99¢
70¢
90¢
97¢

4. You have **85¢**.

90¢
80¢
60¢
75¢

Ring the items you can buy.

5.

6. You have **40¢**.

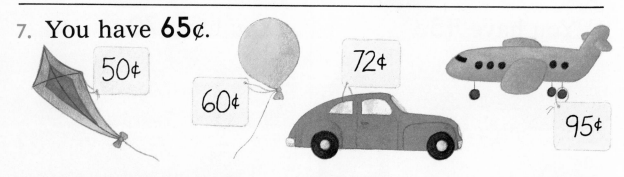

7. You have **65¢**.

8. You have **8** dimes.

9. You have **9** dimes.

TRY THIS: Use play money to show amounts.

QUARTER

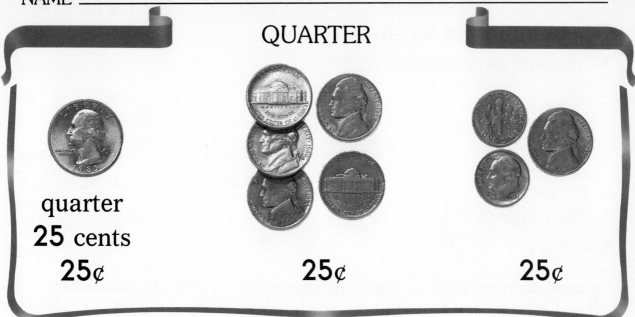

quarter
25 cents
25¢   **25**¢   **25**¢

Ring coins to show **25**¢.

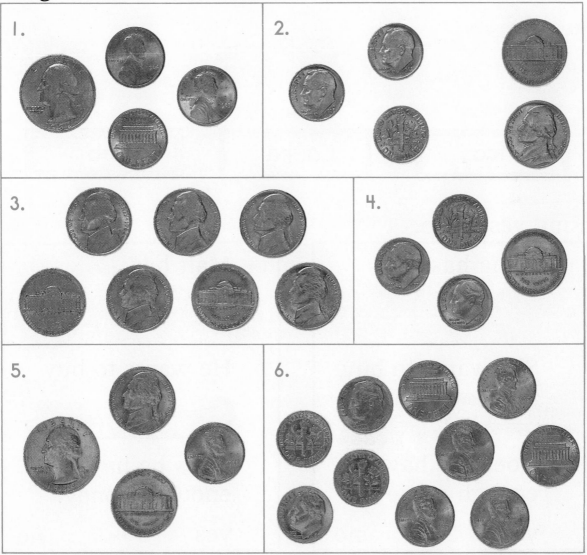

1.

2.

3.

4.

5.

6.

Identifying Value of Quarter   one hundred seventy-nine   **179**

Ring the name to show who can buy an orange.

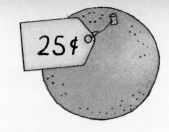

25¢

7.

Steve

8.

Marcia

9.

Jan

10.

Linda

11.

Laura

12.

Bob

Ring yes or no.

13. Anna has

She wants to buy

15¢

Does she have
enough money?

yes   no

14. Matt has

He wants to buy

40¢

Does he have
enough money?

yes   no

Identifying Value of Quarter

COUNTING MONEY

Start with **25¢**.
Then count by tens and fives to find the amount.

Think   **25¢**   **35¢**   **45¢**   **50¢**   _____ **55** ¢

Write the amount.

45¢ in all

1.

25 ¢   **35** ¢   **45** ¢
_____

2.

_____ ¢   _____ ¢   _____ ¢   _____ ¢   _____ ¢

3.

_____ ¢   _____ ¢   _____ ¢   _____ ¢   _____ ¢

4.

_____ ¢   _____ ¢   _____ ¢   _____ ¢   _____ ¢   _____ ¢

Counting Nickels, Dimes, and Quarters

Write the amount.

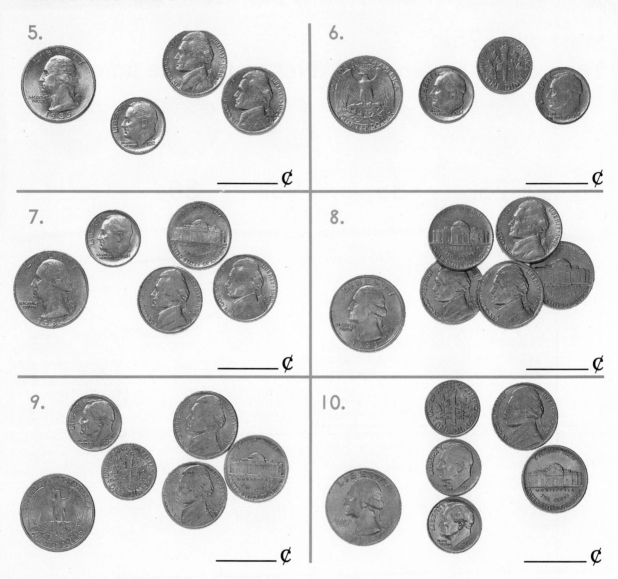

5. _____ ¢

6. _____ ¢

7. _____ ¢

8. _____ ¢

9. _____ ¢

10. _____ ¢

☆ Ring the greater amount.

11. **2** or **5**

12. **8** or **1**

13. **1** or **11**

14. **3** or **10**

15. **3** or **4**

16. **2** or **19**

Counting Nickels, Dimes, and Quarters

COUNTING MONEY

Start with **25¢**.
Then count by tens, fives, and ones
to find the amount.

(Think)　**25¢**　　**35¢**　　**40¢**　　**41¢**　　_42_¢

Write the amount.

1.

_25_ ¢　_35_ ¢　_45_ ¢　_46_ ¢

2.

     (and one more)

_____ ¢　_____ ¢　_____ ¢　_____ ¢　_____ ¢　_____ ¢

3.

_____ ¢　_____ ¢　_____ ¢　_____ ¢　_____ ¢　_____ ¢

4.

_____ ¢　_____ ¢　_____ ¢　_____ ¢　_____ ¢　_____ ¢

Write the amount.

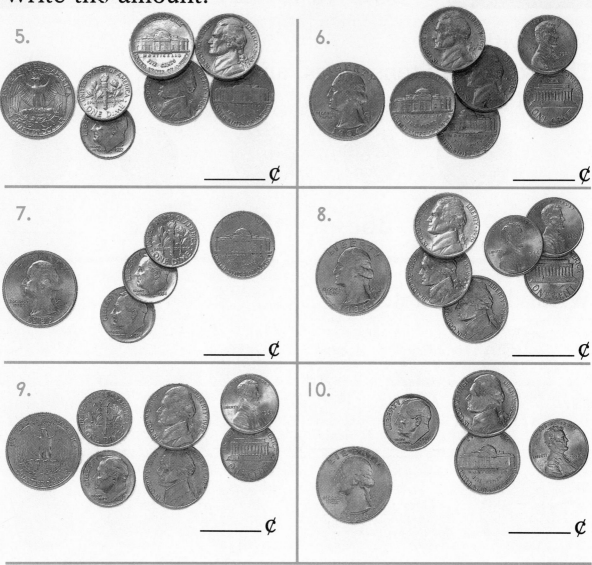

5. _____ ¢

6. _____ ¢

7. _____ ¢

8. _____ ¢

9. _____ ¢

10. _____ ¢

11. Tom has

He buys **35¢**

Ring the coins he has left.

12. Sarah has

She buys **45¢**

Ring the coins she has left.

DISCUSS: Different sets of coins that make 50¢.

COMPARING MONEY

Different sets of coins will buy the toy.

40¢   40¢

Ring the coins to show the amount.

1. 17¢   17¢

2. 23¢   23¢

3. 31¢   31¢

Write the amount. Can you trade the amount? Ring yes or no.

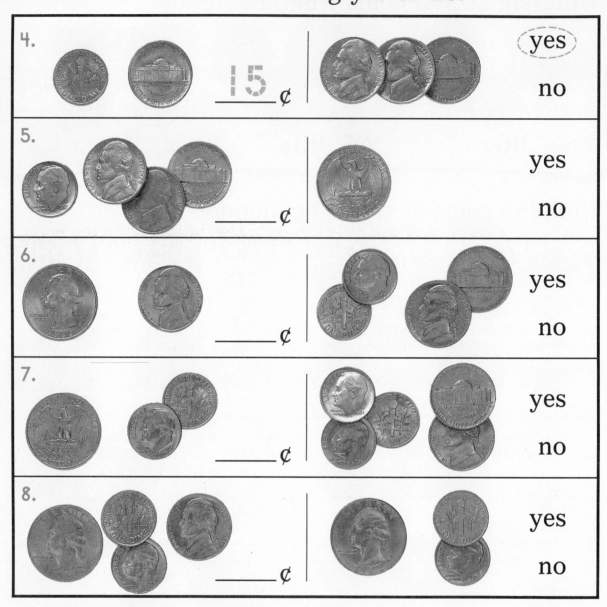

4. _15_ ¢ — (yes) / no

5. _____ ¢ — yes / no

6. _____ ¢ — yes / no

7. _____ ¢ — yes / no

8. _____ ¢ — yes / no

Think of the amount.
If less than **5¢**, color 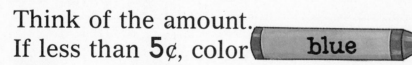 **blue** .

9.
7¢
−4¢
_____

10.
10¢
− 2¢
_____

11.
6¢
−3¢
_____

12.
2¢
+7¢
_____

TRY THIS: Problem Solving Activities, page 399.

PROBLEM SOLVING

Find the number pattern.

2	4	6	8	10	12	14	16

Continue the number pattern.

1. A ones pattern.

   25, 26, 27, 28 **, ____, ____, ____**

2. A twos pattern.

   23, 25, 27, ____, ____, ____, ____

3. A fives pattern.

   45, 50, 55, ____, ____, ____, ____

4. A tens pattern.

   37, 47, 57, ____, ____, ____, ____

5. A pattern that repeats.

   1, 2, 1, 2, 1, 2, ____, ____, ____, ____, ____, ____

Continue the number pattern.

6. **23, 25, 27,** ____, ____, ____, ____

7. **21, 22, 23,** ____, ____, ____, ____

8. **4, 5, 5, 4, 5, 5, 4, 5,** ____, ____, ____, ____

9. **65, 70, 75,** ____, ____, ____, ____, ____

10. **2, 3, 5, 2, 3, 5, 2,** ____, ____, ____, ____, ____

(pages 177–188)

CHECKPOINT 2

Write the amount.

1. ☐ ¢

Continue the number pattern.

2. **1 2 3 1 2 3 1** ☐ ☐ ☐

Extra practice on page 371

Problem Solving

CHAPTER 7 TEST

Count by fives.

1. **5, 10,** _____, _____, _____, _____, _____, _____

Ring the coins to show the amount.

2. **50¢**

Write the amount.

3.    _____ ¢

Write the amount.

4.    _____ ¢

Continue the number pattern.

5. **35, 37, 39,** _____, _____, _____, _____

6. **39, 49, 59,** _____, _____, _____, _____

Extra practice on page 372

MATHEMATICS and HEALTH

You can save money if you buy .

Ring the one that costs less.

1.

   75¢   **69¢**

2.

   80¢   **85¢**

3.

   35¢   **32¢**

4.

   92¢   **93¢**

5.

   79¢   **83¢**

6.

   69¢   **65¢**

Enrichment

Name the coins to make the amount.
Use the number of coins given.

1.	**20¢**	10¢	10¢		
2.	**20¢**	◯	◯	◯	
3.	**25¢**	◯	◯	◯	◯
4.	**25¢**	◯	◯	◯	
5.	**30¢**	◯	◯	◯	
6.	**30¢**	◯	◯	◯	◯ ◯

Logical Reasoning

Name the coins to make
the amount.
Use the number of coins given.

7.	50¢	○	○		
8.	50¢	○	○	○	○
9.	60¢	○	○	○	
10.	60¢	○	○	○	○
11.	75¢	○	○	○	
12.	75¢	○	○	○	○ ○

CUMULATIVE REVIEW

Fill in the ◯ for the correct answer.

How many tens and ones?

1.　　43	2.　　82
Ⓐ **3** tens **4** ones	Ⓐ **8** tens **2** ones
Ⓑ **4** tens **3** ones	Ⓑ **2** tens **8** ones
Ⓒ **4** tens **4** ones	Ⓒ **2** tens **2** ones

Choose the missing numbers.

3. **55**, ___?___, ___?___, **58**	4. **78**, ___?___, ___?___, **81**
Ⓐ **52, 53**	Ⓐ **77, 76**
Ⓑ **57, 56**	Ⓑ **79, 80**
Ⓒ **56, 57**	Ⓒ **80, 90**

Choose the number that is greater.

5. **51**　　**35**	6. **64**　　**68**	7. **62**　　**72**
51　**35**　**15**	**68**　**46**　**64**	**27**　**62**　**72**
Ⓐ　Ⓑ　Ⓒ	Ⓐ　Ⓑ　Ⓒ	Ⓐ　Ⓑ　Ⓒ

Choose the number that is less.

8. **85**　　**43**	9. **57**　　**67**	10. **19**　　**18**
85　**43**　**34**	**57**　**77**　**67**	**81**　**18**　**19**
Ⓐ　Ⓑ　Ⓒ	Ⓐ　Ⓑ　Ⓒ	Ⓐ　Ⓑ　Ⓒ

PLAYTHINGS AT THE PARK

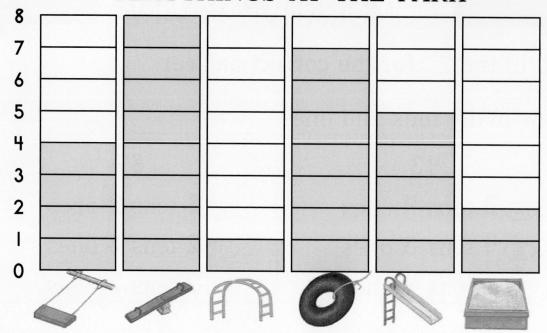

Use the graph to choose the number.

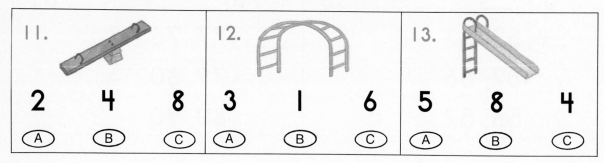

11.	12.	13.
2 (A) 4 (B) 8 (C)	3 (A) 1 (B) 6 (C)	5 (A) 8 (B) 4 (C)

LANGUAGE and VOCABULARY REVIEW

Match the word with the amount.

1. penny   5¢   five cents

2. quarter   10¢   one cent

3. nickel   1¢   ten cents

4. dime   25¢   twenty-five cents

Language and Vocabulary Review

Read with the children:

What time of the day do you think it is?
What do you do in the morning?
What do you do in the afternoon?
What do you do at night?

TIME

THE CLOCK

A **clock** tells us the time.

1. Write the numbers on the clock.

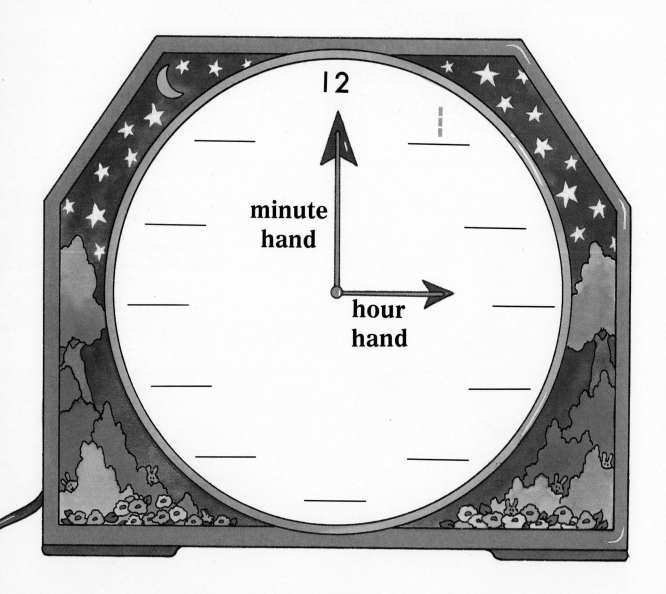

2. The minute hand is on the _____.

3. The hour hand is on the _____.

Identifying Minute and Hour Hands

HOUR

The clock tells us it is **4 o'clock.**

The minute hand is on the __12__.

The hour hand is on the __4__.

What time is it?

1.

__7__ o'clock

_____ o'clock

_____ o'clock

2.

_____ o'clock

_____ o'clock

_____ o'clock

3.

_____ o'clock

_____ o'clock

_____ o'clock

Show the time. Draw the hands.

4.

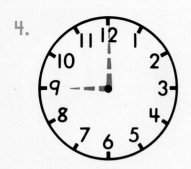
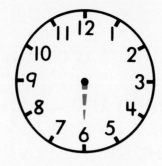

9 o'clock   **6** o'clock   **11** o'clock

5.

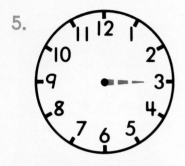

3 o'clock   **7** o'clock   **8** o'clock

☆ Show the time.

6. one hour **later**

7. one hour **earlier**

TRY THIS: Use punchout clocks to show times.

HOUR

Both clocks tell us the time.

9 o'clock   **9** o'clock

What time is it?

1.
| 3:00 | 10:00 | 6:00 |

<u> 3 </u> o'clock   _____ o'clock   _____ o'clock

<u>3:00</u>   ____ : ____   ____ : ____

2.
| 12:00 | 4:00 | 1:00 |

_____ o'clock   _____ o'clock   _____ o'clock

____ : ____   ____ : ____   ____ : ____

3.
| 2:00 | 11:00 | 7:00 |

_____ o'clock   _____ o'clock   _____ o'clock

____ : ____   ____ : ____   ____ : ____

What time is it?

4.

_____ o'clock   _____ o'clock   _____ o'clock

_____ : _____   _____ : _____   _____ : _____

5.

_____ o'clock   _____ o'clock   _____ o'clock

_____ : _____   _____ : _____   _____ : _____

6.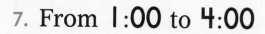

_____ o'clock   _____ o'clock   _____ o'clock

_____ : _____   _____ : _____   _____ : _____

Is it more than two hours?
Ring yes or no.

7. From **1:00** to **4:00**   yes   no

8. From **8:00** to **9:00**   yes   no

9. From **2:00** to **7:00**   yes   no

Telling Time to the Hour

HALF-HOUR

two o'clock
2:00

two thirty
2:30

BOAT RIDES ARE
EVERY HALF HOUR

What time is it?

1.

9:00 9:30

2.

___:___ ___:___

3.

___:___ ___:___

4.

___:___ ___:___

5.

___:___ ___:___

6.

___:___ ___:___

Show the time. Draw the hands.

7.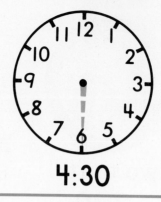

5:30 4:30 3:30

8.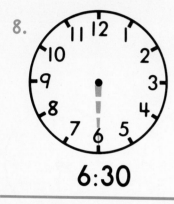

6:30 8:30 2:30

9. Rico went to the store at **8:00**.
Show the time.

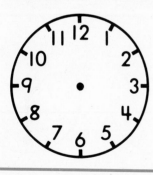 

10. Jill met her friends at **2:00**.
Show the time.

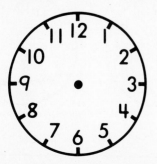 

TRY THIS: Problem Solving Activities, page 400.

HALF-HOUR
Both clocks tell us the time.

twelve thirty
12:30

Ring the clock with the correct time.

1.

2.

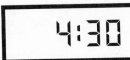   

3.

4.

Match.

5.

`10:30`   (clock)

`2:30`   (clock)

`9:30`   (clock)

`12:30`   (clock)

`3:30`   (clock)

6.

`4:30`   (clock)

`11:30`   (clock)

`1:30`   (clock)

`7:30`   (clock)

`6:30`   (clock)

☆ Ring the correct answer.

7. Your school bus comes at **8:00**.
You get to the bus stop at **7:30**.

Are you   early?   late?   on time?

Telling Time to the Half-Hour

HOUR AND HALF-HOUR

1:00

What time is it?

1.

____:____   ____:____   ____:____   ____:____

2.

____:____   ____:____   ____:____   ____:____

3.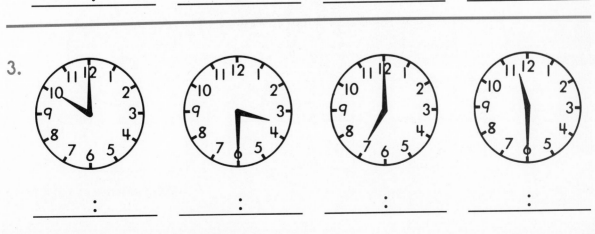

____:____   ____:____   ____:____   ____:____

Show the time. Draw the hands.

4.

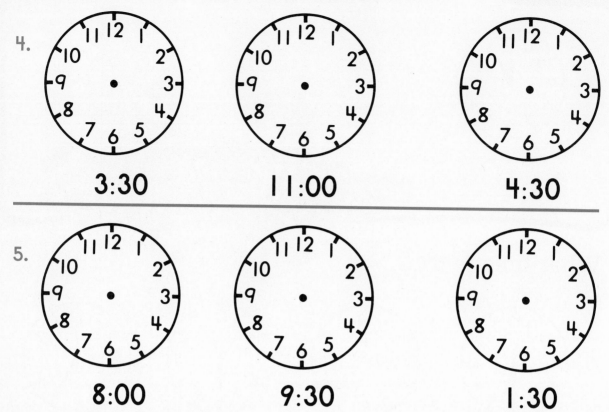

3:30   11:00   4:30

5.

8:00   9:30   1:30

(pages 195–206)

CHECKPOINT 1

What time is it?

:   :   :

Extra practice on page 373

PARTNERS: Tell a story.

PROBLEM SOLVING

Bob had breakfast at **7:00**.
He got to school one hour later.
What time was it?

___8___ o'clock

WEST
SCHOOL

Solve. Write the time.

1.

   Jan began to paint at **3:00**.
   She stopped two hours later.
   What time did she stop?

   _____ o'clock

2.

   Myo went shopping at **2:00**.
   She got home one hour later.
   What time was it?

   _____ o'clock

3.

   Luis started reading at **5:00**.
   He read for two hours.
   What time did he stop?

   _____ o'clock

Solve.

4. Sue began to practice at 10:00.
She finished one hour later.
What time was it?

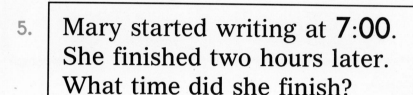

_____ o'clock

5. Mary started writing at 7:00.
She finished two hours later.
What time did she finish?

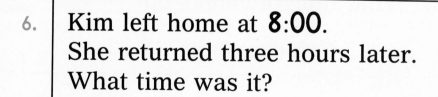

_____ o'clock

6. Kim left home at 8:00.
She returned three hours later.
What time was it?

_____ o'clock

★ 7. Roy started playing at 3:00.
He stopped at 6:00.
How long did he play?

_____ hours

Problem Solving

DAYS OF THE WEEK

February						
Sunday	Monday	Tuesday	Wednesday	Thursday	Friday	Saturday
1	2	3	4	5	6	7
8	9	10	11	12	13	14
15	16	17	18	19	20	21
22	23	24	25	26	27	28

1. How many days are in a week? _____

Ring the next day.

2. Friday	Wednesday	(Saturday)	Sunday
3. Wednesday	Tuesday	Friday	Thursday
4. Saturday	Sunday	Monday	Friday

Ring the day before.

5. Monday	Tuesday	Sunday	Wednesday
6. Tuesday	Wednesday	Sunday	Monday
7. Sunday	Saturday	Monday	Tuesday

Identifying Days of the Week; Calendar

8. Write the missing numbers.

February						
Sunday	Monday	Tuesday	Wednesday	Thursday	Friday	Saturday
1	2		4	5	6	
		10	11			14
	16	17		19	20	21
22			25	26		28

9. How many days are in this month? _____

Use the calendar above.

10. February 6   Friday   Saturday

11. February 15   Saturday   Sunday

12. February 18   Wednesday   Thursday

Think of the number of days.
Is it less than two days?
Ring yes or no.

13. Between Monday and Tuesday   yes   no

14. Between Tuesday and Saturday   yes   no

Identifying Days of the Week; Calendar

MONTHS OF THE YEAR

January	first
February	second
March	third
April	fourth
May	fifth
June	sixth
July	seventh
August	eighth
September	ninth
October	tenth
November	eleventh
December	twelfth

Complete.

1. January is the

   _____

   month of the year.

2. March is the

   _____

   month of the year.

3. May is the

   _____

   month of the year.

4. August is the

   _____

   month of the year.

5. December is the

   _____

   month of the year.

Identifying Months of the Year

Ring the next month.

6.	January	March	(February)	September
7.	March	January	February	April
8.	May	June	July	April
9.	June	May	July	August
10.	September	December	October	August

11. What is the month of your birthday?

_____

12. What month is it now? _____

13. What month comes next? _____.

14. Maria's birthday is in May.
John's birthday is three months later.

What month is John's birthday? _____

15. Tom's birthday is in July.
July is what month of the year?

_____

DISCUSS: The months that make up each season.

PROBLEM SOLVING

HOURS WE WORK

	Lee	Jill	Robert	Carol
homework	1	2	4	3
reading	2	0	1	1
playing	1	2	3	1

Write the number of hours.

1. How many hours does Carol spend

   on homework? __3__ hours

2. How many hours does Jill spend

   on homework? ___ hours

3. How many hours for both? ___ hours

4. How many hours does Lee read? ___ hours

5. How many hours does Robert read? ___ hour

6. How many hours for both? ___ hours

7. How many hours does Jill play? ___ hours

8. How many hours does Robert play? ___ hours

9. How many hours for both? ___ hours

TIMES WE EAT

	Lee	Jill	Robert	Carol
breakfast	8:00	6:30	7:00	7:00
lunch	1:00	11:30	12:00	12:30
dinner	6:00	5:30	6:30	6:00

Write the time.

10. When does Lee eat breakfast? _____:_____

11. When does Robert eat lunch? _____:_____

12. When does Jill eat lunch? _____:_____

13. When does Carol eat dinner? _____:_____

(pages 207–214)

CHECKPOINT 2   Write the number.

1. Mary left home at **9:00**.
   She returned home **3** hours later.
   When did she get home?   [:]

Ring the day that comes just after Tuesday.

2. | Monday | Wednesday | Sunday |

Ring the fourth month of the year.

3. | May | March | April |

Extra practice on page 373

Problem Solving

CHAPTER 8 TEST

What time is it?

1.

_____ o'clock

What time is it?

2.

_____ : _____

Solve.

3. Debbie went for a bike ride at **3:00**.
She finished riding two hours later.
What time did she finish?   _____ o'clock

Ring the one that comes just before.

4.	Thursday	Friday	Tuesday	Wednesday
5.	July	March	June	August

Solve.

TIMES

	Kim	Dusty
leave home for school	8:30	8:00
come home from school	4:00	4:30

6. When does Kim leave for school? _____ : _____

7. When does Dusty come home? _____ : _____

8. Who leaves for school at **8:00**? _____

Extra practice on page 374

MATHEMATICS and SOCIAL STUDIES

This chart shows the number of president's birthdays in each month.

Month	Birthdays
January	4
February	4
March	4
April	4
May	2
June	0
July	3
August	3
September	1
October	6
November	5
December	3

Write the number of birthdays.

1. January ____   March ____   August ____

2. November ____   May ____   April ____

3. December ____   July ____   September ____

4. Which month has the most birthdays? _____

Enrichment

Show the time. Then write the time.

1.

one hour earlier

4 o'clock

one hour later

6 o'clock

2.

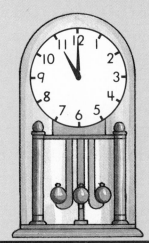

two hours earlier

_____ o'clock

two hours later

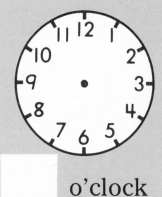

_____ o'clock

3.

four hours earlier

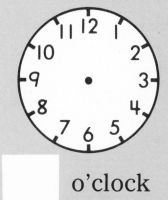

_____ o'clock

four hours later

_____ o'clock

Sunday
Monday
Wednesday
Tuesday
Thursday
Friday
Saturday

Wednesday is **2** days *after* Monday.
Wednesday is **2** days *before* Friday.
Wednesday is *between* Tuesday and Thursday.

Ring the day.

1.	**2** days after Tuesday	(Thursday)	Friday
2.	**3** days after Thursday	Friday	Sunday
3.	**I** day before Saturday	Thursday	Friday
4.	**4** days before Friday	Monday	Sunday
5.	Between Thursday and Saturday	Sunday	Friday
6.	Between Monday and Wednesday	Tuesday	Thursday

7. Ring the days of the weekend.

Sunday   Monday   Tuesday   Wednesday

Thursday   Friday   Saturday

Enrichment: Days Before, After and Between

CUMULATIVE REVIEW

Fill in the ⬭ for the correct answer.

Add.

1. 6 + 4	2. 3 + 6	3. 2 + 8
4 6 10	3 10 9	9 10 6
Ⓐ Ⓑ Ⓒ	Ⓐ Ⓑ Ⓒ	Ⓐ Ⓑ Ⓒ

4.   4
    +4
	5. 7
	    +1
		6. 1
		    +9

8 0 10	8 9 6	8 9 10
Ⓐ Ⓑ Ⓒ	Ⓐ Ⓑ Ⓒ	Ⓐ Ⓑ Ⓒ

Subtract.

7. 7 − 4	8. 8 − 2	9. 10 − 5
2 3 5	6 10 8	6 5 7
Ⓐ Ⓑ Ⓒ	Ⓐ Ⓑ Ⓒ	Ⓐ Ⓑ Ⓒ

10.   9
    −4
	11. 10
	    − 7
		12. 9
		    −3

4 6 5	4 3 5	3 6 9
Ⓐ Ⓑ Ⓒ	Ⓐ Ⓑ Ⓒ	Ⓐ Ⓑ Ⓒ

Choose the numbers in order.

13. 40, 41, 42, __?__, __?__, __?__, __?__, __?__, 48, 49
    Ⓐ 42, 44, 47, 46, 45
    Ⓑ 43, 44, 45, 46, 47
    Ⓒ 41, 43, 46, 44, 47

Choose the numbers that continue the pattern.

14. 4, 5, 6, 4, 5, 6, 4, __?__, __?__, __?__, __?__
    Ⓐ 6, 4, 5, 6, 4
    Ⓑ 6, 7, 8, 6, 7
    Ⓒ 5, 6, 4, 5, 6

LANGUAGE and VOCABULARY REVIEW

Ring the answer.

1. A year has ___ months.   10   (12)

2. There are ___ days in one week.   7   8

3. November is the ___ month of the year.
   eleventh   ninth

4. Sunday comes just before ___.
   Saturday   Monday

COMPUTER
LITERACY

Ring the tool.

1.

2.

3.

4.

5.

6.

Ring what a computer can also do.

1.

2.

3.

4.

5.

6.

7.

8.

Functions of a Computer

Read with the children:

How many blue blocks
do you see?
How many red blocks?
How many green blocks?
How many yellow
blocks?
How many blocks in all?

9

ADDITION AND
SUBTRACTION
FACTS THROUGH 12

ADDING THROUGH 11

$8 + 2 = \underline{10}$ $9 + 2 = \underline{11}$

Add.

1.

$7 + 3 = \underline{\hspace{1cm}}$

2.

$8 + 3 = \underline{\hspace{1cm}}$

3.

$6 + 4 = \underline{\hspace{1cm}}$

4.

 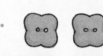   

$7 + 4 = \underline{\hspace{1cm}}$

5. $6 + 5 = \underline{\hspace{1cm}}$ $6 + 4 = \underline{\hspace{1cm}}$ $6 + 3 = \underline{\hspace{1cm}}$

6. $0 + 9 = \underline{\hspace{1cm}}$ $1 + 9 = \underline{\hspace{1cm}}$ $2 + 9 = \underline{\hspace{1cm}}$

7. $2 + 9 = \underline{\hspace{1cm}}$ $2 + 8 = \underline{\hspace{1cm}}$ $2 + 7 = \underline{\hspace{1cm}}$

Addition Facts through 11

ADDING THROUGH 11

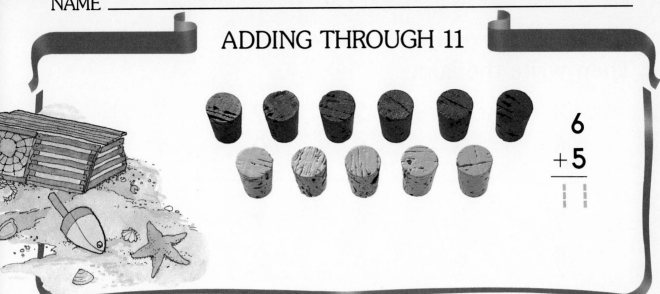

$$\begin{array}{r} 6 \\ +5 \\ \hline \end{array}$$

Add.

1. $\begin{array}{r} 7 \\ +3 \\ \hline \end{array}$

2. $\begin{array}{r} 8 \\ +3 \\ \hline \end{array}$

3. $\begin{array}{r} 8 \\ +2 \\ \hline \end{array}$

4. $\begin{array}{r} 9 \\ +2 \\ \hline \end{array}$

5. $\begin{array}{r} 9 \\ +0 \\ \hline \end{array}$ $\begin{array}{r} 9 \\ +1 \\ \hline \end{array}$ $\begin{array}{r} 9 \\ +2 \\ \hline \end{array}$ $\begin{array}{r} 6 \\ +5 \\ \hline \end{array}$ $\begin{array}{r} 6 \\ +4 \\ \hline \end{array}$ $\begin{array}{r} 6 \\ +3 \\ \hline \end{array}$

6. $\begin{array}{r} 7 \\ +1 \\ \hline \end{array}$ $\begin{array}{r} 7 \\ +2 \\ \hline \end{array}$ $\begin{array}{r} 7 \\ +3 \\ \hline \end{array}$ $\begin{array}{r} 8 \\ +1 \\ \hline \end{array}$ $\begin{array}{r} 8 \\ +2 \\ \hline \end{array}$ $\begin{array}{r} 8 \\ +3 \\ \hline \end{array}$

Use counters to add.
Then write the sum.

7.
3	7	2	9	4	6
+8	+3	+9	+0	+7	+4

8.
2	3	4	7	5	6
+8	+6	+6	+2	+5	+5

9.
9	9	3	8	2	9
+1	+2	+5	+3	+6	+0

10.
8	1	7	8	5	3
+2	+7	+0	+0	+6	+2

Write the sum.

11.

Joe caught **7** fish.
May caught **4** fish.
How many fish
in all?

7 + 4 = _____ fish

12.

Linda caught **6** fish.
May caught **4** fish.
How many fish
in all?

6 + 4 = _____ fish

ADDING THROUGH 12

$5 + 7 =$ __12__

$7 + 5 =$ __12__

Add.

1.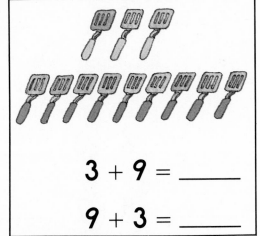

   $3 + 9 =$ _____

   $9 + 3 =$ _____

2.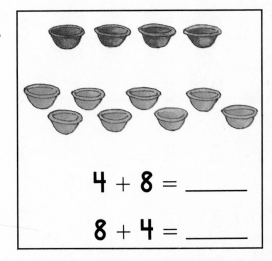

   $4 + 8 =$ _____

   $8 + 4 =$ _____

3.

   $5 + 7 =$ _____

   $7 + 5 =$ _____

4.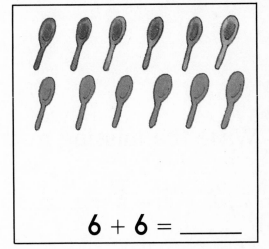

   $6 + 6 =$ _____

5. $6 + 4 =$ _____ $6 + 5 =$ _____ $6 + 6 =$ _____

6. $7 + 5 =$ _____ $7 + 4 =$ _____ $7 + 3 =$ _____

Add.

7. $8 + 2 =$ _____ $8 + 3 =$ _____ $4 + 8 =$ _____

8. $6 + 1 =$ _____ $3 + 9 =$ _____ $4 + 3 =$ _____

9. $7 + 3 =$ _____ $7 + 5 =$ _____ $8 + 4 =$ _____

10. $8 + 1 =$ _____ $3 + 8 =$ _____ $7 + 4 =$ _____

11. $9 + 3 =$ _____ $5 + 7 =$ _____ $9 + 1 =$ _____

12. $4 + 8 =$ _____ $6 + 6 =$ _____ $4 + 6 =$ _____

13. $5 + 5 =$ _____ $2 + 9 =$ _____ $6 + 3 =$ _____

14. $3 + 2 =$ _____ $5 + 7 =$ _____ $4 + 7 =$ _____

☆ Write the missing number.

15. $2 + 9 = 8 +$ _3_   16. $9 + 3 = 7 +$ _____

17. $5 +$ _____ $= 6 + 6$ 18. _____ $+ 8 = 6 + 5$

19. $3 + 5 = 2 +$ _____   20. $4 + 8 =$ _____ $+ 9$

TRY THIS: Use punchouts to show sums.

ADDING THROUGH 12

$$\begin{array}{r} 8 \\ +4 \\ \hline 12 \end{array} \quad \begin{array}{r} 4 \\ +8 \\ \hline 12 \end{array}$$

Add.

1.

$$\begin{array}{r} 7 \\ +5 \\ \hline \end{array} \quad \begin{array}{r} 5 \\ +7 \\ \hline \end{array}$$

2.

$$\begin{array}{r} 9 \\ +3 \\ \hline \end{array} \quad \begin{array}{r} 3 \\ +9 \\ \hline \end{array}$$

3.

$$\begin{array}{r} 8 \\ +4 \\ \hline \end{array} \quad \begin{array}{r} 4 \\ +8 \\ \hline \end{array}$$

4.

$$\begin{array}{r} 6 \\ +6 \\ \hline \end{array}$$

5.

$$\begin{array}{r} 5 \\ +4 \\ \hline \end{array} \quad \begin{array}{r} 6 \\ +4 \\ \hline \end{array} \quad \begin{array}{r} 7 \\ +4 \\ \hline \end{array} \quad \begin{array}{r} 6 \\ +4 \\ \hline \end{array} \quad \begin{array}{r} 7 \\ +4 \\ \hline \end{array} \quad \begin{array}{r} 8 \\ +4 \\ \hline \end{array}$$

6.

$$\begin{array}{r} 9 \\ +3 \\ \hline \end{array} \quad \begin{array}{r} 8 \\ +3 \\ \hline \end{array} \quad \begin{array}{r} 7 \\ +3 \\ \hline \end{array} \quad \begin{array}{r} 8 \\ +3 \\ \hline \end{array} \quad \begin{array}{r} 7 \\ +3 \\ \hline \end{array} \quad \begin{array}{r} 6 \\ +3 \\ \hline \end{array}$$

7. Add.
Color. 10 ■ 11 □ 12 ■

$$\begin{array}{r} 4 \\ +7 \\ \hline \end{array} \quad \begin{array}{r} 9 \\ +3 \\ \hline \end{array} \quad \begin{array}{r} 6 \\ +4 \\ \hline \end{array} \quad \begin{array}{r} 7 \\ +4 \\ \hline \end{array} \quad \begin{array}{r} 8 \\ +4 \\ \hline \end{array} \quad \begin{array}{r} 6 \\ +5 \\ \hline \end{array}$$

$$\begin{array}{r} 4 \\ +8 \\ \hline \end{array} \quad \begin{array}{r} 2 \\ +9 \\ \hline \end{array} \quad \begin{array}{r} 1 \\ +9 \\ \hline \end{array} \quad \begin{array}{r} 8 \\ +3 \\ \hline \end{array} \quad \begin{array}{r} 3 \\ +9 \\ \hline \end{array}$$

$$\begin{array}{r} 7 \\ +5 \\ \hline \end{array} \quad \begin{array}{r} 8 \\ +2 \\ \hline \end{array} \quad \begin{array}{r} 6 \\ +6 \\ \hline \end{array} \quad \begin{array}{r} 3 \\ +8 \\ \hline \end{array} \quad \begin{array}{r} 8 \\ +4 \\ \hline \end{array}$$

(pages 223–230)

CHECKPOINT 1

Add.

1.
$$\begin{array}{r} 5 \\ +5 \\ \hline \end{array} \quad \begin{array}{r} 7 \\ +5 \\ \hline \end{array} \quad \begin{array}{r} 8 \\ +2 \\ \hline \end{array} \quad \begin{array}{r} 9 \\ +2 \\ \hline \end{array} \quad \begin{array}{r} 6 \\ +6 \\ \hline \end{array} \quad \begin{array}{r} 3 \\ +8 \\ \hline \end{array}$$

2. $5 + 6 =$ ☐ $4 + 7 =$ ☐ $3 + 9 =$ ☐

Extra practice on page 375

Addition Facts through 12

PROBLEM SOLVING

Sue wants **6** horns.

She has **3** horns.

How many more horns does she need?

_3_ horns

Draw pictures to show how many more are needed. Then write the answer.

1. John needs **8** plates.

   He has **3** plates.
   How many more
   plates does he need?

   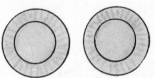

   _____ plates

2. Maria needs **10** balloons.

   She has **4** balloons.
   How many more balloons
   does she need?

   _____ balloons

3. Diana wants **9** apples.

   She already has **4** apples.
   How many more
   does she need?

   _____ apples

Drawing a Picture

Draw pictures to show how many more
are needed. Then write the answer.

4. Mrs. Thomas wants
   9 flowers.

   She has **7** flowers.
   How many more
   flowers does she need?

   _____ flowers

5. Tim needs **9** hats.

   He already bought **3** hats.
   How many more hats
   should he buy?

   _____ hats

6. Mr. Jones needs **10** cups.

   He has **3** cups.
   How many more cups
   does he need?

   _____ cups

7. Pam wants **8** spoons.

   She has **4** spoons.
   How many more spoons
   does she need?

   _____ spoons

Problem Solving

SUBTRACTING FROM 11

$11 - 5 = \underline{6}$

$11 - 6 = \underline{5}$

Subtract.

1.

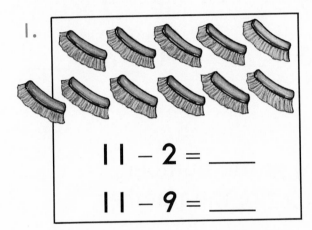

$11 - 2 = \underline{\hphantom{00}}$

$11 - 9 = \underline{\hphantom{00}}$

2.

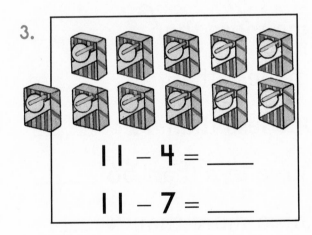

$11 - 3 = \underline{\hphantom{00}}$

$11 - 8 = \underline{\hphantom{00}}$

3.

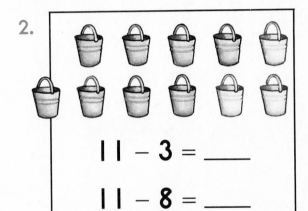

$11 - 4 = \underline{\hphantom{00}}$

$11 - 7 = \underline{\hphantom{00}}$

4.

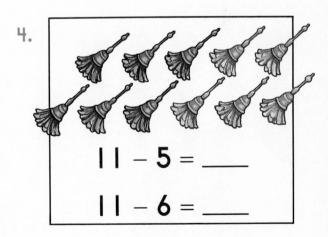

$11 - 5 = \underline{\hphantom{00}}$

$11 - 6 = \underline{\hphantom{00}}$

5. $11 - 6 = \underline{\hphantom{00}}$ $11 - 5 = \underline{\hphantom{00}}$ $11 - 4 = \underline{\hphantom{00}}$

6. $11 - 8 = \underline{\hphantom{00}}$ $11 - 7 = \underline{\hphantom{00}}$ $11 - 6 = \underline{\hphantom{00}}$

7. $11 - 2 = \underline{\hphantom{00}}$ $11 - 3 = \underline{\hphantom{00}}$ $11 - 4 = \underline{\hphantom{00}}$

Subtract.

8. $11 - 2 =$ _____ $11 - 5 =$ _____ $8 - 7 =$ _____

9. $11 - 7 =$ _____ $11 - 8 =$ _____ $11 - 6 =$ _____

10. $10 - 9 =$ _____ $10 - 2 =$ _____ $9 - 7 =$ _____

11. $6 - 2 =$ _____ $10 - 5 =$ _____ $8 - 5 =$ _____

12. $11 - 3 =$ _____ $11 - 4 =$ _____ $10 - 4 =$ _____

13. $9 - 9 =$ _____ $10 - 7 =$ _____ $9 - 7 =$ _____

14. $11 - 9 =$ _____ $10 - 3 =$ _____ $10 - 6 =$ _____

Think of the number.
Then write the number.

15. One more than **8** _____

16. One less than **17** _____

17. One less than **12** _____

18. Three less than **56** _____

19. Three more than **4** _____

20. Four more than **37** _____

21. Four less than **9** _____

22. Two less than **28** _____

PARTNERS: Make up problems. Use counters to solve. Discuss the answers.

SUBTRACTING FROM 11

$$11¢$$
$$- \ \ 3¢$$
$$8¢$$

Tell a story. Then subtract.

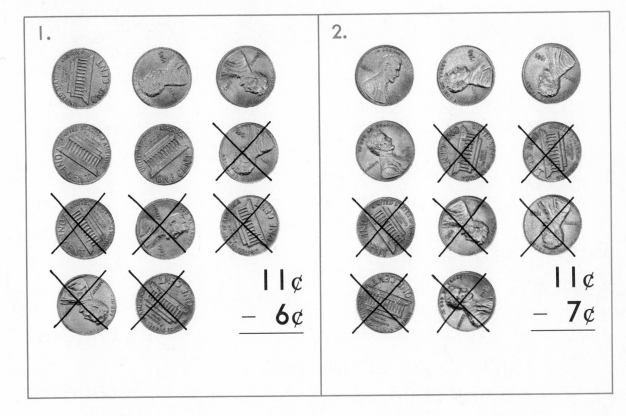

1.

$$11¢$$
$$- \ \ 6¢$$

2.

$$11¢$$
$$- \ \ 7¢$$

3.
$$11¢ \quad 11¢ \qquad 11¢ \quad 11¢ \qquad 11¢ \quad 11¢$$
$$- \ 2¢ \ - \ 9¢ \qquad - \ 3¢ \ - \ 8¢ \qquad - \ 6¢ \ - \ 5¢$$

4.
$$11¢ \quad 11¢ \qquad 11¢ \quad 11¢ \qquad 11¢ \quad 11¢$$
$$- \ 4¢ \ - \ 7¢ \qquad - \ 6¢ \ - \ 5¢ \qquad - \ 2¢ \ - \ 9¢$$

Subtract. Complete the table.

5.

−3	
11	8
10	
9	

6.

−6	
11	
9	
10	

7.

−5	
9	
10	
11	

8.

−7	
11	
9	
10	

9.

−8	
9	
10	
11	

10.

−9	
11	
10	
9	

Write + or − in the ☐.
Then add or subtract.

11. There are 11 children
on a bus. 5 get off the bus.
How many children
are still on the bus?

11 children
☐
5 children
──────
children

12. There are 8 children
on a boat. 3 more children
get on. How many children
are now on the boat?

8 children
☐
3 children
──────
children

Subtraction Facts through 11

SUBTRACTING FROM 12

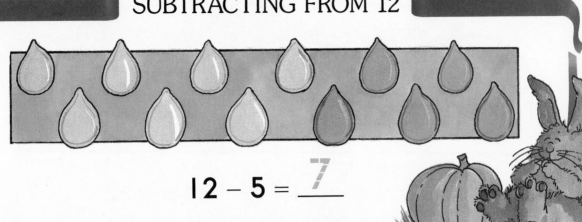

$$12 - 5 = \underline{7}$$

Subtract.

1.

$$12 - 3 = \underline{}$$

$$12 - 9 = \underline{}$$

2.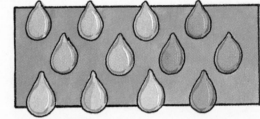

$$12 - 4 = \underline{}$$

$$12 - 8 = \underline{}$$

3.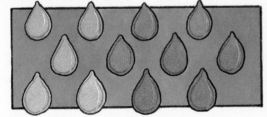

$$12 - 7 = \underline{}$$

$$12 - 5 = \underline{}$$

4.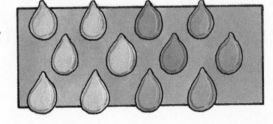

$$12 - 6 = \underline{}$$

5. $12 - 3 = \underline{}$ $12 - 4 = \underline{}$ $12 - 5 = \underline{}$

6. $12 - 9 = \underline{}$ $12 - 8 = \underline{}$ $12 - 7 = \underline{}$

7. $12 - 6 = \underline{}$ $12 - 7 = \underline{}$ $12 - 8 = \underline{}$

8. Subtract.

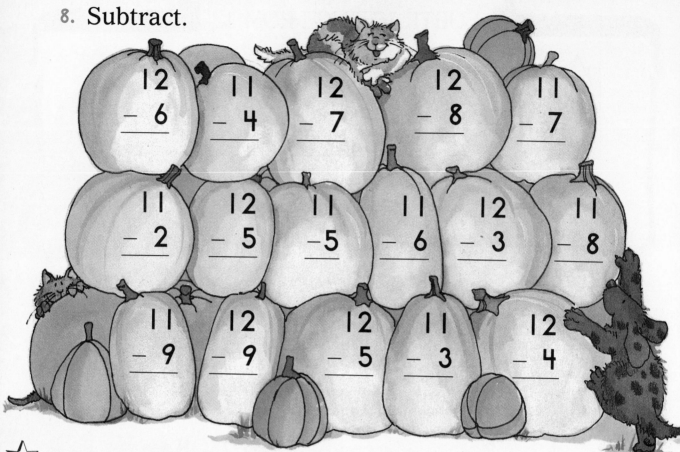

$$12 - 6$$ $$11 - 4$$ $$12 - 7$$ $$12 - 8$$ $$11 - 7$$

$$11 - 2$$ $$12 - 5$$ $$11 - 5$$ $$11 - 6$$ $$12 - 3$$ $$11 - 8$$

$$11 - 9$$ $$12 - 9$$ $$12 - 5$$ $$11 - 3$$ $$12 - 4$$

☆ Add or subtract. Write the numbers.

9.

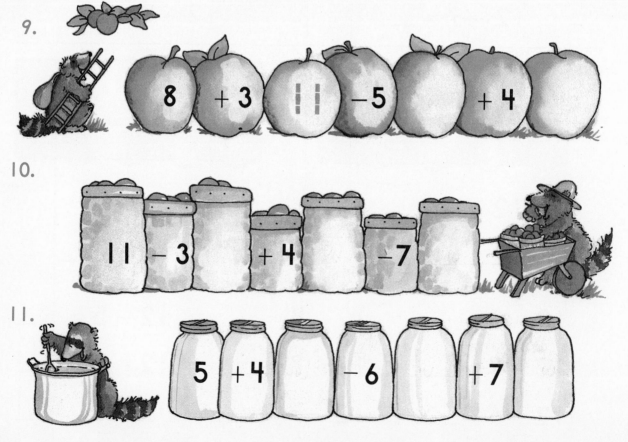

$$8 \quad +3 \quad 11 \quad -5 \quad \quad +4$$

10.

$$11 \quad -3 \quad \quad +4 \quad \quad -7$$

11.

$$5 \quad +4 \quad \quad -6 \quad \quad +7$$

TRY THIS: Problem Solving Activities, page 401.

FACT FAMILIES

$2 + 9 =$ ___11___

$11 - 9 =$ ___2___

$9 + 2 =$ ___11___

$11 - 2 =$ ___9___

Add or subtract.

1. $5 + 6 =$ _____

   $11 - 6 =$ _____

   $6 + 5 =$ _____

   $11 - 5 =$ _____

2. $5 + 7 =$ _____

   $12 - 7 =$ _____

   $7 + 5 =$ _____

   $12 - 5 =$ _____

3. $3 + 9 =$ _____

   $12 - 9 =$ _____

   $9 + 3 =$ _____

   $12 - 3 =$ _____

4. $4 + 8 =$ _____

   $12 - 8 =$ _____

   $8 + 4 =$ _____

   $12 - 4 =$ _____

5. $4 + 7 =$ _____

   $11 - 7 =$ _____

   $7 + 4 =$ _____

   $11 - 4 =$ _____

6. $3 + 8 =$ _____

   $11 - 8 =$ _____

   $8 + 3 =$ _____

   $11 - 3 =$ _____

Add or subtract.

7.
$$\begin{array}{r} 11 \\ -\ 4 \\ \hline \end{array}$$
$$\begin{array}{r} 12 \\ -\ 8 \\ \hline \end{array}$$
$$\begin{array}{r} 4 \\ +8 \\ \hline \end{array}$$
$$\begin{array}{r} 8 \\ +3 \\ \hline \end{array}$$
$$\begin{array}{r} 9 \\ +3 \\ \hline \end{array}$$
$$\begin{array}{r} 11 \\ -\ 6 \\ \hline \end{array}$$

8.
$$\begin{array}{r} 3 \\ +9 \\ \hline \end{array}$$
$$\begin{array}{r} 12 \\ -\ 6 \\ \hline \end{array}$$
$$\begin{array}{r} 4 \\ +7 \\ \hline \end{array}$$
$$\begin{array}{r} 9 \\ +2 \\ \hline \end{array}$$
$$\begin{array}{r} 6 \\ +5 \\ \hline \end{array}$$
$$\begin{array}{r} 9 \\ -2 \\ \hline \end{array}$$

9.
$$\begin{array}{r} 5 \\ +6 \\ \hline \end{array}$$
$$\begin{array}{r} 8 \\ +4 \\ \hline \end{array}$$
$$\begin{array}{r} 11 \\ -\ 2 \\ \hline \end{array}$$
$$\begin{array}{r} 12 \\ -\ 5 \\ \hline \end{array}$$
$$\begin{array}{r} 7 \\ +4 \\ \hline \end{array}$$
$$\begin{array}{r} 11 \\ -\ 8 \\ \hline \end{array}$$

10.
$$\begin{array}{r} 12 \\ -\ 4 \\ \hline \end{array}$$
$$\begin{array}{r} 2 \\ +9 \\ \hline \end{array}$$
$$\begin{array}{r} 12 \\ -\ 9 \\ \hline \end{array}$$
$$\begin{array}{r} 11 \\ -\ 7 \\ \hline \end{array}$$
$$\begin{array}{r} 5 \\ +7 \\ \hline \end{array}$$
$$\begin{array}{r} 4 \\ +6 \\ \hline \end{array}$$

11.
$$\begin{array}{r} 12 \\ -\ 5 \\ \hline \end{array}$$
$$\begin{array}{r} 3 \\ +8 \\ \hline \end{array}$$
$$\begin{array}{r} 6 \\ +3 \\ \hline \end{array}$$
$$\begin{array}{r} 12 \\ -\ 7 \\ \hline \end{array}$$
$$\begin{array}{r} 4 \\ +3 \\ \hline \end{array}$$
$$\begin{array}{r} 10 \\ -\ 5 \\ \hline \end{array}$$

Think of the number.
Then write the number.

12. Two more than **35** _____

13. One less than **29** _____

14. Four more than **73** _____

15. Two less than **68** _____

16. Two less than **56** _____

Fact Families

PROBLEM SOLVING

7 bears are sleeping.
5 bears are eating.
How many bears in all?

```
      7
 +    5
   1 2  bears
```

Solve.

1. There are **11** rabbits.
    Then **5** run away.
    How many rabbits
    are there now?

    □

    rabbits

2. **6** squirrels are in the tree.
    6 are on the ground.
    How many squirrels
    are there?

    □

    squirrels

3. **8** birds are on a rock.
    Then **5** fly away.
    How many birds are
    now on the rock?

    □

    birds

Solve.

4. A squirrel has 11 acorns.
It eats **7** of them.
How many acorns
does it have now?

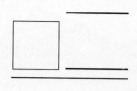

acorns

5. There are **7** deer
in the meadow.
4 more deer join them.
Now how many deer
are there?

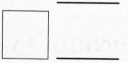

deer

(pages 231–242)
CHECKPOINT 2

Subtract.

1.
$$11 - 5 \qquad 12 - 6 \qquad 11 - 2$$

2. $12 - 5 = \boxed{}$ $11 - 8 = \boxed{}$

Write + or − in the $\boxed{}$.
Then write the answer.

$$\boxed{} \begin{array}{r} 6 \\ 5 \end{array}$$

3. Debbie has **6** marbles.
Sue has **5** marbles.
How many marbles in all?

$\boxed{}$ marbles

Extra practice on page 375

DISCUSS: The different fact families for 12.

CHAPTER 9 TEST

Add.

1.

3	7	3	2	6	4
+9	+5	+8	+9	+5	+8

Draw pictures to show how many more are needed. Then write the answer.

2. Ann wants **7** trees.
   She has planted **2** trees.
   How many more does she need? ____ trees

Subtract.

3.

11	12	11	12	11	12
− 7	− 4	− 3	− 6	− 5	− 8

Solve.

4. Allen has **6** pens.
   He buys **5** more pens.
   How many does he have now?

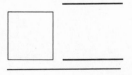

pens

Extra practice on page 376

MATHEMATICS and READING

A letter carrier puts letters in order.
Help put these letters in order.
Begin with the lowest number on the street.
Match.

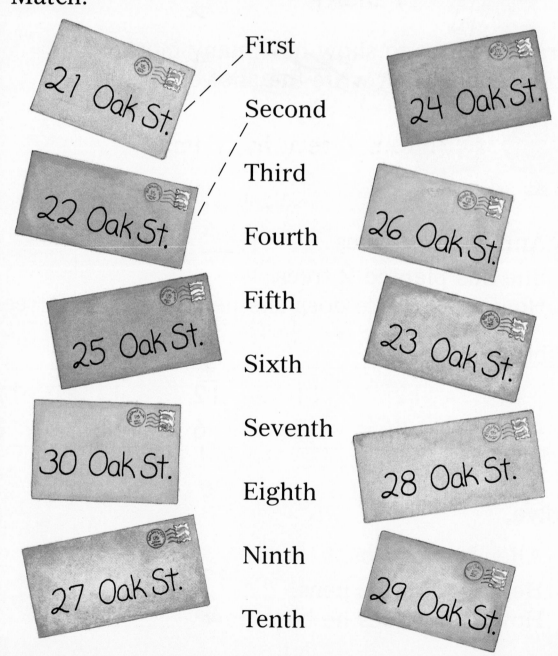

First

21 Oak St.

Second

24 Oak St.

Third

22 Oak St.

Fourth

26 Oak St.

Fifth

25 Oak St.

23 Oak St.

Sixth

Seventh

30 Oak St.

28 Oak St.

Eighth

Ninth

27 Oak St.

29 Oak St.

Tenth

Enrichment

You can check
subtraction
by adding.

$$\begin{array}{r} 8 \\ -2 \\ \hline 6 \end{array} \qquad \begin{array}{r} 6 \\ +2 \\ \hline 8 \end{array}$$

Subtract. Check by adding.

1. $\begin{array}{r} 6 \\ -3 \\ \hline \end{array}$ $\begin{array}{r} 3 \\ +3 \\ \hline \end{array}$

2. $\begin{array}{r} 7 \\ -4 \\ \hline \end{array}$ $\begin{array}{r} 3 \\ +4 \\ \hline \end{array}$

3. $\begin{array}{r} 9 \\ -3 \\ \hline \end{array}$ $\begin{array}{r} \\ + \\ \hline \end{array}$

4. $\begin{array}{r} 8 \\ -2 \\ \hline \end{array}$ $\begin{array}{r} \\ + \\ \hline \end{array}$

5. $\begin{array}{r} 12 \\ -\ 5 \\ \hline \end{array}$ $\begin{array}{r} \\ + \\ \hline \end{array}$

6. $\begin{array}{r} 10 \\ -\ 6 \\ \hline \end{array}$ $\begin{array}{r} \\ + \\ \hline \end{array}$

7. $\begin{array}{r} 11 \\ -\ 4 \\ \hline \end{array}$ $\begin{array}{r} \\ + \\ \hline \end{array}$

8. $\begin{array}{r} 12 \\ -\ 8 \\ \hline \end{array}$ $\begin{array}{r} \\ + \\ \hline \end{array}$

Ring the sum if it is incorrect.
Then write the correct sum.

9. $5 + 3 = (9)$

8
_____

10. $6 + 6 = 12$

_____

11. $9 + 3 = 11$

_____

12. $2 + 8 = 11$

_____

13. $7 + 5 = 12$

_____

14. $3 + 8 = 11$

_____

15. $4 + 5 = 10$

_____

16. $5 + 6 = 11$

_____

17. $4 + 7 = 12$

_____

18. $3 + 9 = 11$

_____

Enrichment: Checking Addition

CUMULATIVE REVIEW

Fill in the ⬭ for the correct answer.

Choose the amount.

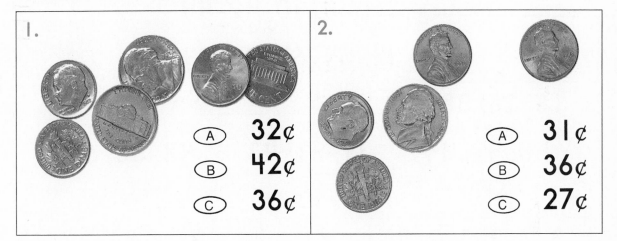

1.

- (A) 32¢
- (B) 42¢
- (C) 36¢

2.

- (A) 31¢
- (B) 36¢
- (C) 27¢

Choose the amount.

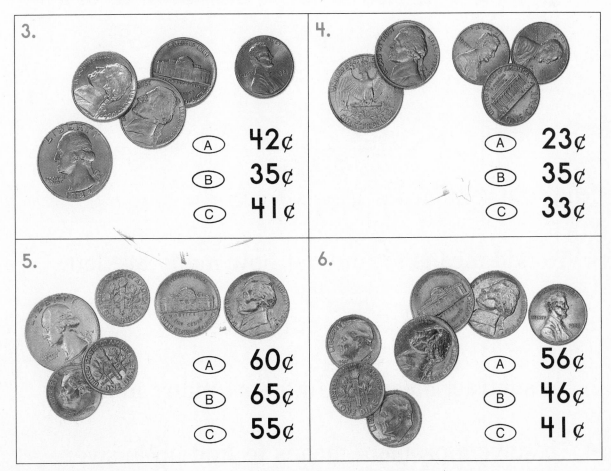

3.

- (A) 42¢
- (B) 35¢
- (C) 41¢

4.

- (A) 23¢
- (B) 35¢
- (C) 33¢

5.

- (A) 60¢
- (B) 65¢
- (C) 55¢

6.

- (A) 56¢
- (B) 46¢
- (C) 41¢

Choose the numbers that continue the pattern.

7. 30, 32, 34, ___?___, ___?___, ___?___, ___?___, ___?___

    Ⓐ 35, 36, 37, 38, 39

    Ⓑ 36, 38, 40, 42, 44

    Ⓒ 44, 54, 64, 74, 84

8. 18, 28, 38, ___?___, ___?___, ___?___

    40, 42, 44   39, 41, 43   48, 58, 68

     Ⓐ   Ⓑ   Ⓒ

9. 3, 2, 2, 3, 2, 2, 3, ___?___, ___?___, ___?___, ___?___, ___?___

    2, 2, 3, 2, 2   3, 3, 2, 3, 3   2, 3, 2, 3, 2

     Ⓐ   Ⓑ   Ⓒ

LANGUAGE and VOCABULARY REVIEW

Ring the sentence if it is correct.

1. To add means to find out how many are left.

2. In $9 - 3 = 6$, 6 is the difference.

3. To subtract means to find how many in all.

4. To solve a problem means to find an answer.

Read with the children:

The rider wants to know how high the horse jumped.
Can you think of ways to measure how high the horse jumped?

10

MEASUREMENT

LONGER AND SHORTER

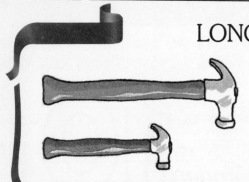 The 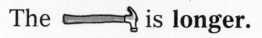 is **longer.**

The 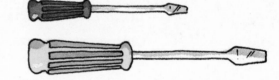 is **shorter.**

Ring the object that is longer.

1.

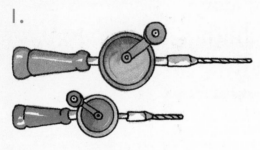

2.

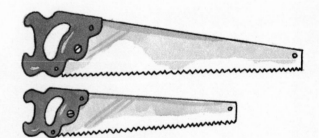

3.

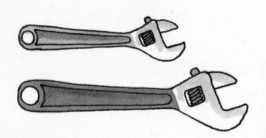

4.

Ring the object that is shorter.

5.

  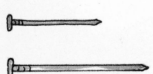

6.

7.

8.

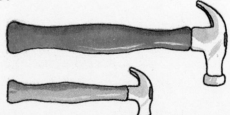

Comparing Lengths

MEASURING LENGTH

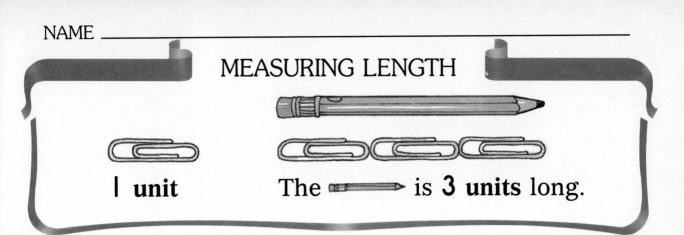

1 unit   The ⬤▬▶ is **3 units** long.

How long is the object?

1.

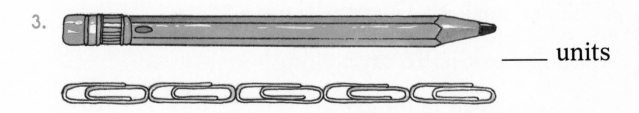

4 ___ units

2.

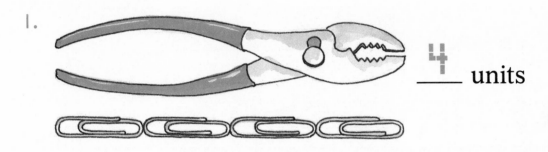

___ units

3.

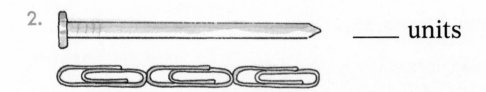

___ units

4.

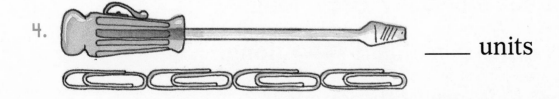

___ units

How long is the object?

5.  _____ units

6. 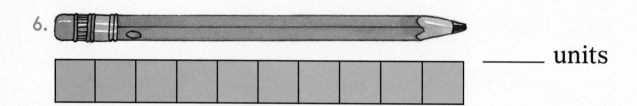 _____ units

7. 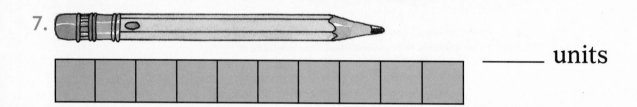 _____ units

8. 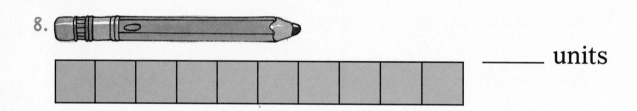 _____ units

9. Tina's desk is **37** 🔗 long.

Sue's desk is **46** 🔗 long.

Whose desk is longer? _____

10. Bill has a pencil **7** 🔗 long.

His other pencil is **4** 🔗 long.

How long are both pencils? _____

TRY THIS: Problem Solving Activities, page 402.

CENTIMETER

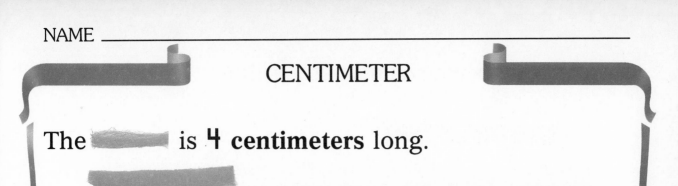

The ▬ is **4 centimeters** long.

| 1 | 2 | 3 | 4 | 5 | 6 | 7 | 8 | 9 | 10 | 11 | 12 | 13 |
centimeters

How long is the object?

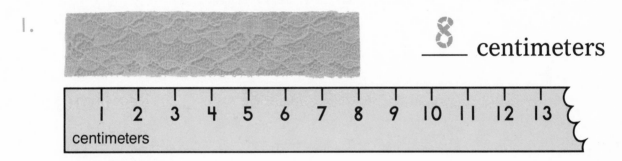

1. _8_ centimeters

| 1 | 2 | 3 | 4 | 5 | 6 | 7 | 8 | 9 | 10 | 11 | 12 | 13 |
centimeters

2. ____ centimeters

| 1 | 2 | 3 | 4 | 5 | 6 | 7 | 8 | 9 | 10 | 11 | 12 | 13 |
centimeters

3. ____ centimeters

| 1 | 2 | 3 | 4 | 5 | 6 | 7 | 8 | 9 | 10 | 11 | 12 | 13 |
centimeters

4. ____ centimeters

| 1 | 2 | 3 | 4 | 5 | 6 | 7 | 8 | 9 | 10 | 11 | 12 | 13 |
centimeters

Measure with your centimeter ruler.

5.

___ centimeters

6.

___ centimeters

7.

___ centimeters

8.

___ centimeters

9.

___ centimeters

Is the object longer than **3** centimeters?
Ring yes or no.

10.

yes   no

11.

yes   no

TRY THIS: Use rulers to measure objects.

MORE AND LESS

The  holds
more than the .

The  holds
less than the  .

Ring the object that holds more.

1.

2.

3.

Ring the object that holds less.

4.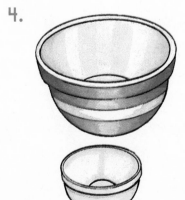

5.

6.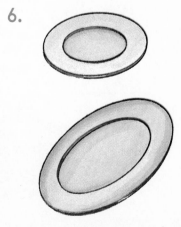

Identifying More and Less

Ring the object that holds more.
✓ the object that holds less.

7.

8.

9.

10.

11.

12.

☆ Ring the object that holds the **most.**
✓ the object that holds the **least.**

13.

14.

15.

16.

Identifying More and Less

LITER

I liter   The mug holds **less** than a liter.   The pail holds **more** than a liter.

Does it hold more or less than a liter?

1.

more

(less)

2.

more

less

3.

more

less

4.

more

less

5.

more

less

6.

more

less

Ring the objects that hold more than a liter.
✓ the objects that hold less than a liter.

I liter

7.

8.

9.

10.

11.

12.

13.

14.

15.

16.

17.

Write the answer.

18. Sara made **4** liters of juice.
    Al made **3** more liters of juice.

    How many liters in all? _____ liters

19. Ching put **7** liters of water
    in the tub. The tub holds
    10 liters. How many more
    liters can he put in?

    _____ liters

Liter

NAME ______________________________

HEAVIER AND LIGHTER

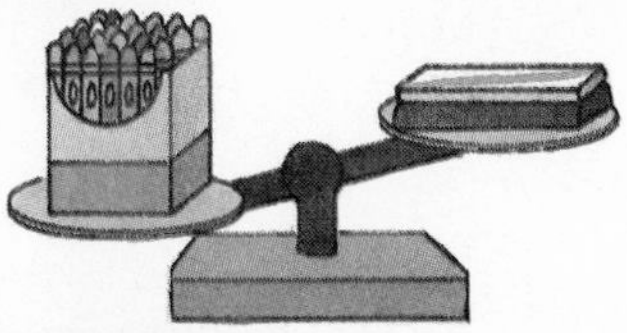

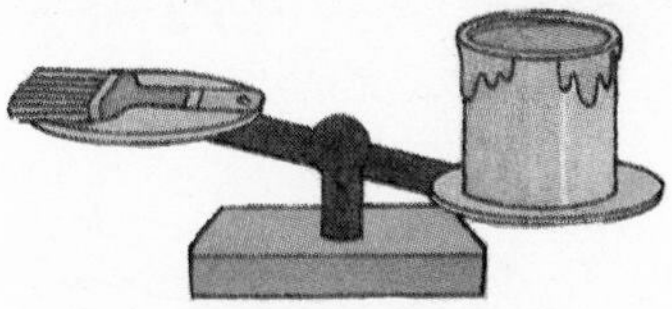

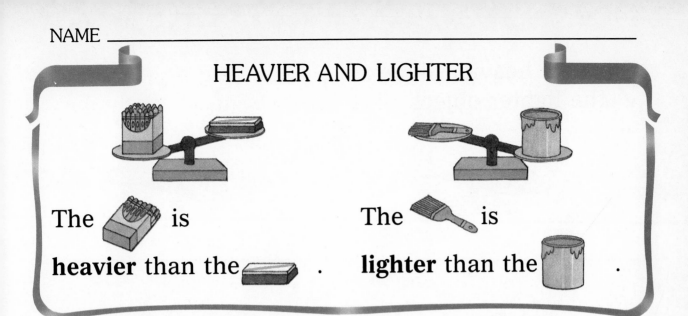

The 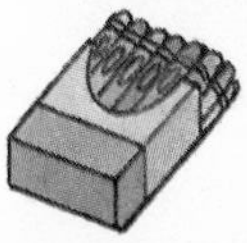 is **heavier** than the 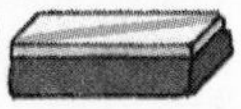 .

The 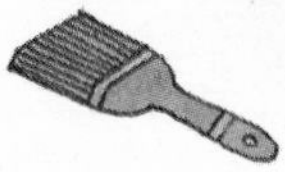 is **lighter** than the 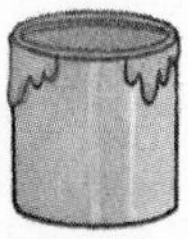 .

Ring the object that is heavier.

1.

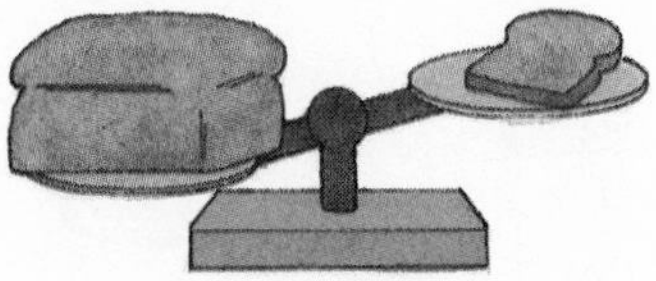

2.

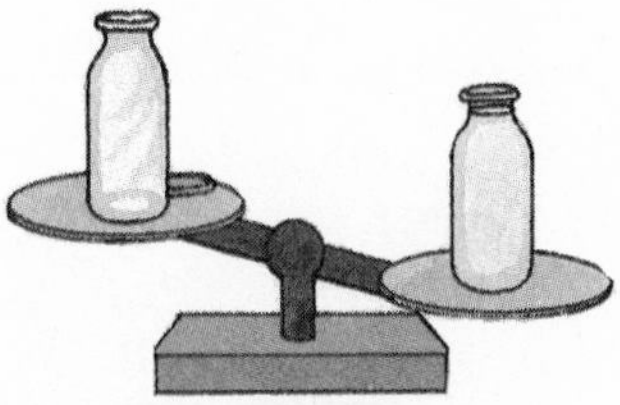

3.

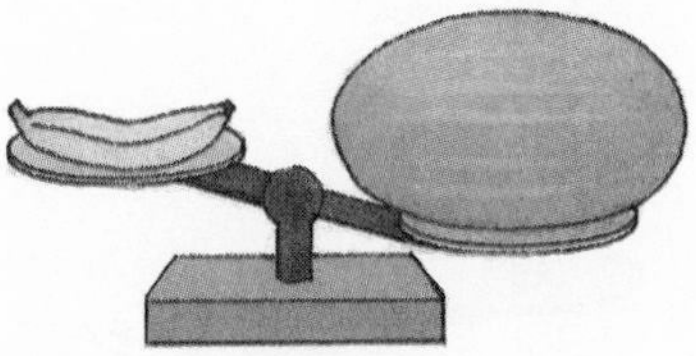

4.

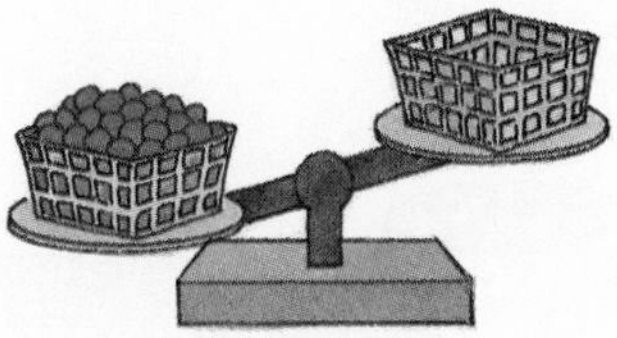

Ring the object that is lighter.

5.

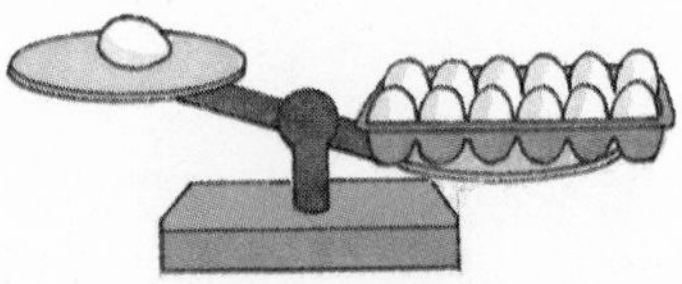

6.

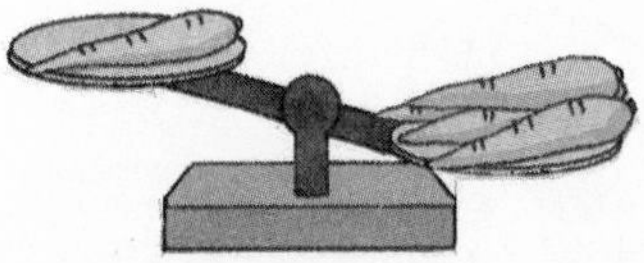

7.

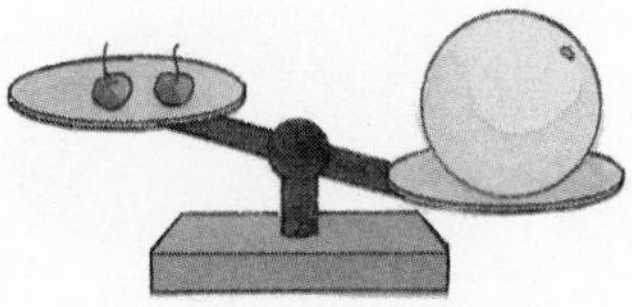

8.

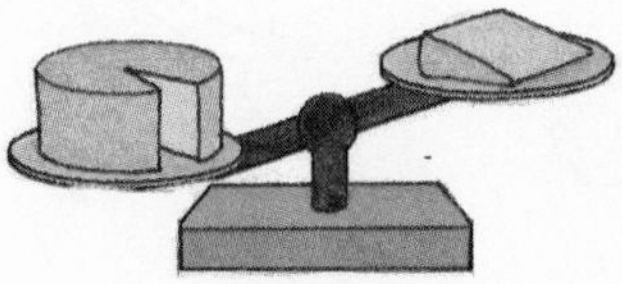

Ring the heavier object.
✓ the lighter object.

9.

10.

11.

12.

13.

14.

15.

16.

☆ Ring the **heaviest.** ✓ the **lightest.**

17.

18.

19.

20.

PARTNERS: Find two objects. Tell which is lighter.

KILOGRAM

The fruit is
1 **kilogram.**

How many kilograms?

1.

_3_ kilograms

2.

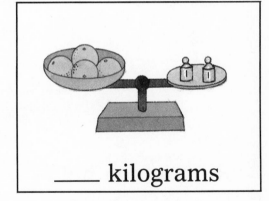

_____ kilogram

3.

_____ kilograms

4.

_____ kilograms

5.

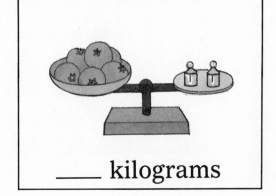

_____ kilograms

6.

_____ kilograms

How many kilograms?

7.

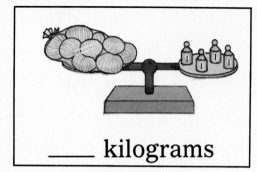

____ kilograms

8.

____ kilogram

9.

____ kilograms

10.

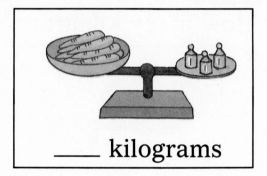

____ kilograms

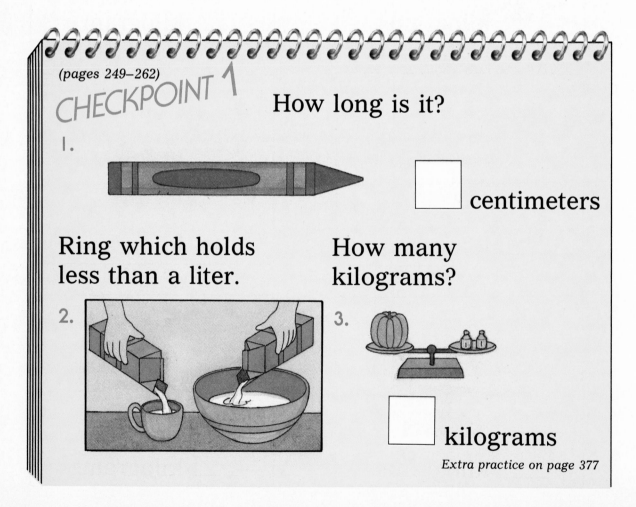

(pages 249–262)

CHECKPOINT 1

How long is it?

1.

☐ centimeters

Ring which holds less than a liter.

2.

How many kilograms?

3.

☐ **kilograms**

Extra practice on page 377

Kilogram

PROBLEM SOLVING

BEACH ITEMS

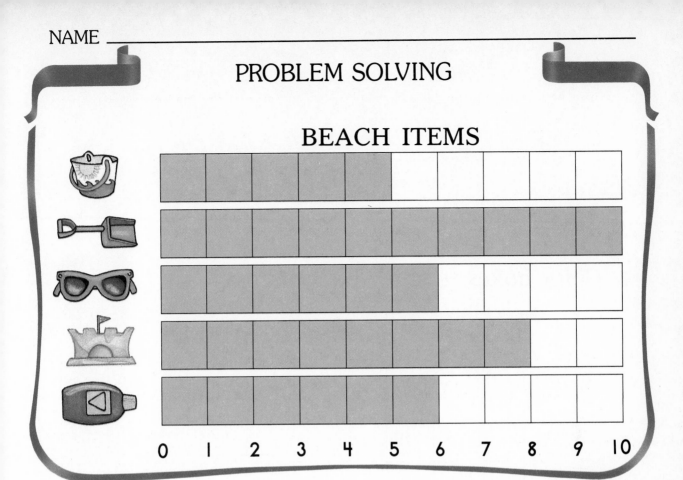

Use the graph. Write the number.

1. How many  ? ___10___

2. How many 🏰 ? _____

3. How many 🕶 ? _____

4. How many more 🕶 than 🪣 ? _____

5. How many more 🥄 than 🧴 ? _____

6. How many fewer 🏰 than 🥄 ? _____

7. Color boxes to show how many.

NUMBER OF SHELLS

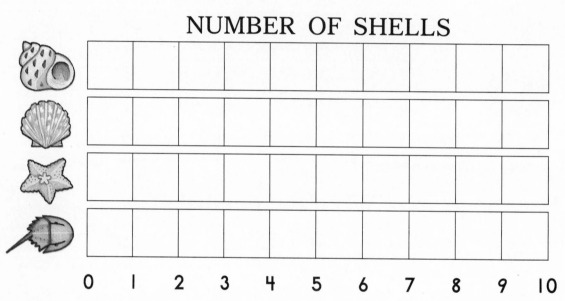

Use your graph. Write the number.

8. How many ? ___   **9.** How many ? ___

10. How many ? ___   **11.** How many ? ___

12. How many more than ? ___

13. How many more than ? ___

Problem Solving

INCH

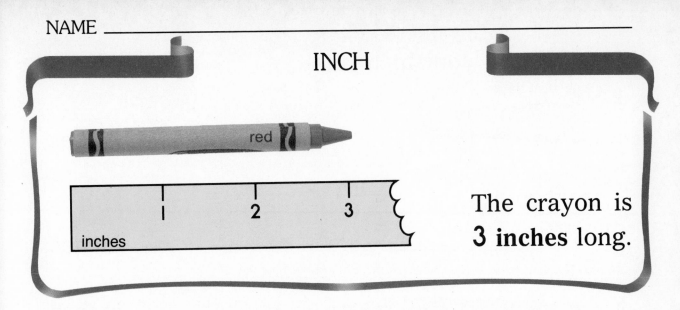

The crayon is **3 inches** long.

How long is the object?

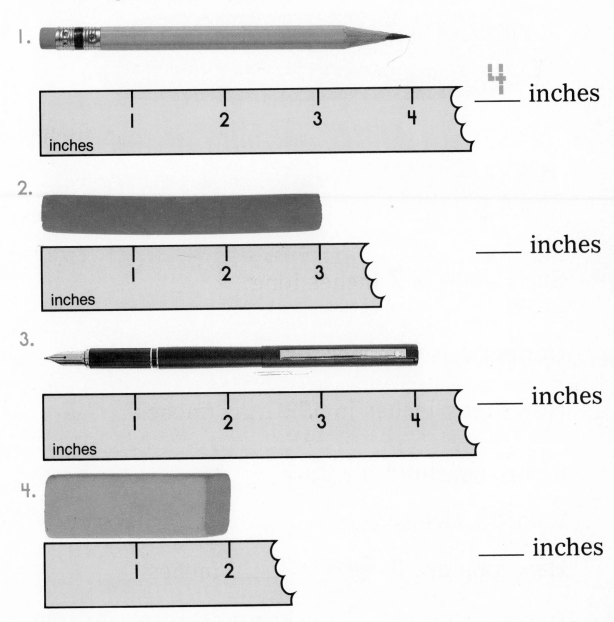

1. _4_ inches

2. ___ inches

3. ___ inches

4. ___ inches

Measure with your inch ruler.

5.  _____ inches

6.  _____ inches

7.  _____ inches

8.

_____ inches

9. _____ inches

10. Sue's ➤ is **7** inches long.

Her ▭➤ is **5** inches long.

How many inches in all? _____ inches

11. Pedro measured his ✂ .

It was **5** inches long.

How long are **3** ✂ ? _____ inches

DISCUSS: Compare the lengths of the children's feet.

CUP, PINT, AND QUART

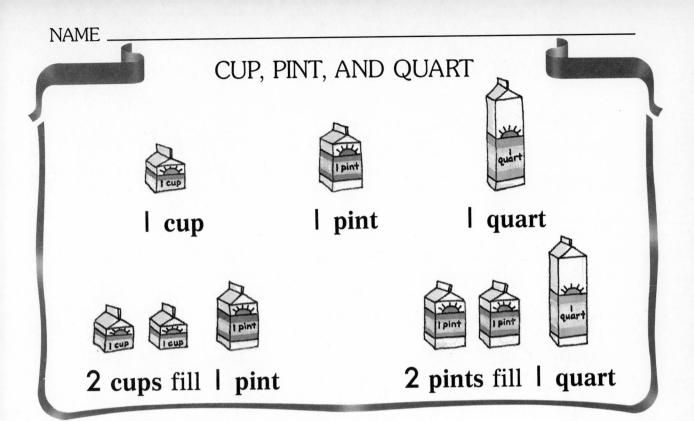

| cup | | pint | | quart

2 cups fill **| pint**   **2 pints** fill **| quart**

Color the number you can fill.

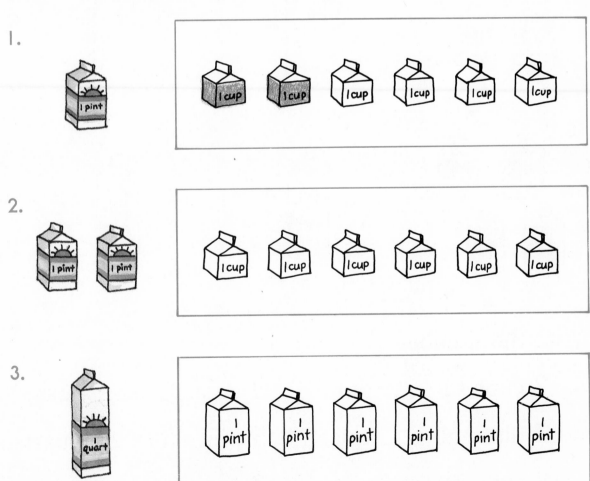

1.

2.

3.

Color the number you can fill.

4.

5.

6.

7.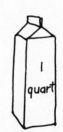

⭐ Write the number.

8. **2** cups fill _____ pint.   **4** cups fill _____ pints.

9. **2** pints fill _____ quart.   **4** pints fill _____ quarts.

10. **4** cups fill _____ pints.   **8** cups fill _____ quarts.

Cup, Pint, and Quart

POUND

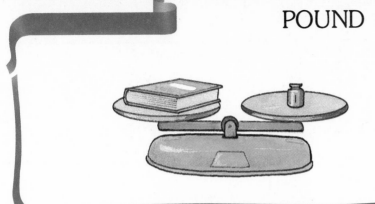

The book weighs
1 pound.

How many pounds?

1.

__2__ pounds

2.

____ pounds

3.

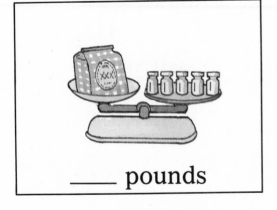

____ pounds

4.

____ pounds

5.

____ pounds

6.

____ pounds

How many pounds?

7.

_____ pounds

8.

_____ pounds

9.

_____ pounds

10.

_____ pounds

11.

_____ pound

12.

_____ pounds

Think of the sum.
Is it more than 10? Ring yes or no.

13. **8 + 4**   (yes)   no   **5 + 6**   yes   no

14. **11 + 4**   yes   no   **6 + 3**   yes   no

15. **10 + 2**   yes   no   **4 + 7**   yes   no

Pound

PROBLEM SOLVING

  Use a  to find out how **long** the rope is.

 Use a to find out how much the berries **weigh.**

 Use a to find out how much the vase **holds.**

Ring the one you would use.

1. You want to know the cost of grapes.
   They are sold by the pound.

   You would use

2. You are making a hat.
   You need paper **10** inches long.

   You would use

3. There will be **8** children at the party.
   How many quarts of punch will you need?

   You would use

Ring the one you would use.

4. Each card is **4** inches long.
How many pieces of paper
will you need?

You would use

5. You are making soup.
You need a pint of water.
You would use

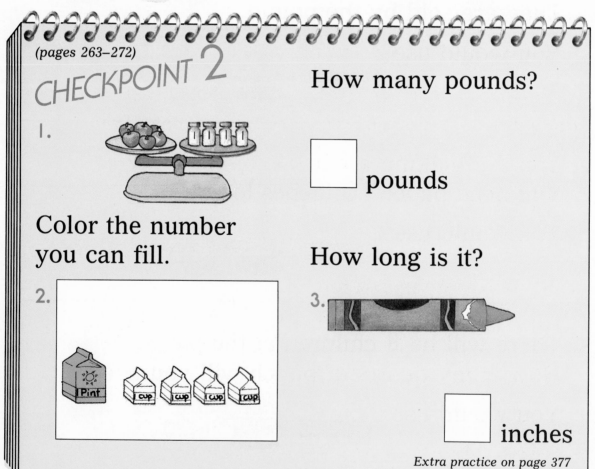

(pages 263–272)

CHECKPOINT 2

How many pounds?

1.

☐ pounds

Color the number
you can fill.

How long is it?

2.

3.

☐ inches

Extra practice on page 377

Problem Solving

CHAPTER 10 TEST

Ring which holds more?

1.

How many?

2.

____ kilograms

How many?

3.

____ pounds

How long?

4.

____ centimeters

5.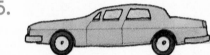

____ inches

Write the number.   CRAYONS

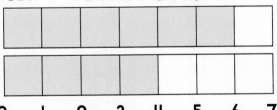

0   1   2   3   4   5   6   7

6. How many more than ? ____

Color the number you can fill.

7.

Extra practice on page 378

MATHEMATICS and SCIENCE

You use a **thermometer** to measure temperature. This thermometer reads **20 degrees.**

Write the temperature.

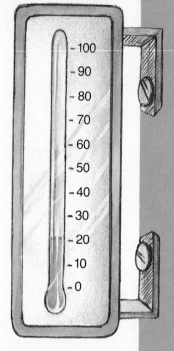

1.
- 100
- 90
- 80
- 70
- 60
- 50
- 40
- 30
- 20
- 10
- 0

_____ degrees

2.
- 100
- 90
- 80
- 70
- 60
- 50
- 40
- 30
- 20
- 10
- 0

_____ degrees

3.
- 100
- 90
- 80
- 70
- 60
- 50
- 40
- 30
- 20
- 10
- 0

_____ degrees

4. Match.

Enrichment

You use a **centimeter** to measure small objects.

You use a **meter** to measure large objects.

A meter is
100 centimeters.

Which is the better measure to use?
Ring meter or centimeter.

1.

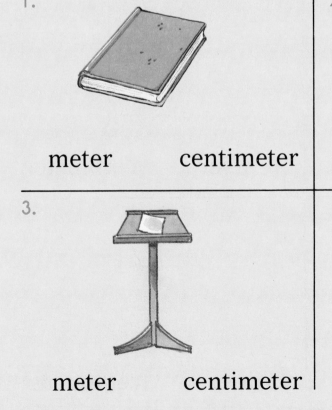

meter   centimeter

2.

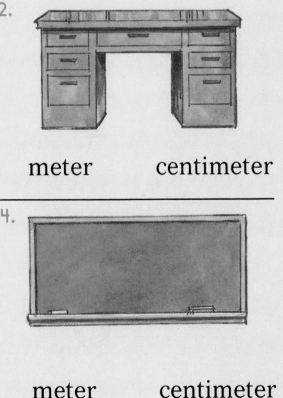

meter   centimeter

3.

meter   centimeter

4.

meter   centimeter

Which is the better measure to use?
Ring meter or centimeter.

5.

meter   centimeter

6.

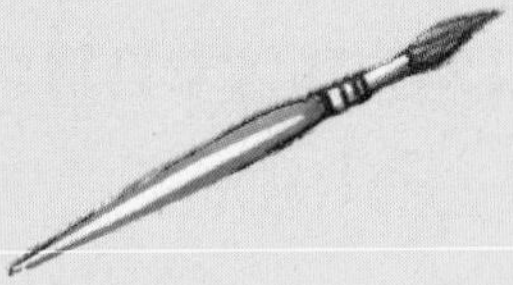

meter   centimeter

7.

meter   centimeter

8.

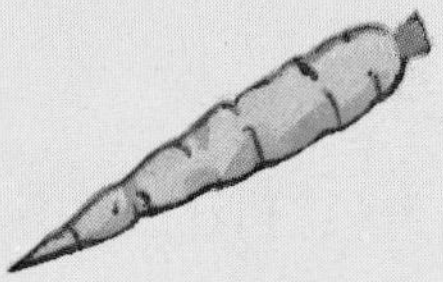

meter   centimeter

9.

meter   centimeter

10.

meter   centimeter

11.

meter   centimeter

12.

meter   centimeter

Meter

NAME _____

 CUMULATIVE REVIEW

Fill in the ◯ for the correct answer.

Choose the number of tens and ones.

1. **57**	2. **93**
Ⓐ **5** tens **5** ones	Ⓐ **3** tens **9** ones
Ⓑ **7** tens **5** ones	Ⓑ **9** tens **3** ones
Ⓒ **5** tens **7** ones	Ⓒ **3** tens **3** ones

Choose the missing numbers.

3.

33, _?_, _?_, _?_, 37

33, 34, 35   **34, 35, 36**   **34, 37, 38**

　Ⓐ　　　　　　　　Ⓑ　　　　　　　　Ⓒ

Choose the number that is greater.

4. **42** **54**	Ⓐ **24** Ⓑ **42** Ⓒ **54**	5. **87** **85**	Ⓐ **87** Ⓑ **58** Ⓒ **85**

Choose the number that is less.

6. **13** **11**	Ⓐ **13** Ⓑ **11** Ⓒ **31**	7. **26** **27**	Ⓐ **26** Ⓑ **62** Ⓒ **27**

Use the chart to solve.

CIRCUS TIMES

	Mon.	Tues.	Wed.
Circus begins	1:00	3:30	8:00
Circus ends	3:00	5:30	10:00

8. What time does the circus begin on Wednesday?

Ⓐ 1:00   Ⓑ 10:00   Ⓒ 8:00

9. On what day does the circus end at 5:30?

Ⓐ Monday   Ⓑ Tuesday   Ⓒ Wednesday

LANGUAGE and VOCABULARY REVIEW

Ring the answer.

1. A __?__ holds less than a pint.

quart   (cup)

2. The car is __?__ than the bus.

heavier   lighter

3. A __?__ shows inches.

ruler   scale

4. The book is 1 __?__.

liter   kilogram

Read with the children:

Suppose you want to buy walnuts for **53**¢ and peanuts for **21**¢. How many dimes and pennies is that in all?

ADDITION AND SUBTRACTION TWO DIGIT NUMBERS

ADDING TENS

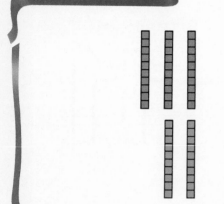

tens	ones
3	0
+ 2	0
5	0

3 tens
+2 tens
5 tens

1. Add.

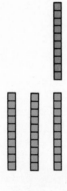

1 tens
+3 tens
___ tens

tens	ones
1	0
+ 3	0

2.

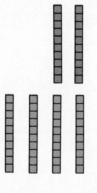

2 tens
+4 tens
___ tens

tens	ones
2	0
+ 4	0

3. 3 tens   30
   +2 tens   +20

   ___ tens

4. 2 tens   20
   +5 tens   +50

   ___ tens

5. 4 tens   40
   +5 tens   +50

   ___ tens

6. 4 tens   40
   +4 tens   +40

   ___ tens

Adding Multiples of Ten

ADDING TWO DIGITS

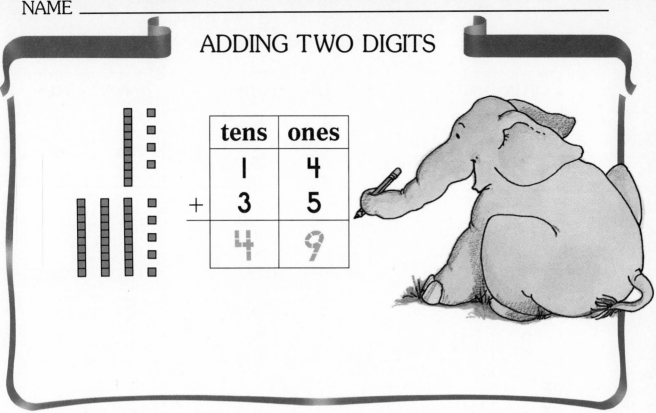

tens	ones
1	4
+ 3	5
4	9

Add the ones. Then add the tens.

1.

tens	ones
1	3
+ 2	1

2.

tens	ones
2	3
+ 3	6

3.

tens	ones
1	4
+ 2	5

4.

tens	ones
3	2
+ 3	5

Add the ones. Then add the tens.

5.

tens	ones
3	2
+ 4	3

tens	ones
3	5
+ 2	4

tens	ones
6	2
+ 2	3

6.

tens	ones
3	4
+ 3	4

tens	ones
2	6
+ 1	2

tens	ones
5	1
+ 4	1

7.

tens	ones
3	7
+ 2	2

tens	ones
5	3
+ 2	2

tens	ones
1	4
+ 1	5

Think. $30 + 20 = 50$

Then add. $30 + 22 = 52$

8. $20 + 20 = 40$

$20 + 21 = \underline{\hspace{1cm}}$

9. $30 + 40 = 70$

$30 + 47 = \underline{\hspace{1cm}}$

10. $10 + 40 = 50$

$10 + 46 = \underline{\hspace{1cm}}$

11. $30 + 30 = 60$

$30 + 35 = \underline{\hspace{1cm}}$

TRY THIS: Use punchouts to show addition.

ADDING TWO DIGITS

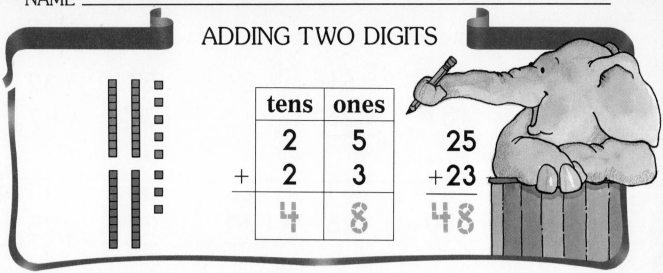

tens	ones
2	5
+ 2	3
4	8

25
+23
48

Add the ones. Then add the tens.

1.

tens	ones
2	3
+ 1	5

23
+15

2.

tens	ones
3	2
+ 2	4

32
+24

3.

tens	ones
3	4
+ 3	4

34
+34

4.

tens	ones
1	5
+ 4	2

15
+42

5.

36	71	78	32	41	52
+52	+20	+21	+16	+35	+36

6.

75	48	52	78	32	61
+13	+21	+30	+20	+67	+34

Add. Use punchouts to help you.

7.
$$\begin{array}{r}23\\+15\\\hline\end{array}$$
$$\begin{array}{r}11\\+57\\\hline\end{array}$$
$$\begin{array}{r}61\\+26\\\hline\end{array}$$
$$\begin{array}{r}24\\+32\\\hline\end{array}$$
$$\begin{array}{r}57\\+31\\\hline\end{array}$$
$$\begin{array}{r}32\\+47\\\hline\end{array}$$

8.
$$\begin{array}{r}43\\+46\\\hline\end{array}$$
$$\begin{array}{r}59\\+40\\\hline\end{array}$$
$$\begin{array}{r}64\\+25\\\hline\end{array}$$
$$\begin{array}{r}26\\+70\\\hline\end{array}$$
$$\begin{array}{r}50\\+37\\\hline\end{array}$$
$$\begin{array}{r}43\\+25\\\hline\end{array}$$

9.
$$\begin{array}{r}12\\+47\\\hline\end{array}$$
$$\begin{array}{r}29\\+50\\\hline\end{array}$$
$$\begin{array}{r}43\\+21\\\hline\end{array}$$
$$\begin{array}{r}65\\+31\\\hline\end{array}$$
$$\begin{array}{r}56\\+31\\\hline\end{array}$$
$$\begin{array}{r}82\\+17\\\hline\end{array}$$

10.
$$\begin{array}{r}32\\+67\\\hline\end{array}$$
$$\begin{array}{r}81\\+12\\\hline\end{array}$$
$$\begin{array}{r}40\\+52\\\hline\end{array}$$
$$\begin{array}{r}31\\+14\\\hline\end{array}$$
$$\begin{array}{r}61\\+27\\\hline\end{array}$$
$$\begin{array}{r}37\\+21\\\hline\end{array}$$

11.
$$\begin{array}{r}23\\+61\\\hline\end{array}$$
$$\begin{array}{r}45\\+12\\\hline\end{array}$$
$$\begin{array}{r}52\\+37\\\hline\end{array}$$
$$\begin{array}{r}26\\+50\\\hline\end{array}$$
$$\begin{array}{r}42\\+25\\\hline\end{array}$$
$$\begin{array}{r}36\\+51\\\hline\end{array}$$

Write the numbers.

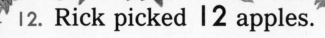

12. Rick picked **12** apples.

John picked **32** apples.

How many in all?

$$\begin{array}{r}12\\+32\\\hline\end{array}$$

apples

Adding Two-Digit Numbers

ADDING TWO DIGITS

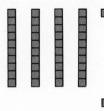

tens	ones	
4	1	41
+	6	+ 6
4	7	47

Add.

1.

tens	ones
2	2
+	7

22
+ 7

2.

tens	ones
	3
+ 7	5

3
+75

3.

tens	ones
3	4
+	5

34
+ 5

4.

tens	ones
6	8
+	1

68
+ 1

5.
36   25   67   4   32   42
+ 3 + 2 + 2 +45 + 6 + 5

6.
17   5   72   82   26   91
+ 2 +53 + 6 + 4 + 3 + 5

Add.

7.   31   92   63   96   64   4
   + 7   + 4   +22   + 2   +33   +81
   ----   ----   ----   ----   ----   ----

8.   43   85   74   3   45   37
   + 3   +12   + 5   +22   + 1   + 2
   ----   ----   ----   ----   ----   ----

9.   56   22   2   36   32   33
   + 3   +77   +17   +52   + 6   + 5
   ----   ----   ----   ----   ----   ----

10. 51   42   57   22   4   14
   +32   + 7   +30   + 6   +35   + 2
   ----   ----   ----   ----   ----   ----

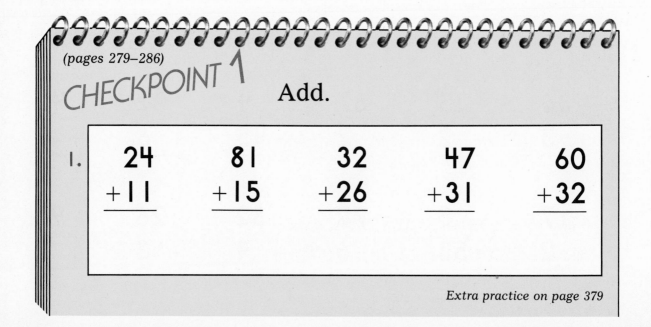

(pages 279–286)

CHECKPOINT 1   Add.

1.   24   81   32   47   60
   +11   +15   +26   +31   +32
   ----   ----   ----   ----   ----

Extra practice on page 379

TRY THIS: Problem Solving Activities, page 403.

NAME _____

Write the numbers. Then solve.

1. George bought a mop and a duster. How much did he spend?

$$50¢$$
$$+\ 42¢$$
$$92¢$$

2. Mrs. Smith needs a duster and soap. How much do both cost?

$$\underline{}$$
$$+\ \underline{}$$

3. Nancy wants to buy a broom and soap. How much money does she need?

$$\underline{}$$
$$+\ \underline{}$$

4. Mr. Garcia bought a bucket and a broom. How much did he spend?

$$\underline{}$$
$$+\ \underline{}$$

Write the numbers. Then solve.

5. Mrs. Smith wants to buy
a fish and a bear. How much
will both cost?

_____
+ _____
_____

6. Roberta bought a duck
and a bear. How much
did she spend?

_____
+ _____
_____

7. Mr. Lee wants to buy a dog
and a fish. How much
money does he need?

_____
+ _____
_____

8. Eric has **75**¢.
Can he buy a cat and a bear?
Ring yes or no.

_____
+ _____
_____

yes   no

PARTNERS: Make up problems. Use play
money to solve. Discuss the answers.

SUBTRACTING TENS

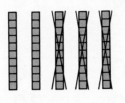

5 tens
−3 tens
_____
2 tens

tens	ones
5	0
− 3	0
2	0

Subtract.

1.

4 tens
−2 tens
_____
tens

tens	ones
4	0
− 2	0

2.

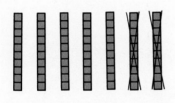

7 tens
−2 tens
_____
tens

tens	ones
7	0
− 2	0

3.　**3** tens　　**30**
　　−1 tens　　**−10**
　　　_____　_____
　　　tens

4.　**8** tens　　**80**
　　−5 tens　　**−50**
　　　_____　_____
　　　tens

5.　**5** tens　　**50**
　　−2 tens　　**−20**
　　　_____　_____
　　　tens

6.　**9** tens　　**90**
　　−7 tens　　**−70**
　　　_____　_____
　　　tens

Subtract.

7.	80 −40	40 −30	70 −30	40 −20	90 −70	30 −10

8.	50 −30	30 −10	70 −40	80 −60	50 −30	40 −20

9.	90 −50	40 −30	50 −20	30 −20	60 −30	70 −20

10.	40 −30	60 −20	70 −40	30 −30	90 −60	80 −50

Write + or − in the ☐ .
Then add or subtract.

11. The Smith family drove
74 miles on Monday.
They drove 23 miles on Tuesday.
How many miles did they drive?

☐ 74
23

miles

Subtracting Multiples of Ten

SUBTRACTING TWO DIGITS

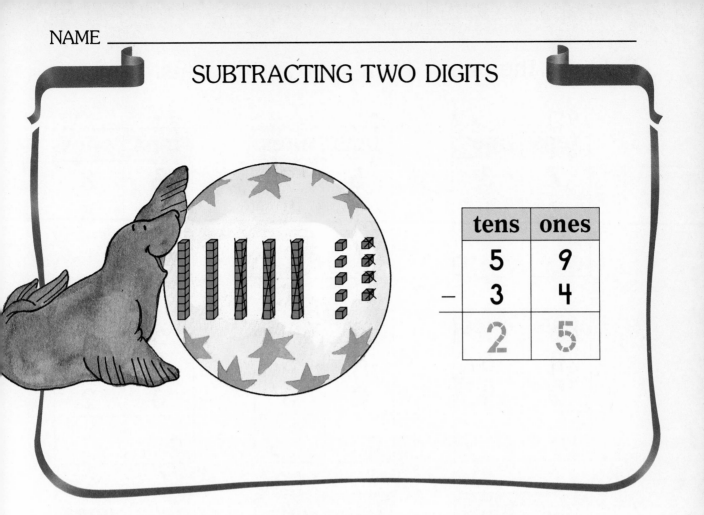

tens	ones
5	9
− 3	4
2	5

Subtract the ones. Then subtract the tens.

1.

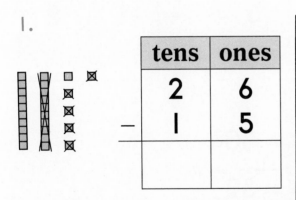

tens	ones
2	6
− 1	5

2.

tens	ones
3	7
− 2	4

3.

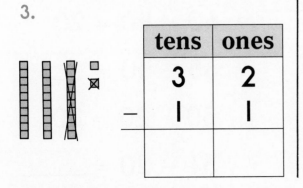

tens	ones
3	2
− 1	1

4.

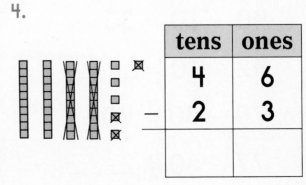

tens	ones
4	6
− 2	3

Subtract the ones. Then subtract the tens.

5.

tens	ones
7	3
− 3	1

tens	ones
5	9
− 1	4

tens	ones
6	8
− 4	5

6.

tens	ones
3	6
− 2	4

tens	ones
4	5
− 2	3

tens	ones
5	7
− 3	2

7.

tens	ones
5	9
− 2	7

tens	ones
8	7
− 6	3

tens	ones
7	9
− 1	2

Think. $50 - 20 = 30$

Then subtract. $52 - 20 = 32$

8. $40 - 10 = 30$

$42 - 10 = \underline{\qquad}$

9. $60 - 40 = 20$

$65 - 40 = \underline{\qquad}$

10. $70 - 30 = 40$

$77 - 30 = \underline{\qquad}$

11. $50 - 20 = 30$

$51 - 20 = \underline{\qquad}$

Subtracting Two-Digit Numbers

SUBTRACTING TWO DIGITS

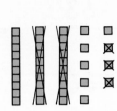

tens	ones
3	9
− 2	3
1	6

39
−23
16

Subtract the ones. Then subtract the tens.

1.

tens	ones
7	8
− 5	3

78
−53

2.

tens	ones
8	6
− 2	5

86
−25

3.

tens	ones
6	8
− 2	5

68
−25

4.

tens	ones
4	7
− 1	3

47
−13

5.

52	37	68	96	78	85
−21	−10	−32	−43	−37	−21

6.

72	98	21	67	78	95
−51	−32	−10	−35	−32	−21

Subtract the ones. Then subtract the tens.

7. $\begin{array}{r} 95 \\ -22 \\ \hline \end{array}$ $\begin{array}{r} 79 \\ -27 \\ \hline \end{array}$ $\begin{array}{r} 85 \\ -31 \\ \hline \end{array}$ $\begin{array}{r} 46 \\ -10 \\ \hline \end{array}$ $\begin{array}{r} 98 \\ -63 \\ \hline \end{array}$ $\begin{array}{r} 87 \\ -25 \\ \hline \end{array}$

8. $\begin{array}{r} 99 \\ -21 \\ \hline \end{array}$ $\begin{array}{r} 79 \\ -48 \\ \hline \end{array}$ $\begin{array}{r} 94 \\ -60 \\ \hline \end{array}$ $\begin{array}{r} 37 \\ -24 \\ \hline \end{array}$ $\begin{array}{r} 66 \\ -23 \\ \hline \end{array}$ $\begin{array}{r} 68 \\ -35 \\ \hline \end{array}$

9. $\begin{array}{r} 86 \\ -24 \\ \hline \end{array}$ $\begin{array}{r} 64 \\ -42 \\ \hline \end{array}$ $\begin{array}{r} 54 \\ -30 \\ \hline \end{array}$ $\begin{array}{r} 37 \\ -16 \\ \hline \end{array}$ $\begin{array}{r} 78 \\ -46 \\ \hline \end{array}$ $\begin{array}{r} 65 \\ -24 \\ \hline \end{array}$

10. $\begin{array}{r} 97 \\ -32 \\ \hline \end{array}$ $\begin{array}{r} 43 \\ -32 \\ \hline \end{array}$ $\begin{array}{r} 89 \\ -31 \\ \hline \end{array}$ $\begin{array}{r} 85 \\ -62 \\ \hline \end{array}$ $\begin{array}{r} 75 \\ -52 \\ \hline \end{array}$ $\begin{array}{r} 57 \\ -43 \\ \hline \end{array}$

11. $\begin{array}{r} 36 \\ -21 \\ \hline \end{array}$ $\begin{array}{r} 55 \\ -31 \\ \hline \end{array}$ $\begin{array}{r} 62 \\ -21 \\ \hline \end{array}$ $\begin{array}{r} 98 \\ -81 \\ \hline \end{array}$ $\begin{array}{r} 37 \\ -16 \\ \hline \end{array}$ $\begin{array}{r} 89 \\ -63 \\ \hline \end{array}$

☆ Rewrite. Then add or subtract.

12. 56 − 24

13. 62 + 21

14. 36 + 23

Subtracting Two-Digit Numbers

SUBTRACTING TWO DIGITS

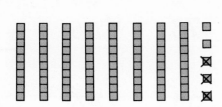

tens	ones
8	5
−	3
8	2

85
− 3
82

Subtract.

1.

tens	ones
2	9
−	8

29
− 8

2.

tens	ones
9	8
−	3

98
− 3

3.

tens	ones
7	6
−	5

76
− 5

4.

tens	ones
5	7
−	2

57
− 2

5.
```
  27      86      57      78      89      95
−  3    −  4    −  3    −  6    − 72    −  3
```

6.
```
  96      37      68      19      28      87
−  2    − 16    −  3    −  3    −  5    −  3
```

Subtract.

7.
$$\begin{array}{r} 49 \\ -\ 3 \\ \hline \end{array}$$
$$\begin{array}{r} 85 \\ -\ 1 \\ \hline \end{array}$$
$$\begin{array}{r} 56 \\ -\ 2 \\ \hline \end{array}$$
$$\begin{array}{r} 75 \\ -23 \\ \hline \end{array}$$
$$\begin{array}{r} 58 \\ -\ 6 \\ \hline \end{array}$$
$$\begin{array}{r} 26 \\ -\ 3 \\ \hline \end{array}$$

8.
$$\begin{array}{r} 97 \\ -\ 3 \\ \hline \end{array}$$
$$\begin{array}{r} 77 \\ -15 \\ \hline \end{array}$$
$$\begin{array}{r} 38 \\ -\ 5 \\ \hline \end{array}$$
$$\begin{array}{r} 64 \\ -\ 3 \\ \hline \end{array}$$
$$\begin{array}{r} 48 \\ -\ 2 \\ \hline \end{array}$$
$$\begin{array}{r} 89 \\ -55 \\ \hline \end{array}$$

9.
$$\begin{array}{r} 68 \\ -\ 7 \\ \hline \end{array}$$
$$\begin{array}{r} 56 \\ -14 \\ \hline \end{array}$$
$$\begin{array}{r} 37 \\ -\ 2 \\ \hline \end{array}$$
$$\begin{array}{r} 29 \\ -\ 3 \\ \hline \end{array}$$
$$\begin{array}{r} 68 \\ -37 \\ \hline \end{array}$$
$$\begin{array}{r} 95 \\ -\ 2 \\ \hline \end{array}$$

10.
$$\begin{array}{r} 92 \\ -11 \\ \hline \end{array}$$
$$\begin{array}{r} 55 \\ -\ 3 \\ \hline \end{array}$$
$$\begin{array}{r} 27 \\ -\ 2 \\ \hline \end{array}$$
$$\begin{array}{r} 38 \\ -16 \\ \hline \end{array}$$
$$\begin{array}{r} 46 \\ -\ 4 \\ \hline \end{array}$$
$$\begin{array}{r} 78 \\ -\ 5 \\ \hline \end{array}$$

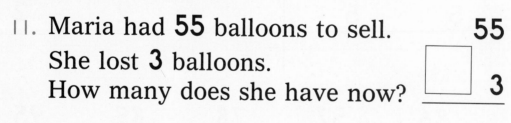

Write + or − in the ☐ .
Then add or subtract.

11. Maria had **55** balloons to sell.
She lost **3** balloons.
How many does she have now?

$$\begin{array}{r} 55 \\ \Box\ 3 \\ \hline \end{array}$$

12. Jason had **35** marbles.
He bought **13** more marbles.
How many marbles
does he have now?

$$\begin{array}{r} 35 \\ \Box\ 13 \\ \hline \end{array}$$

Subtracting Two-Digit Numbers.

ADD, SUBTRACT MONEY

48¢
−22¢
26¢

Tell a story. Then add or subtract.

1.

23¢
+11¢

2.

66¢
−21¢

3.

47¢
−12¢

4.

35¢
+21¢

Use play money. Add or subtract.

5.
| 33¢ | 84¢ | 50¢ | 79¢ | 58¢ |
| +36¢ | −52¢ | +40¢ | − 3¢ | −35¢ |

6.
| 53¢ | 39¢ | 98¢ | 34¢ | 46¢ |
| +32¢ | +20¢ | −65¢ | +53¢ | +32¢ |

7.
| 67¢ | 69¢ | 23¢ | 74¢ | 40¢ |
| −23¢ | −35¢ | +26¢ | −42¢ | +30¢ |

8.
| 59¢ | 32¢ | 34¢ | 13¢ | 55¢ |
| −13¢ | +47¢ | +42¢ | +41¢ | +12¢ |

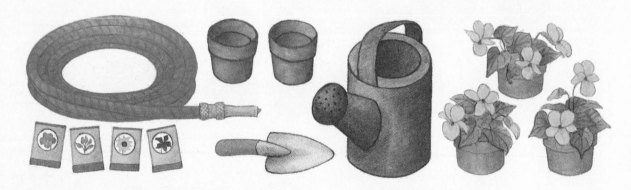

⭐ Write numbers to make the sum
or difference.

9.

1 5			
+ 6 4	− ☐ ☐	+ ☐ ☐	− ☐ ☐
7 9	6 8	4 6	3 2

DISCUSS: Different sets of coins that make 75¢.

PROBLEM SOLVING

Molly has **26¢**.
She spends **12¢**.
How much does she have left?

$$\begin{array}{r} 26¢ \\ -\ 12¢ \\ \hline 14¢ \end{array}$$

Write the numbers.
Then add or subtract.

1. Jeff has **25¢**.
   He gets **20¢** more.
   How much does he have in all?

2. Chris had **32¢**.
   He saves **46¢** more.
   How much does he have?

3. Barbara had **76¢**.
   She spends **45¢**.
   How much does she have left?

Write the numbers. Then add or subtract.

4. Bill had **53¢**.
   Then he saved **36¢**.
   How much does he have?

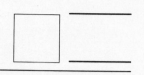

5. David had **46¢**.
   He gave **32¢** to Chris.
   How much does David have?

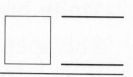

(pages 287–300)

CHECKPOINT 2

Write the numbers.
Then add or subtract.

1. Lupita had **45¢**.
   She gave **21¢** to Jim.
   How much does
   she have now?

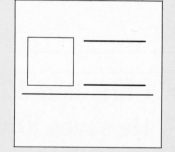

Subtract.

2.
```
 89    67    79
-31   -26   -48
```

Add or subtract.

3.
```
 52¢    75¢
+41¢   -40¢
```

Extra practice on page 379

Problem Solving

CHAPTER 11 TEST

Add.

1.
$$
\begin{array}{cccccc}
35 & 26 & 50 & 37 & 56 & 17 \\
+34 & +12 & +40 & +22 & +31 & +82 \\
\hline
\end{array}
$$

Write the numbers. Then solve.

2. Paul wants to buy marbles and jacks. How much money does he need?

☐ ___
  ___

Subtract.

3.
$$
\begin{array}{cccccc}
58 & 46 & 70 & 79 & 45 & 68 \\
-23 & -31 & -40 & -12 & -23 & -45 \\
\hline
\end{array}
$$

Add or subtract.

4.
$$
\begin{array}{cccccc}
58¢ & 65¢ & 37¢ & 79¢ & 50¢ & 53¢ \\
-35¢ & +32¢ & -12¢ & -\ 3¢ & +40¢ & +32¢ \\
\hline
\end{array}
$$

Write the numbers. Then add or subtract.

5. Kathy had **76¢**.
   She spent **34¢**.
   How much does she have now?

Extra Practice on page 380

MATHEMATICS and HEALTH

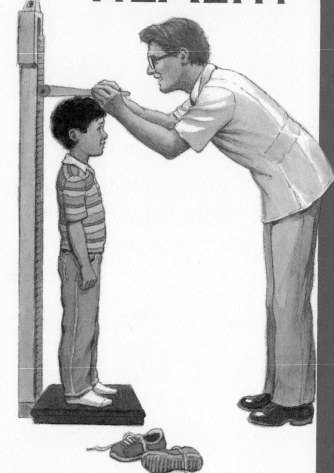

A nurse measures your height. He may use a measuring stick like this.

Write the number.

1. Eurico is **46** inches tall. Last year he was **41** inches tall. How much taller is he now? _____ inches

2. Susan is **44** inches tall. Janet is **3** inches taller than Susan. How tall is Janet? _____ inches

3. Two years ago Kate was **40** inches tall. She grew **6** inches. How tall is she now? _____ inches

Mathematics and Health

Enrichment

30 31 32 33 34 35 36 37 38 39 40

32 is nearer **30** than **40**.   **37** is nearer **40** than **30**.

30 is the ten nearest **32**.   **40** is the ten nearest **37**.

Write the ten nearest the number.

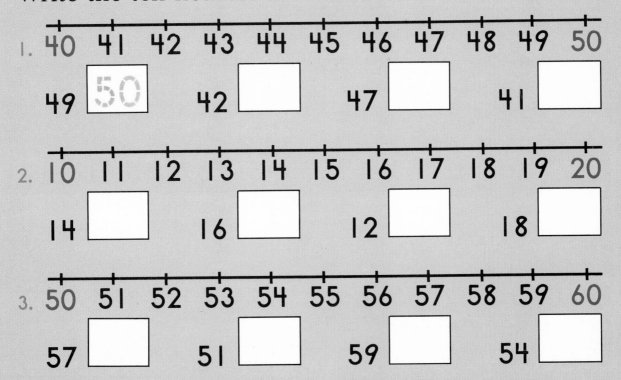

1. 40 41 42 43 44 45 46 47 48 49 50

49 [50]   42 [ ]   47 [ ]   41 [ ]

2. 10 11 12 13 14 15 16 17 18 19 20

14 [ ]   16 [ ]   12 [ ]   18 [ ]

3. 50 51 52 53 54 55 56 57 58 59 60

57 [ ]   51 [ ]   59 [ ]   54 [ ]

When we find the nearest ten
of a number, that number is
rounded.

22, rounded to the nearest ten, is **20**.
28, rounded to the nearest ten, is **30**.

Round to the nearest ten.

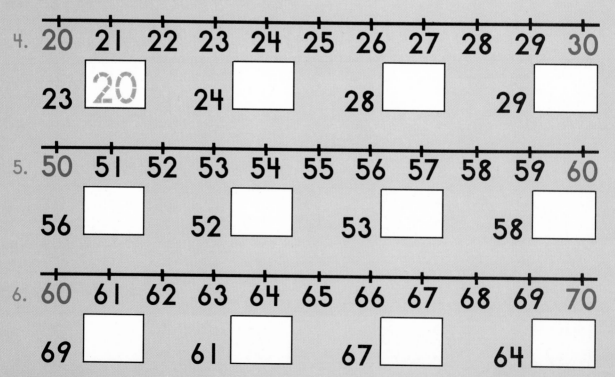

4.

| 20 | 21 | 22 | 23 | 24 | 25 | 26 | 27 | 28 | 29 | 30 |

23 [20]   24 [ ]   28 [ ]   29 [ ]

5.

| 50 | 51 | 52 | 53 | 54 | 55 | 56 | 57 | 58 | 59 | 60 |

56 [ ]   52 [ ]   53 [ ]   58 [ ]

6.

| 60 | 61 | 62 | 63 | 64 | 65 | 66 | 67 | 68 | 69 | 70 |

69 [ ]   61 [ ]   67 [ ]   64 [ ]

Enrichment: Rounding

CUMULATIVE REVIEW

Fill in the ⬭ for the correct answer.

Choose the correct example.

1. Jane had **5¢**. She spent **3¢**. How much does she have now?	Ⓐ **5¢ + 3¢** Ⓑ **3¢ + 5¢** Ⓒ **5¢ – 3¢**
2. Michael had **4¢**. He saved **5¢** more. How much does he have now?	Ⓐ **4¢ + 5¢** Ⓑ **5¢ – 4¢** Ⓒ **9¢ – 5¢**

Solve.

3. Anita has **6** pennies.
She needs **9** pennies.
How many more pennies
does she need?

Ⓐ

Ⓑ

Ⓒ

Add or subtract.

4. **9 + 3** 10 11 12 Ⓐ Ⓑ Ⓒ	5. **7 + 4** 11 10 12 Ⓐ Ⓑ Ⓒ	6. **6 + 6** 11 12 10 Ⓐ Ⓑ Ⓒ
7. **11 – 3** 7 8 6 Ⓐ Ⓑ Ⓒ	8. **12 – 8** 4 5 6 Ⓐ Ⓑ Ⓒ	9. **11 – 7** 3 5 4 Ⓐ Ⓑ Ⓒ

How long?

10.

(A) **6** centimeters

(B) **7** centimeters

(C) **8** centimeters

11.

(A) **6** centimeters

(B) **7** centimeters

(C) **5** centimeters

LANGUAGE and VOCABULARY REVIEW

Match

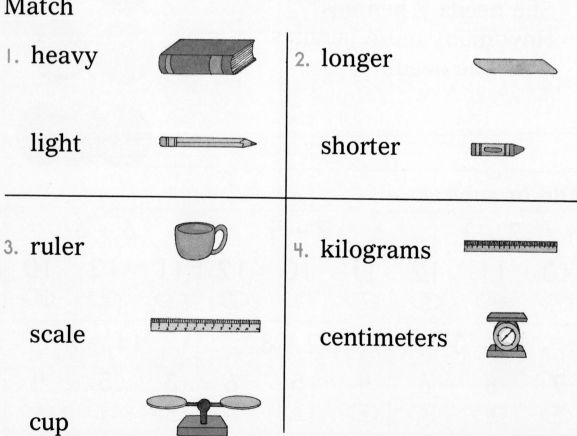

1. heavy

   light

2. longer

   shorter

3. ruler

   scale

   cup

4. kilograms

   centimeters

Language and Vocabulary Review

COMPUTER
LITERACY

Number each story in order.

1.

2.

Follow the steps to draw the picture.

3.

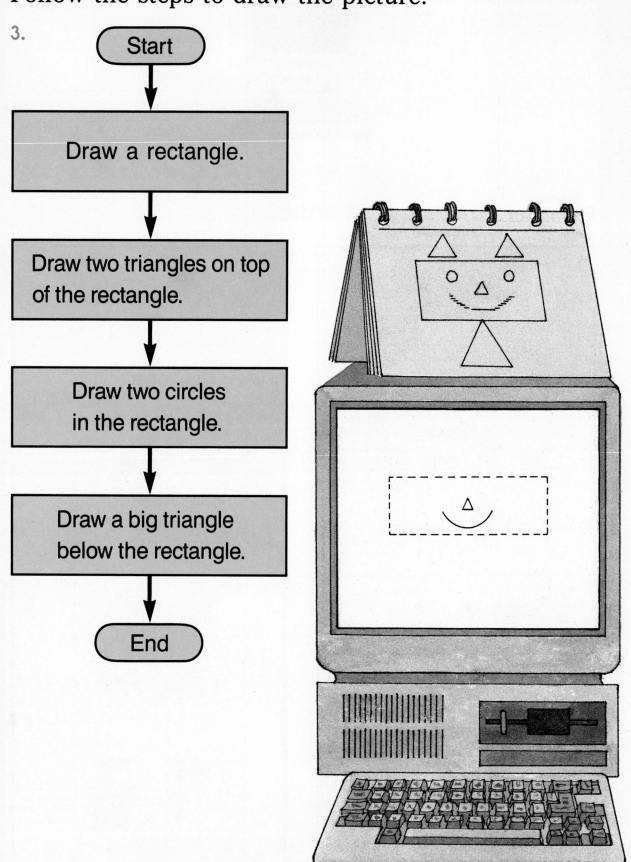

Start

Draw a rectangle.

Draw two triangles on top of the rectangle.

Draw two circles in the rectangle.

Draw a big triangle below the rectangle.

End

Flowcharting

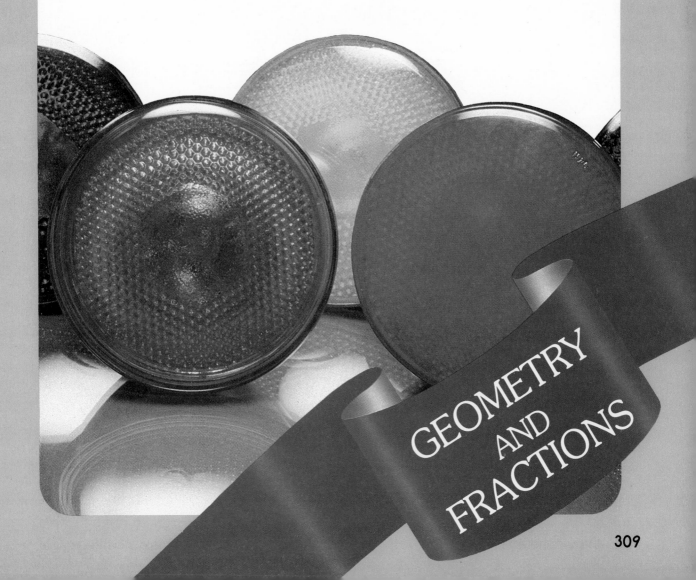

12

Read with the children:

What is the shape of the red lights?
Could the yellow light be a circle?
What other shapes can you find in your classroom?

GEOMETRY AND FRACTIONS

309

TRIANGLE AND RECTANGLE

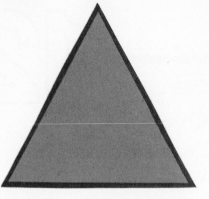

This is a **triangle**.
It has 3 sides.

This is a **rectangle**.
It has 4 sides.

1. Color triangles ▨ .

2. Color rectangles ▨ .

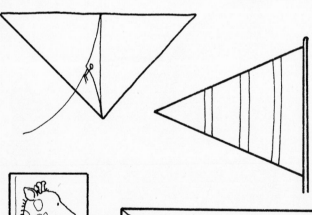

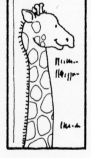

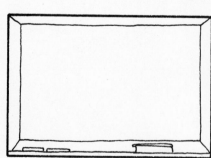

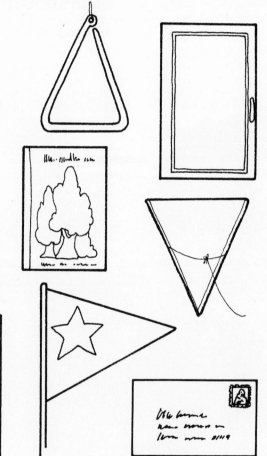

3. How many triangles? ____

4. How many rectangles? ____

Identifying Triangle and Rectangle

CIRCLE AND SQUARE

This is a **circle**.
It has no sides.

This is a **square**.
It has **4** sides.
The sides are
the same length.

1. Ring the circles.

2. ✓ the squares.

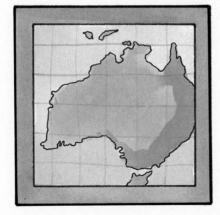

3. How many circles? ____

4. How many squares? ____

Identifying Circle and Square

5. Color circles ■.

6. Color squares ■.

7. Color the 🐦.

inside ■
outside ▢
on ■

TRY THIS: Problem Solving Activities, page 404.

CUBE AND CYLINDER

This is a **cube**.
It has **6** flat sides.
It cannot roll.

This is a **cylinder**.
It has **2** flat sides.
It can roll.

1. Ring the cubes.
2. ✓ the cylinders.

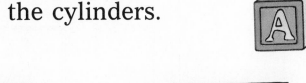

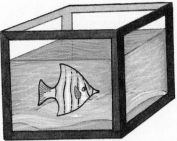

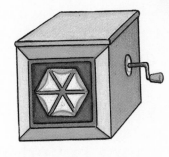

3. How many cubes? ____

4. How many cylinders? ____

Identifying Cube and Cylinder

5. Color cubes ■ .
6. Color cylinders ■ .

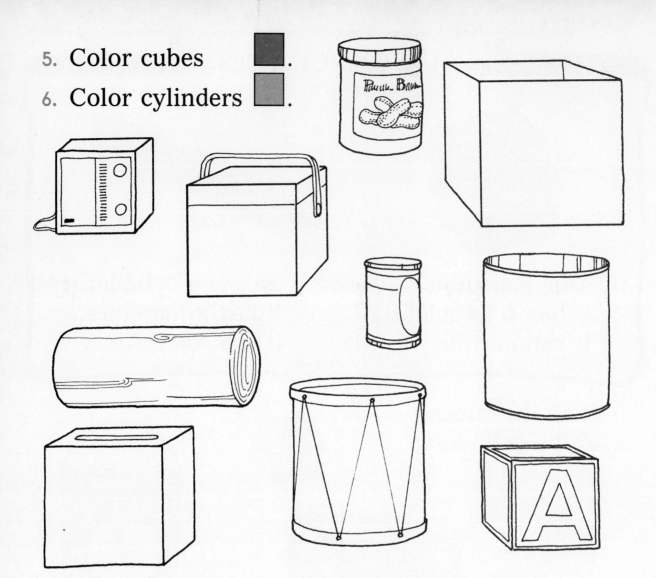

Read the graph.
Then write the number.

SHAPES

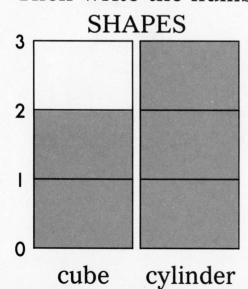

7. How many cubes? ____

8. How many cylinders? ____

9. How many more cylinders than cubes? ____

Identifying Cube and Cylinder

SPHERE AND CONE

This is a **sphere**.
It has no flat sides.
It can roll.

This is a **cone**.
It has one flat side.
It can roll.

1. Ring the spheres.
2. ✓ the cones.

3. How many spheres? ____

4. How many cones? ____

Identifying Sphere and Cone

Ring the shapes that match.

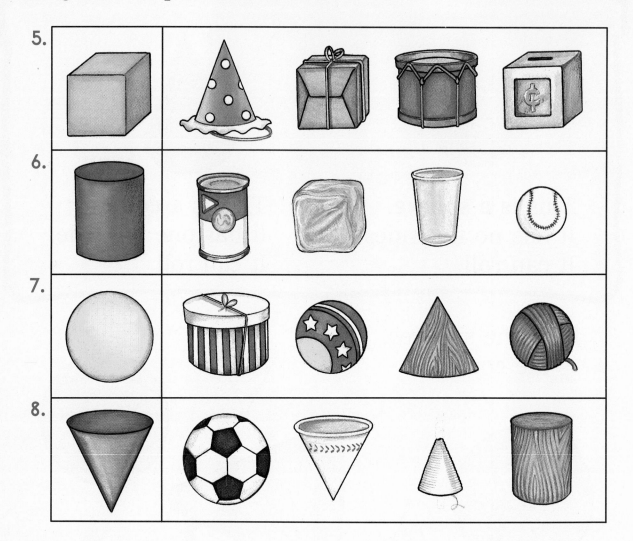

5.

6.

7.

8.

$$10 + 0 = 10 \qquad 25 + 0 = 25$$

Write the sum.

9. $12 + 0 =$ _____ $36 + 0 =$ _____ $42 + 0 =$ _____

10. $74 + 0 =$ _____ $67 + 0 =$ _____ $57 + 0 =$ _____

11. $89 + 0 =$ _____ $23 + 0 =$ _____ $94 + 0 =$ _____

DISCUSS: Objects that look like spheres and cones.

PROBLEM SOLVING

Carlos found different shapes at home.
Then he made a graph.

SHAPES CARLOS FOUND

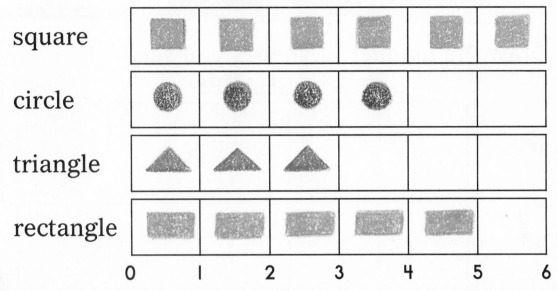

How many did Carlos find?

1. square ___6___   circle ___

   triangle ___   rectangle ___

Ring the shape he found more often.

2. square   or   circle   3. rectangle   or   square

4. circle   or   triangle   5. triangle   or   rectangle

Ring the shape he found less often.

6. circle   or   rectangle   7. triangle   or   square

8. rectangle   or   square   9. circle   or   triangle

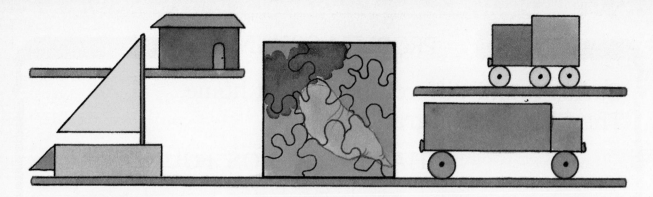

10. Draw the number of shapes you see.

SHAPES

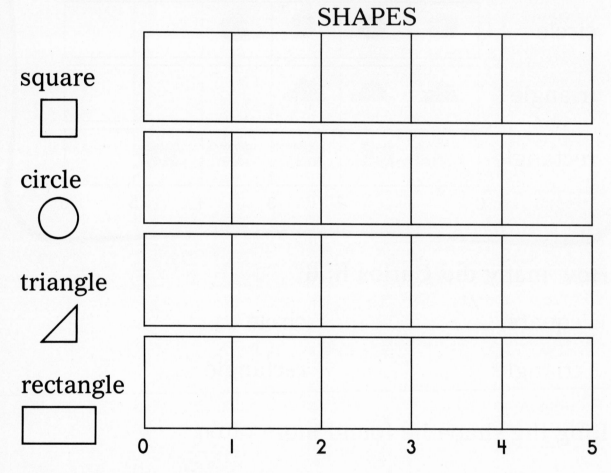

square

circle

triangle

rectangle

0   1   2   3   4   5

Write the number.

11. How many squares? ____

12. How many rectangles? ____

13. How many circles? ____

14. How many triangles? ____

Problem Solving

PARTS THAT MATCH

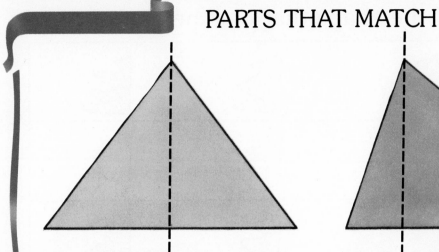

If you fold this shape, the two parts would match.

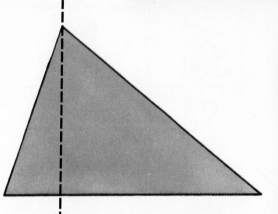

If you fold this shape, the two parts would not match.

Ring the shape if the parts match.

1.

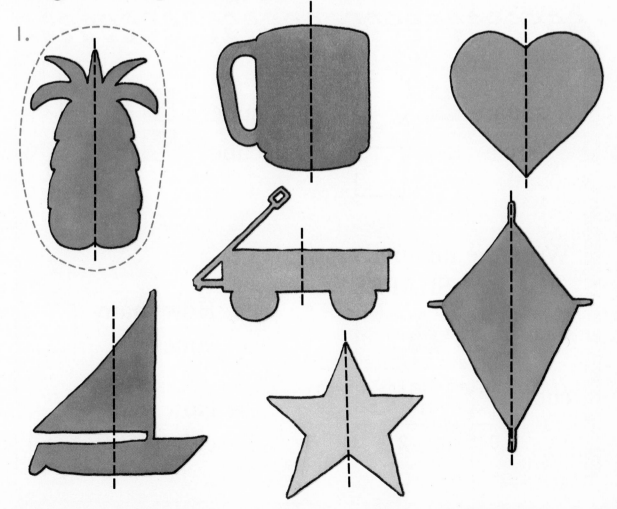

Identifying Symmetrical Shapes

Ring the part of the shape that matches.

2.

3.

4.

5.

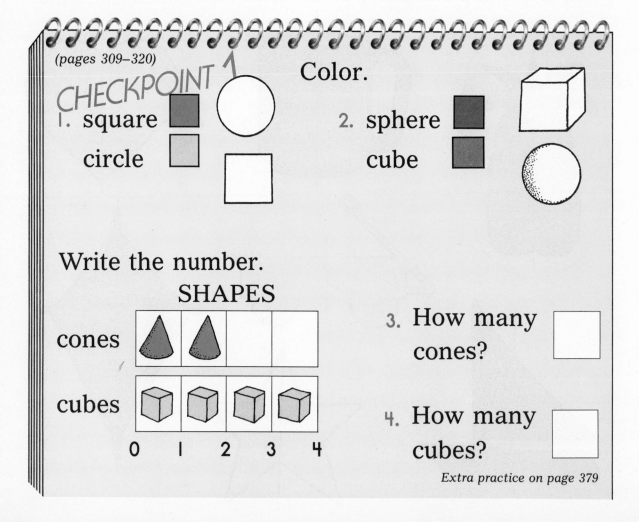

(pages 309–320)

CHECKPOINT 1

Color.

1. square
   circle

2. sphere
   cube

Write the number.

SHAPES

cones

cubes

0   1   2   3   4

3. How many cones?

4. How many cubes?

Extra practice on page 379

Identifying Symmetrical Shapes

EQUAL PARTS

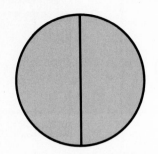

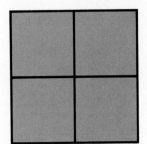

This circle has **2 equal parts**.

This square has **4 equal parts**.

Ring the shape that has equal parts.

1.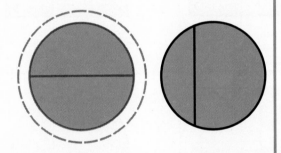

2.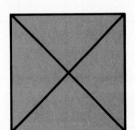

3.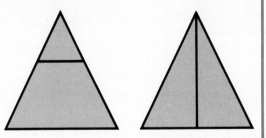

4.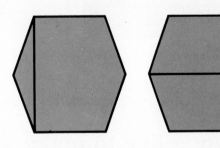

5.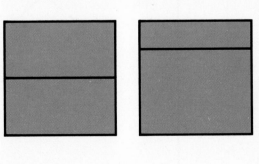

6.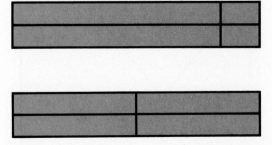

Write the number of equal parts.

7.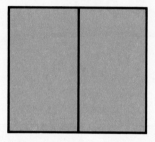

2 ̲ ̲ ̲ ̲

8.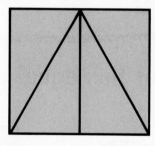

̲ ̲ ̲ ̲

9.

̲ ̲ ̲ ̲

10.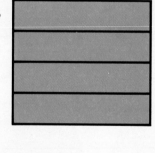

̲ ̲ ̲ ̲

11.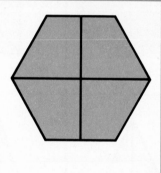

̲ ̲ ̲ ̲

12.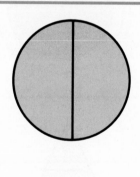

̲ ̲ ̲ ̲

13.

̲ ̲ ̲ ̲

14.

̲ ̲ ̲ ̲

15.

̲ ̲ ̲ ̲

⭐ Draw a line to make **2** equal parts.

16.

17.

18.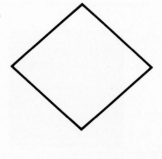

TRY THIS: Use punchouts to show equal parts.

ONE HALF

There are **2** equal parts.
I part is red.

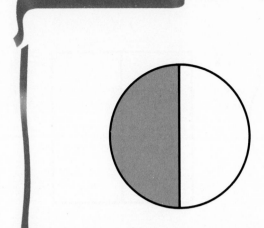

one half $\frac{1}{2}$

Ring the shapes that show one half.

1.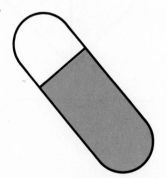

2.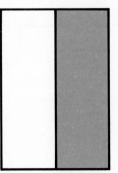

3.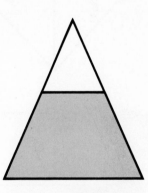

4.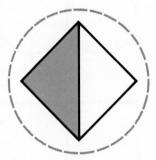

5.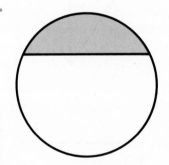

6.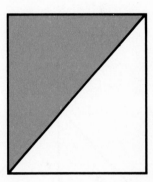

7.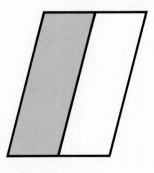

8.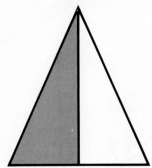

9.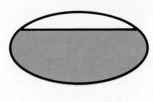

Color $\frac{1}{2}$.

10.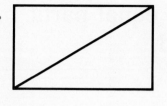

11.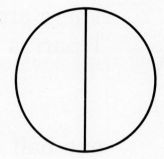

12.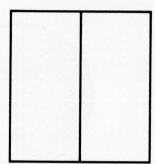

13.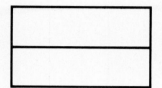

14.

15.

16.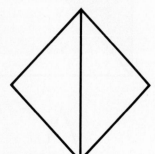

17.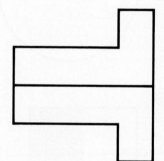

18.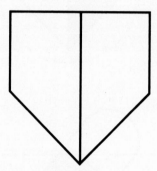

$9 - 0 = 9$　　　　$35 - 0 = 35$

Write the difference.

19. $12 - 0 =$ _____　$23 - 0 =$ _____　$78 - 0 =$ _____

20. $56 - 0 =$ _____　$37 - 0 =$ _____　$97 - 0 =$ _____

　　　　Identifying One Half

ONE THIRD

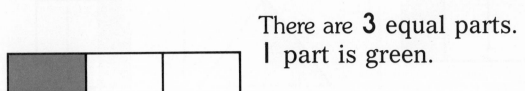

There are **3** equal parts.
I part is green.

one third $\frac{1}{3}$

Ring the shapes that show one third.

1.

2.

3.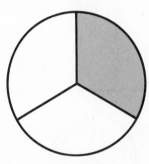

4.

5.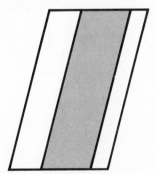

6.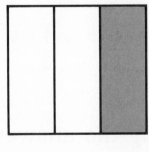

7.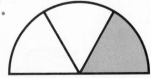

8.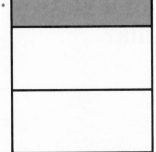

9.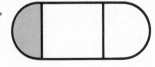

Ring $\frac{1}{2}$ or $\frac{1}{3}$.

10.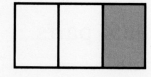

$\frac{1}{2}$ ⊘$\frac{1}{3}$

11.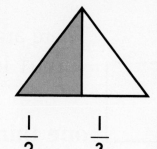

$\frac{1}{2}$ $\frac{1}{3}$

12.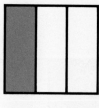

$\frac{1}{2}$ $\frac{1}{3}$

13.

$\frac{1}{2}$ $\frac{1}{3}$

14.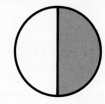

$\frac{1}{2}$ $\frac{1}{3}$

15.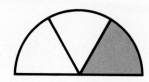

$\frac{1}{2}$ $\frac{1}{3}$

16.

$\frac{1}{2}$ $\frac{1}{3}$

17.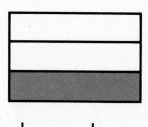

$\frac{1}{2}$ $\frac{1}{3}$

18.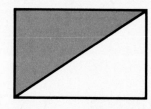

$\frac{1}{2}$ $\frac{1}{3}$

Ring the answer.

19. Sarah had half of a glass of milk.
Juan had a third of a glass of milk.
Who had more milk?

Sarah   Juan

Identifying One Third

ONE FOURTH

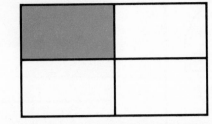 There are **4** equal parts.
1 part is blue.

one fourth $\frac{1}{4}$

Ring the shapes that show one fourth.

1.

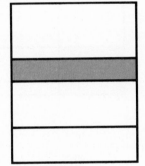

2.

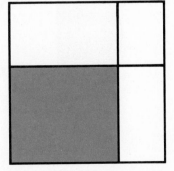

3.

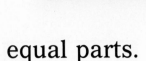

4.

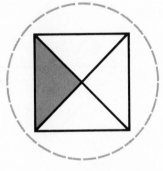

5.

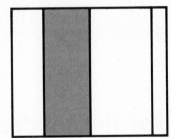

6.

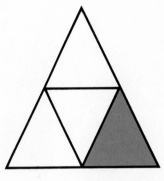

7.

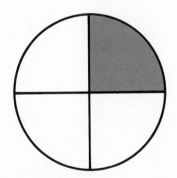

8.

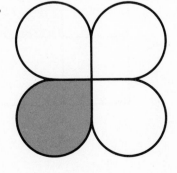

9.

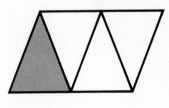

Identifying One Fourth

Ring $\frac{1}{2}$, $\frac{1}{3}$, or $\frac{1}{4}$.

10.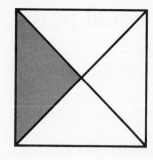

$\frac{1}{2}$ $\frac{1}{3}$ $\left(\frac{1}{4}\right)$

11.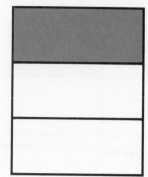

$\frac{1}{2}$ $\frac{1}{3}$ $\frac{1}{4}$

12.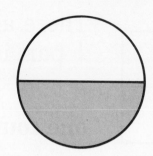

$\frac{1}{2}$ $\frac{1}{3}$ $\frac{1}{4}$

13.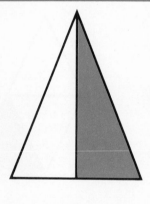

$\frac{1}{2}$ $\frac{1}{3}$ $\frac{1}{4}$

14.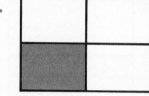

$\frac{1}{2}$ $\frac{1}{3}$ $\frac{1}{4}$

15.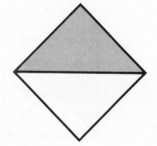

$\frac{1}{2}$ $\frac{1}{3}$ $\frac{1}{4}$

⭐ Write the fraction for the shaded part.

16.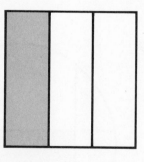

———

17.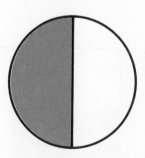

———

18.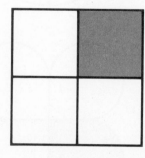

———

PARTNERS: Use punchouts to show $\frac{1}{2}$, $\frac{1}{3}$, and $\frac{1}{4}$.

PROBLEM SOLVING

Tina can buy carrots or squash. She does not want squash.

What does she buy?

carrots _____

Solve.

1. Jane was **6** years old two years ago.
   How old is Jane?

   _____

2. Micki is not as tall as James.
   She is taller than Amy.
   Who is the shortest?

   _____

3. Carl is **10** years old.
   Susan is **4** years younger.
   How old is Susan?

   _____

4. Rick has **6¢**.
   Jim has **5¢** more than Rick.
   How much money does Jim have? _____

5. Alex is **8** years old.
   Amanda is two years older.
   How old is Amanda? _____

⭐ 6. Think of this number.
   It is greater than **18** and less than **27**.
   There is no **2** in this number.
   What is the number? _____

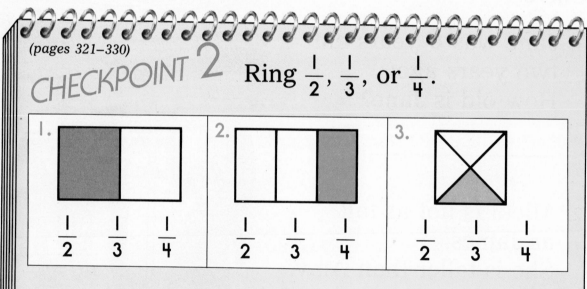

(pages 321–330)

CHECKPOINT 2   Ring $\frac{1}{2}$, $\frac{1}{3}$, or $\frac{1}{4}$.

1. $\frac{1}{2}$ $\frac{1}{3}$ $\frac{1}{4}$

2. $\frac{1}{2}$ $\frac{1}{3}$ $\frac{1}{4}$

3. $\frac{1}{2}$ $\frac{1}{3}$ $\frac{1}{4}$

Write the answer.

4. Juan has two hats.
   They are blue and red.
   He is not wearing the blue hat.
   What color hat is he wearing?

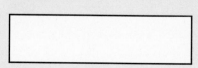

Extra practice on page 379

Problem Solving

CHAPTER 12 TEST

Color.

1. triangle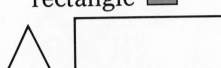
   rectangle

Color.

2. cylinder
   cone

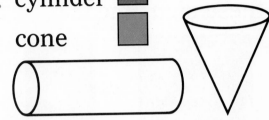

Write the number.

FRUIT

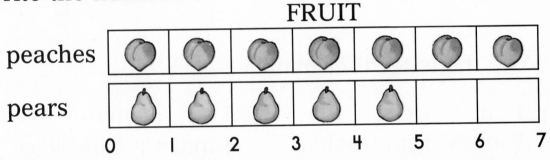

peaches

pears

0   1   2   3   4   5   6   7

3. How many peaches?

____ peaches

4. How many pears?

____ pears

Ring $\frac{1}{2}$, $\frac{1}{3}$, or $\frac{1}{4}$.

5.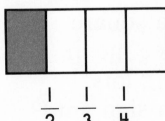

$\frac{1}{2}$ $\frac{1}{3}$ $\frac{1}{4}$

6.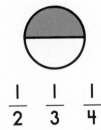

$\frac{1}{2}$ $\frac{1}{3}$ $\frac{1}{4}$

7.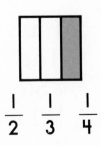

$\frac{1}{2}$ $\frac{1}{3}$ $\frac{1}{4}$

Write the number.

8. Sue was **4** years old three years ago.

   How old is she now? _____

Extra practice on page 380

MATHEMATICS and SOCIAL STUDIES

Do you know what
these signs mean?

A

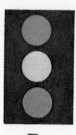
B

C

D

Write the letter that matches each clue.

1. I am a circle.
I mark train tracks.
Which sign am I?

_____

2. I am a square.
I mark a safe place
to ride a bike.
Which sign am I?

_____

3. I have **3** circles.
The red circle means
"Stop."
Which sign am I?

_____

4. I am a square.
You see me in
parking lots.
Which sign am I?

_____

Math and Social Studies

Enrichment

One half of **4**
is **2**

One third of **9**
is **3**

One fourth of
4 is **1**

Color one half.

1.

2.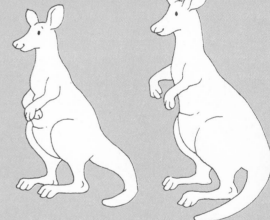

3.

4.

Color one third.

5.

6.

Color one fourth.

7.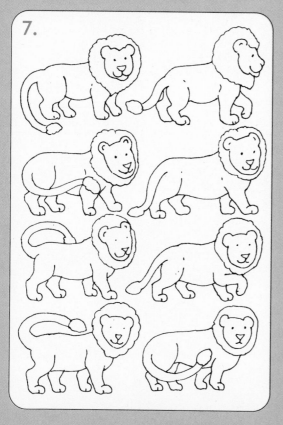

8.

Enrichment: Fractions and Sets

CUMULATIVE REVIEW

Fill in the ⬭ for the correct answer.

What is the amount?

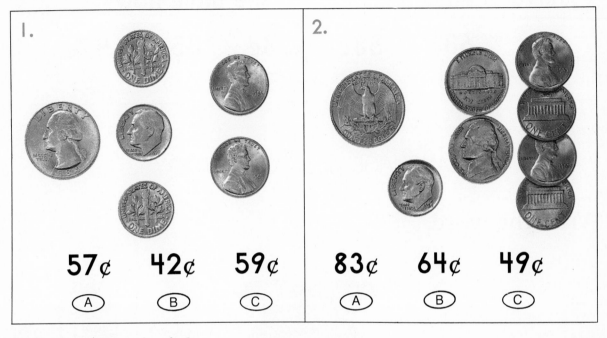

1.		
57¢	42¢	59¢
Ⓐ	Ⓑ	Ⓒ

2.		
83¢	64¢	49¢
Ⓐ	Ⓑ	Ⓒ

What time is it?

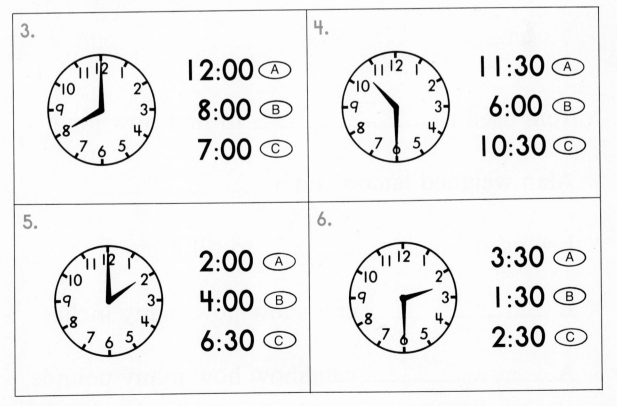

3.

12:00 Ⓐ

8:00 Ⓑ

7:00 Ⓒ

4.

11:30 Ⓐ

6:00 Ⓑ

10:30 Ⓒ

5.

2:00 Ⓐ

4:00 Ⓑ

6:30 Ⓒ

6.

3:30 Ⓐ

1:30 Ⓑ

2:30 Ⓒ

How much?

7. Bill has **35**¢. He saved **23**¢ more. How much does he have in all?	8. Janet has **87**¢. She lost **52**¢. How much does she have now?
48¢ (A) **63**¢ (B) **58**¢ (C)	**28**¢ (A) **35**¢ (B) **47**¢ (C)

LANGUAGE and VOCABULARY REVIEW

Write the word.

ruler   scale   cup

1. Tom used a _____ to find how long.

2. Alan weighed lemons on a _____.

3. Lee used a _____ to fill a pint.

4. A _____ can show how many inches.

5. A _____ can show how many pounds.

Language and Vocabulary Review

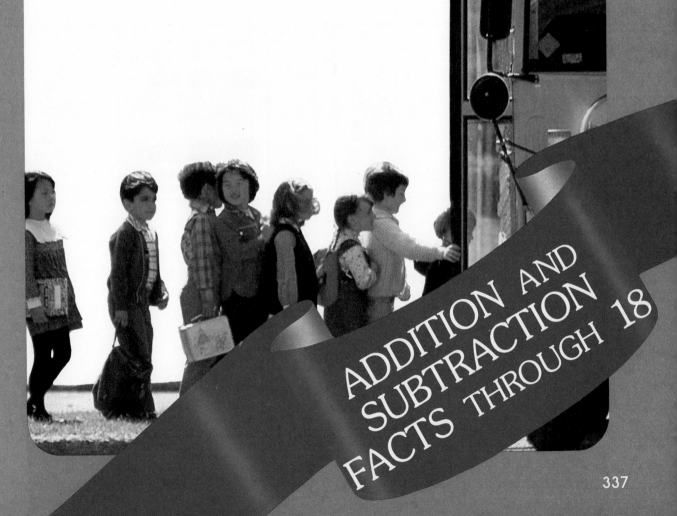

Read with the children:

How many children are getting on the bus? If **6** children are already on the bus, how many children are there in all?

13

ADDING THROUGH 15

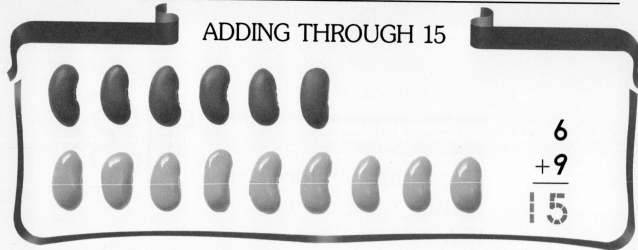

$$\begin{array}{r} 6 \\ +9 \\ \hline 15 \end{array}$$

Tell a story. Then add.

1.

$$\begin{array}{r} 8 \\ +7 \\ \hline \end{array}$$

2.

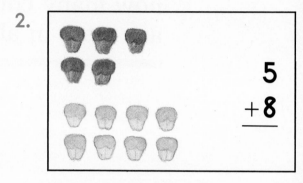

$$\begin{array}{r} 5 \\ +8 \\ \hline \end{array}$$

3.

$$\begin{array}{r} 6 \\ +8 \\ \hline \end{array}$$

4.

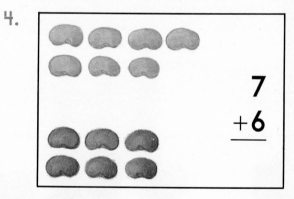

$$\begin{array}{r} 7 \\ +6 \\ \hline \end{array}$$

5.
$$\begin{array}{r} 7 \\ +7 \\ \hline \end{array} \quad \begin{array}{r} 9 \\ +6 \\ \hline \end{array} \quad \begin{array}{r} 8 \\ +6 \\ \hline \end{array} \quad \begin{array}{r} 7 \\ +8 \\ \hline \end{array} \quad \begin{array}{r} 9 \\ +4 \\ \hline \end{array} \quad \begin{array}{r} 5 \\ +9 \\ \hline \end{array}$$

6.
$$\begin{array}{r} 4 \\ +9 \\ \hline \end{array} \quad \begin{array}{r} 6 \\ +7 \\ \hline \end{array} \quad \begin{array}{r} 9 \\ +5 \\ \hline \end{array} \quad \begin{array}{r} 8 \\ +5 \\ \hline \end{array} \quad \begin{array}{r} 6 \\ +9 \\ \hline \end{array} \quad \begin{array}{r} 8 \\ +6 \\ \hline \end{array}$$

Addition Facts through 15

ADDING THROUGH 18

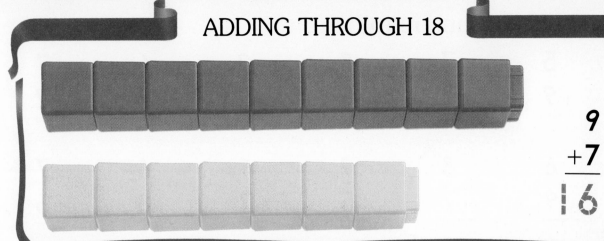

$$\begin{array}{r} 9 \\ +7 \\ \hline 16 \end{array}$$

Tell a story. Then add.

1.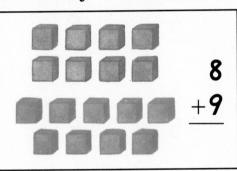

$$\begin{array}{r} 8 \\ +9 \\ \hline \end{array}$$

2.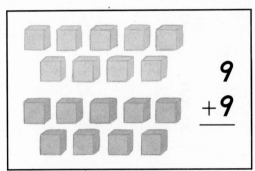

$$\begin{array}{r} 9 \\ +9 \\ \hline \end{array}$$

3.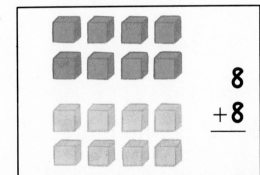

$$\begin{array}{r} 8 \\ +8 \\ \hline \end{array}$$

4.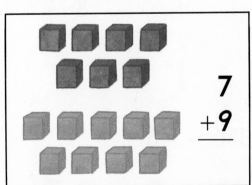

$$\begin{array}{r} 7 \\ +9 \\ \hline \end{array}$$

5.
$$\begin{array}{r} 7 \\ +9 \\ \hline \end{array} \quad \begin{array}{r} 8 \\ +9 \\ \hline \end{array} \quad \begin{array}{r} 9 \\ +9 \\ \hline \end{array} \quad \begin{array}{r} 9 \\ +8 \\ \hline \end{array} \quad \begin{array}{r} 8 \\ +8 \\ \hline \end{array} \quad \begin{array}{r} 7 \\ +8 \\ \hline \end{array}$$

6.
$$\begin{array}{r} 7 \\ +7 \\ \hline \end{array} \quad \begin{array}{r} 8 \\ +7 \\ \hline \end{array} \quad \begin{array}{r} 9 \\ +7 \\ \hline \end{array} \quad \begin{array}{r} 5 \\ +8 \\ \hline \end{array} \quad \begin{array}{r} 6 \\ +8 \\ \hline \end{array} \quad \begin{array}{r} 7 \\ +8 \\ \hline \end{array}$$

Add. Use counters to help.

7.
$$5 \atop +9$$ 　 $$7 \atop +8$$ 　 $$8 \atop +6$$ 　 $$9 \atop +9$$ 　 $$6 \atop +7$$ 　 $$7 \atop +7$$

8.
$$6 \atop +9$$ 　 $$8 \atop +7$$ 　 $$9 \atop +5$$ 　 $$9 \atop +7$$ 　 $$6 \atop +8$$ 　 $$7 \atop +6$$

9.
$$4 \atop +9$$ 　 $$9 \atop +6$$ 　 $$4 \atop +8$$ 　 $$7 \atop +5$$ 　 $$8 \atop +9$$ 　 $$6 \atop +4$$

10.
$$5 \atop +8$$ 　 $$9 \atop +4$$ 　 $$6 \atop +6$$ 　 $$8 \atop +5$$ 　 $$7 \atop +9$$ 　 $$9 \atop +8$$

11.
$$4 \atop +9$$ 　 $$8 \atop +8$$ 　 $$7 \atop +9$$ 　 $$3 \atop +8$$ 　 $$9 \atop +6$$ 　 $$7 \atop +8$$

Think. 6 + 6

$$6 \atop +6 \over 12$$

6 + 7 is one more.

$$6 \atop +7 \over 13$$

Add.

12.
$$8 \atop +8$$ 　 $$8 \atop +9$$

13.
$$7 \atop +7$$ 　 $$7 \atop +8$$

14.
$$5 \atop +5$$ 　 $$5 \atop +6$$

Addition Facts through 18

PROBLEM SOLVING

Ryan bought **4** tickets.
Paul bought **5** tickets.
Ann bought **3** tickets.
Together they bought
__12__ tickets.

Solve.

1. Melanie had **3** rides on the slide.
Sue had **4** rides.
John had **6** rides.
Together they had

_____ rides.

2. Jamie won **5** animals.
Matthew won **3** boats.
Jeanne won **4** clowns.
Together they won

_____ prizes.

3. There are **4** red cars.
There are **3** yellow cars.
There are **7** green cars.
Together there are

_____ cars.

Solve.

4. Jack sold **6** cups of juice.
Andrea sold **3** cups.
Penny sold **9** cups.
Together they sold

_____ cups.

5. Luis won **2** blue ribbons.
Susan won **3** blue ribbons.
Will won **5** blue ribbons.
Together they won

_____ blue ribbons.

6. The Andersons showed
2 cows, **4** goats,
and **7** lambs.
Together they showed

_____ animals.

7. Terry saw **6** white horses.
Tom saw **3** black horses.
Raoul saw **7** brown horses.
Together they saw

_____ horses.

TRY THIS: Use counters to show sums.

SUBTRACTING FROM 15

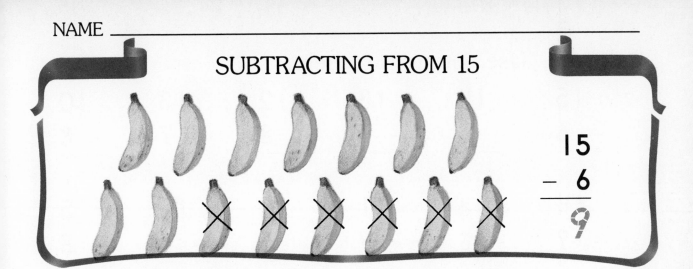

$$\begin{array}{r} 15 \\ -6 \\ \hline 9 \end{array}$$

Tell a story. Then subtract.

1.

$$\begin{array}{r} 14 \\ -7 \\ \hline \end{array}$$

2.

$$\begin{array}{r} 13 \\ -4 \\ \hline \end{array}$$

3.

$$\begin{array}{r} 15 \\ -7 \\ \hline \end{array}$$

4.

$$\begin{array}{r} 14 \\ -9 \\ \hline \end{array}$$

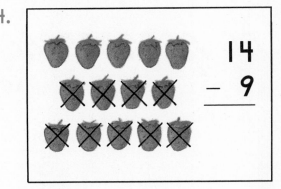

5.
$$\begin{array}{r} 15 \\ -9 \\ \hline \end{array} \qquad \begin{array}{r} 15 \\ -8 \\ \hline \end{array} \qquad \begin{array}{r} 15 \\ -7 \\ \hline \end{array} \qquad \begin{array}{r} 14 \\ -6 \\ \hline \end{array} \qquad \begin{array}{r} 14 \\ -7 \\ \hline \end{array} \qquad \begin{array}{r} 14 \\ -8 \\ \hline \end{array}$$

6.
$$\begin{array}{r} 13 \\ -4 \\ \hline \end{array} \qquad \begin{array}{r} 13 \\ -5 \\ \hline \end{array} \qquad \begin{array}{r} 13 \\ -6 \\ \hline \end{array} \qquad \begin{array}{r} 12 \\ -7 \\ \hline \end{array} \qquad \begin{array}{r} 12 \\ -8 \\ \hline \end{array} \qquad \begin{array}{r} 12 \\ -9 \\ \hline \end{array}$$

Subtract. Use counters to help.

7.
$$\begin{array}{r} 15 \\ -\ 6 \\ \hline \end{array}$$
$$\begin{array}{r} 14 \\ -\ 5 \\ \hline \end{array}$$
$$\begin{array}{r} 13 \\ -\ 4 \\ \hline \end{array}$$
$$\begin{array}{r} 12 \\ -\ 8 \\ \hline \end{array}$$
$$\begin{array}{r} 13 \\ -\ 7 \\ \hline \end{array}$$
$$\begin{array}{r} 10 \\ -\ 8 \\ \hline \end{array}$$

8.
$$\begin{array}{r} 14 \\ -\ 9 \\ \hline \end{array}$$
$$\begin{array}{r} 13 \\ -\ 8 \\ \hline \end{array}$$
$$\begin{array}{r} 11 \\ -\ 9 \\ \hline \end{array}$$
$$\begin{array}{r} 10 \\ -\ 5 \\ \hline \end{array}$$
$$\begin{array}{r} 13 \\ -\ 6 \\ \hline \end{array}$$
$$\begin{array}{r} 15 \\ -\ 8 \\ \hline \end{array}$$

9.
$$\begin{array}{r} 15 \\ -\ 7 \\ \hline \end{array}$$
$$\begin{array}{r} 12 \\ -\ 7 \\ \hline \end{array}$$
$$\begin{array}{r} 14 \\ -\ 6 \\ \hline \end{array}$$
$$\begin{array}{r} 13 \\ -\ 5 \\ \hline \end{array}$$
$$\begin{array}{r} 11 \\ -\ 9 \\ \hline \end{array}$$
$$\begin{array}{r} 10 \\ -\ 7 \\ \hline \end{array}$$

10.
$$\begin{array}{r} 12 \\ -\ 8 \\ \hline \end{array}$$
$$\begin{array}{r} 13 \\ -\ 9 \\ \hline \end{array}$$
$$\begin{array}{r} 14 \\ -\ 8 \\ \hline \end{array}$$
$$\begin{array}{r} 12 \\ -\ 6 \\ \hline \end{array}$$
$$\begin{array}{r} 14 \\ -\ 7 \\ \hline \end{array}$$
$$\begin{array}{r} 15 \\ -\ 9 \\ \hline \end{array}$$

(pages 337–344)

CHECKPOINT 1

Add or subtract.

1.
$$\begin{array}{r} 8 \\ +5 \\ \hline \end{array}$$
$$\begin{array}{r} 15 \\ -\ 8 \\ \hline \end{array}$$
$$\begin{array}{r} 12 \\ -\ 9 \\ \hline \end{array}$$
$$\begin{array}{r} 4 \\ +9 \\ \hline \end{array}$$
$$\begin{array}{r} 11 \\ -\ 5 \\ \hline \end{array}$$

Solve.

2. Jessica picked **4** red,
5 yellow, and **3** orange flowers.

She picked ⬜ flowers in all.

Extra practice on page 383

Subtraction Facts through 15

SUBTRACTING FROM 18

$$18 - 9 = 9$$

Tell a story. Then subtract.

1.
$$17 - 8 = $$

2.
$$16 - 9 = $$

3.
$$18 - 9 = $$

4.
$$16 - 8 = $$

5.
$$17 - 9 \qquad 16 - 9 \qquad 15 - 9 \qquad 15 - 8 \qquad 16 - 8 \qquad 17 - 8$$

6.
$$16 - 9 \qquad 17 - 9 \qquad 18 - 9 \qquad 16 - 7 \qquad 16 - 8 \qquad 16 - 9$$

7. Subtract.
   Color. 6   7 ⬜ 8 ⬜ 9 ⬜

$$14 - 6$$

$$17 - 8$$

$$17 - 9$$

$$15 - 9$$

$$16 - 7$$

$$15 - 6$$

$$15 - 7$$

$$18 - 9$$

$$16 - 7$$

$$14 - 7$$

$$16 - 9$$

$$17 - 8$$

$$15 - 8$$

$$16 - 8$$

$$14 - 8$$

$$14 - 5$$

☆ **Write the missing number.**

8.

$$\begin{array}{r} 5 \\ + \boxed{} \\ \hline 11 \end{array} \quad \begin{array}{r} 8 \\ + \boxed{} \\ \hline 14 \end{array} \quad \begin{array}{r} \boxed{} \\ + 7 \\ \hline 13 \end{array} \quad \begin{array}{r} 6 \\ + \boxed{} \\ \hline 15 \end{array} \quad \begin{array}{r} \boxed{} \\ + 9 \\ \hline 12 \end{array} \quad \begin{array}{r} \boxed{} \\ + 7 \\ \hline 16 \end{array}$$

TRY THIS: Problem Solving Activities, page 405.

FACT FAMILIES

If you know $5 + 9 = \underline{14}$

Then you know $14 - 5 = \underline{9}$

$9 + 5 = \underline{14}$

$14 - 9 = \underline{5}$

14

5   9

Add or subtract.

1.
7   15   8

$7 + 8 = \underline{\hspace{1cm}}$

$15 - 8 = \underline{\hspace{1cm}}$

$8 + 7 = \underline{\hspace{1cm}}$

$15 - 7 = \underline{\hspace{1cm}}$

2.
6   13   7

$6 + 7 = \underline{\hspace{1cm}}$

$13 - 7 = \underline{\hspace{1cm}}$

$7 + 6 = \underline{\hspace{1cm}}$

$13 - 6 = \underline{\hspace{1cm}}$

3.
6   14   8

$6 + 8 = \underline{\hspace{1cm}}$

$14 - 8 = \underline{\hspace{1cm}}$

$8 + 6 = \underline{\hspace{1cm}}$

$14 - 6 = \underline{\hspace{1cm}}$

4.
6   15   9

$6 + 9 = \underline{\hspace{1cm}}$

$15 - 9 = \underline{\hspace{1cm}}$

$9 + 6 = \underline{\hspace{1cm}}$

$15 - 6 = \underline{\hspace{1cm}}$

Add or subtract.

5.

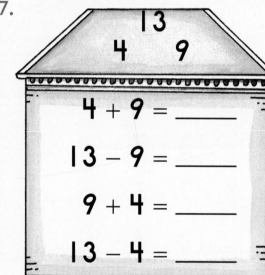

$5 + 8 =$ _____

$13 - 8 =$ _____

$8 + 5 =$ _____

$13 - 5 =$ _____

6.

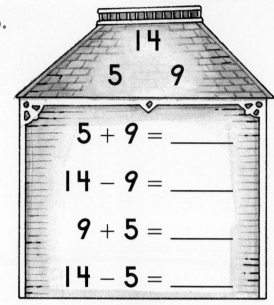

$5 + 9 =$ _____

$14 - 9 =$ _____

$9 + 5 =$ _____

$14 - 5 =$ _____

7.

$4 + 9 =$ _____

$13 - 9 =$ _____

$9 + 4 =$ _____

$13 - 4 =$ _____

8.

$4 + 8 =$ _____

$12 - 8 =$ _____

$8 + 4 =$ _____

$12 - 4 =$ _____

Solve.

9. Mike had **14** balloons. He sold **8**.

How many does he have left? _____ balloons

10. Janet walked **8** blocks to the store.
Then she walked **7** blocks to the park.

How many blocks did she walk? _____ blocks

Fact Families through 15

FACT FAMILIES

9	8	17

_8_ + _9_ = 17   _17_ - _9_ = 8

_9_ + _8_ = 17   _17_ - _8_ = 9

Complete the fact families.

1.
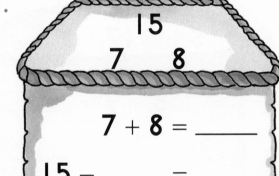

15

7   8

7 + 8 = ____

15 - ____ = ____

8 + ____ = ____

15 - ____ = ____

2.

16

7   9

7 + 9 = ____

16 - ____ = ____

9 + ____ = ____

16 - ____ = ____

3.

17

8   9

8 + 9 = ____

17 - ____ = ____

9 + ____ = ____

17 - ____ = ____

4.

15

6   9

6 + 9 = ____

15 - ____ = ____

9 + ____ = ____

15 - ____ = ____

Complete the fact families.

5.
7   16   9

$7 + 9 =$ ____

$16 -$ ____ $=$ ____

$9 +$ ____ $=$ ____

$16 -$ ____ $=$ ____

6.
6   13   7

$6 + 7 =$ ____

$13 -$ ____ $=$ ____

$7 +$ ____ $=$ ____

$13 -$ ____ $=$ ____

7.
7   15   8

$7 + 8 =$ ____

$15 -$ ____ $=$ ____

$8 +$ ____ $=$ ____

$15 -$ ____ $=$ ____

8.
8   17   9

$8 + 9 =$ ____

$17 -$ ____ $=$ ____

$9 +$ ____ $=$ ____

$17 -$ ____ $=$ ____

Think. $6 + 6$

$$\begin{array}{r} 6 \\ +6 \\ \hline 12 \end{array}$$

$6 + 5$ is one less.

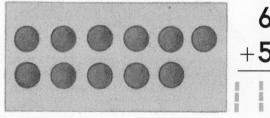

$$\begin{array}{r} 6 \\ +5 \\ \hline 11 \end{array}$$

Add.

9.
$$\begin{array}{r} 8 \\ +8 \\ \hline \end{array} \quad \begin{array}{r} 8 \\ +7 \\ \hline \end{array}$$

10.
$$\begin{array}{r} 7 \\ +7 \\ \hline \end{array} \quad \begin{array}{r} 7 \\ +6 \\ \hline \end{array}$$

11.
$$\begin{array}{r} 9 \\ +9 \\ \hline \end{array} \quad \begin{array}{r} 9 \\ +8 \\ \hline \end{array}$$

PARTNERS: Use counters to show different fact families for 15.

PROBLEM SOLVING

Write the numbers. Then solve.

1. Nancy spends **8¢** for a top.
   Anna spends **6¢** for a doll.
   Together they spend ___14¢___.

$$\begin{array}{r} 8¢ \\ +\ 6¢ \\ \hline 14¢ \end{array}$$

2. Michael has **13¢**.
   He spends **6¢** for a ball.

   How much does he have left? _____

3. Elizabeth spends **3¢** for a book.
   She spends **9¢** for a truck.

   How much does she spend? _____

4. Lindsay has **18¢**.
   He spends **9¢** for a jack-in-the-box.

   How much does he have now? _____

Write the numbers. Then solve.

5. Robert buys three items. He spends
   6¢ for a pencil, **7**¢ for a pen,
   and **3**¢ for an eraser.

   How much does he spend in all? _____

6. Christie has **12**¢.
   She spends **6**¢ for a car.

   How much does she have left? _____

7. Simon spends **8**¢ for a book.
   Luke spends **8**¢ for a toy.

   Together they spend _____.

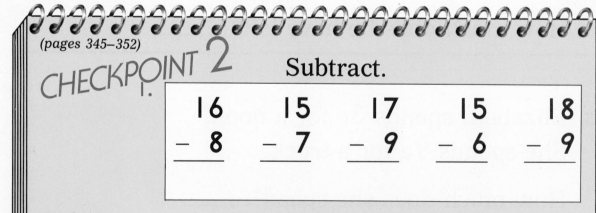

(pages 345–352)

CHECKPOINT 2

Subtract.

1.

16	15	17	15	18
− 8	− 7	− 9	− 6	− 9

Solve.

2. Jason bought a notebook for **9**¢
   and a pencil for **6**¢.
   How much were both items?

Extra practice on page 383

DISCUSS: The children's favorite toys. Make a
graph.

CHAPTER 13 TEST

Add.

1.
7	6	8	5	9	7
+6	+6	+7	+6	+4	+5

Write the number.

2. Cindy won **3** red ribbons, **7** blue ribbons,
   and **4** yellow ribbons.
   How many ribbons did she win in all?

   _____ ribbons

Subtract.

3.
14	16	15	12	13	17
− 6	− 9	− 6	− 4	− 7	− 9

Write the numbers. Then add or subtract.

4. Joe spent **8¢** for a ball.
   Lydia spent **6¢** for a bucket.
   How much did they spend together?

   _____
   [ ] _____

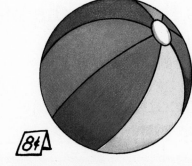

Extra practice on page 384

MATHEMATICS and PHYSICAL EDUCATION

The graph shows how many 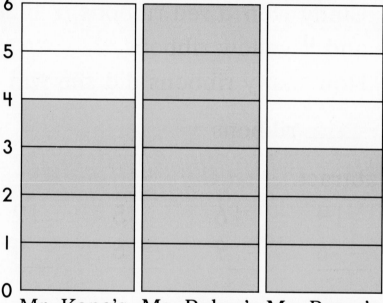 each first grade class won.

BLUE RIBBONS WON

1. How many 🏅 did each class win?

Mr. Kane's ____ Ms. Baker's ____ Ms. Perez's ____

2. Ring the class that won the most 🏅.

   Mr. Kane's   Ms. Baker's   Ms. Perez's

3. How many ribbons did the classes win in all? ____

Enrichment

Write the number.

1.

2 + 2 = ____ 4

2 groups of **2 = ____** 4

2.

2 + 2 + 2 = ____

3 groups of **2 = ____**

3.

3 + 3 = ____

2 groups of **3 = ____**

4.

3 + 3 + 3 = ____

3 groups of **3 = ____**

5.

4 + 4 = ____

2 groups of **4 = ____**

6.

4 + 4 + 4 = ____

3 groups of **4 = ____**

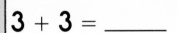

Write the number.

7.

$2 + 2 + 2 + 2 = $ _____

4 groups of **2** = _____

8.

$3 + 3 + 3 + 3 = $ _____

4 groups of **3** = _____

9.

$5 + 5 + 5 = $ _____

3 groups of **5** = _____

10.

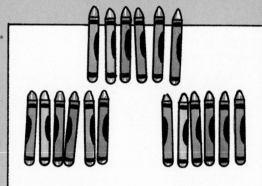

$6 + 6 + 6 = $ _____

3 groups of **6** = _____

11.

$3 + 3 + 3 + 3 + 3 = $ _____

5 groups of **3** = _____

Enrichment: Multiplication Readiness

CUMULATIVE REVIEW

Fill in the ⬭ for the correct answer.

Add or subtract.

1.	2.	3.
84¢ −53¢	13¢ +43¢	35¢ +22¢
48¢ 31¢ 37¢	56¢ 50¢ 46¢	33¢ 57¢ 48¢
Ⓐ Ⓑ Ⓒ	Ⓐ Ⓑ Ⓒ	Ⓐ Ⓑ Ⓒ

How much?

4. Tom had **50¢**. He saved **26¢** more. How much does he have now?	5. Susan had **96¢**. She spent **73¢**. How much does she have left?
78¢ 76¢ 34¢	23¢ 59¢ 29¢
Ⓐ Ⓑ Ⓒ	Ⓐ Ⓑ Ⓒ

Which is the square?   Which is the cylinder?

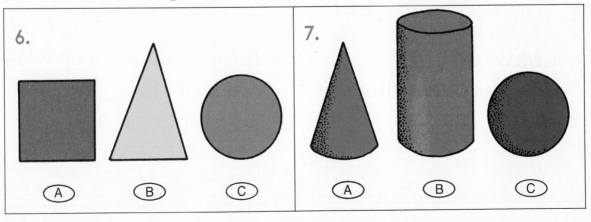

6.   Ⓐ   Ⓑ   Ⓒ   7.   Ⓐ   Ⓑ   Ⓒ

Which shows the shaded part?

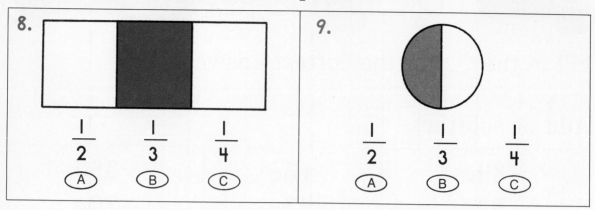

8.
$\dfrac{1}{2}$ Ⓐ $\dfrac{1}{3}$ Ⓑ $\dfrac{1}{4}$ Ⓒ

9.
$\dfrac{1}{2}$ Ⓐ $\dfrac{1}{3}$ Ⓑ $\dfrac{1}{4}$ Ⓒ

LANGUAGE and VOCABULARY REVIEW

Solve the riddle.
Write the word.

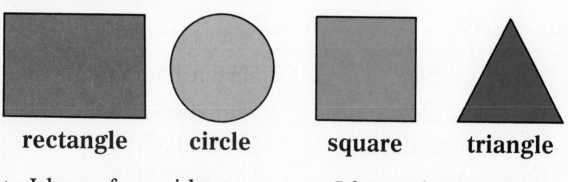

rectangle   **circle**   **square**   **triangle**

1. I have four sides.
   Each side is the
   same length.

2. I have three sides.

_____

3. I have no sides.
   I am a round shape.

4. I have four sides.
   Two of the sides
   are longer than
   the other two.

_____

Language and Vocabulary Review

EXTRA PRACTICE

CHAPTER 1

FOR USE AFTER CHECKPOINT 1

Write the number.

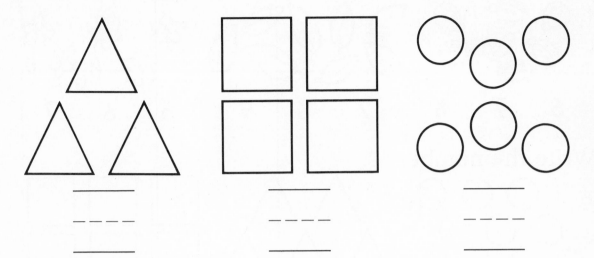

_ _

FOR USE AFTER CHECKPOINT 2

Write the number.

1.   2.

_____ ¢   _____ ¢

3.

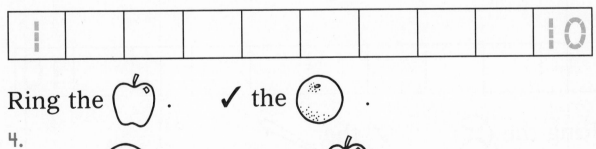

Ring the .   ✓ the .

4.

Ring the number.

1.

6   7   8   7   8   9   5   6   7

Write the number.

2.

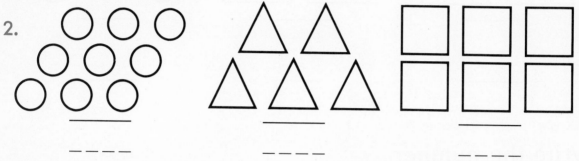

_____   _____   _____

- - - -   - - - -   - - - -

_____   _____   _____

3.   4.

_____ ¢   _____ ¢

5.

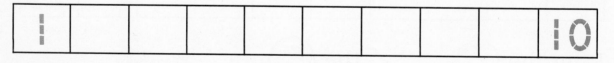

| 1 | | | | | | | | 10 |

Ring the 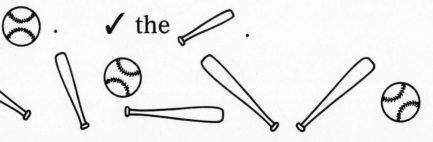 . ✔ the .

6.

EXTRA PRACTICE   CHAPTER 2

Add.

1. $2 + 1 =$ ____ $3 + 2 =$ ____ $4 + 2 =$ ____

2. $3 + 2 =$ ____ $4 + 3 =$ ____ $2 + 3 =$ ____

3. $2 + 2 =$ ____ $1 + 1 =$ ____ $5 + 2 =$ ____

4. $6 + 1 =$ ____ $5 + 1 =$ ____ $4 + 1 =$ ____

Add.

1.
$$\begin{array}{c} 3 \\ +1 \\ \hline \end{array} \qquad \begin{array}{c} 4 \\ +0 \\ \hline \end{array} \qquad \begin{array}{c} 5 \\ +2 \\ \hline \end{array} \qquad \begin{array}{c} 2 \\ +4 \\ \hline \end{array} \qquad \begin{array}{c} 3 \\ +0 \\ \hline \end{array} \qquad \begin{array}{c} 1 \\ +5 \\ \hline \end{array}$$

2. $0 + 3 =$ ____ $1 + 3 =$ ____ $2 + 0 =$ ____

3. $3 + 4 =$ ____ $3 + 2 =$ ____ $6 + 0 =$ ____

Write the number.

4.

____ + ____ = ____ in all

Add.

1. 1 + 3 = ___   2 + 0 = ___   2 + 4 = ___

2. 3 + 2 = ___   5 + 1 = ___   1 + 1 = ___

3. 6 + 0 = ___   4 + 1 = ___   3 + 3 = ___

4. $\begin{array}{r} 5 \\ +0 \\ \hline \end{array}$ $\begin{array}{r} 2 \\ +2 \\ \hline \end{array}$ $\begin{array}{r} 1 \\ +2 \\ \hline \end{array}$ $\begin{array}{r} 3 \\ +3 \\ \hline \end{array}$ $\begin{array}{r} 1 \\ +5 \\ \hline \end{array}$ $\begin{array}{r} 0 \\ +1 \\ \hline \end{array}$

5. $\begin{array}{r} 2 \\ +3 \\ \hline \end{array}$ $\begin{array}{r} 4 \\ +0 \\ \hline \end{array}$ $\begin{array}{r} 5 \\ +1 \\ \hline \end{array}$ $\begin{array}{r} 2 \\ +1 \\ \hline \end{array}$ $\begin{array}{r} 2 \\ +3 \\ \hline \end{array}$ $\begin{array}{r} 4 \\ +2 \\ \hline \end{array}$

6. $\begin{array}{r} 6 \\ +0 \\ \hline \end{array}$ $\begin{array}{r} 1 \\ +1 \\ \hline \end{array}$ $\begin{array}{r} 4 \\ +1 \\ \hline \end{array}$ $\begin{array}{r} 3 \\ +2 \\ \hline \end{array}$ $\begin{array}{r} 5 \\ +0 \\ \hline \end{array}$ $\begin{array}{r} 2 \\ +4 \\ \hline \end{array}$

Write the number.

7.

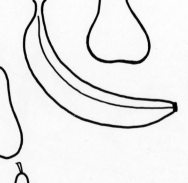

 ___ + ___ = ___ in all

EXTRA PRACTICE   CHAPTER 3

FOR USE AFTER CHECKPOINT 1

Add.

1. $5 + 4 =$ _____ $6 + 2 =$ _____ $3 + 6 =$ _____

2. $4 + 3 =$ _____ $7 + 1 =$ _____ $2 + 7 =$ _____

3.
$$\begin{array}{c} 3 \\ +5 \\ \hline \end{array} \qquad \begin{array}{c} 4 \\ +4 \\ \hline \end{array} \qquad \begin{array}{c} 3 \\ +2 \\ \hline \end{array} \qquad \begin{array}{c} 9 \\ +0 \\ \hline \end{array} \qquad \begin{array}{c} 5 \\ +3 \\ \hline \end{array} \qquad \begin{array}{c} 0 \\ +8 \\ \hline \end{array}$$

FOR USE AFTER CHECKPOINT 2

Add.

1. $3 + 5 =$ _____ $3 + 7 =$ _____ $8 + 0 =$ _____

2.
$$\begin{array}{c} 4 \\ +6 \\ \hline \end{array} \qquad \begin{array}{c} 1 \\ +8 \\ \hline \end{array} \qquad \begin{array}{c} 9 \\ +0 \\ \hline \end{array} \qquad \begin{array}{c} 5 \\ +5 \\ \hline \end{array} \qquad \begin{array}{c} 3 \\ +5 \\ \hline \end{array} \qquad \begin{array}{c} 7 \\ +3 \\ \hline \end{array}$$

3.
$$\begin{array}{c} 6 \\ 1 \\ +2 \\ \hline \end{array} \qquad \begin{array}{c} 1 \\ 3 \\ +4 \\ \hline \end{array} \qquad \begin{array}{c} 5 \\ 0 \\ +2 \\ \hline \end{array} \qquad \begin{array}{c} 1 \\ 7 \\ +2 \\ \hline \end{array} \qquad \begin{array}{c} 5 \\ 1 \\ +4 \\ \hline \end{array} \qquad \begin{array}{c} 5 \\ 1 \\ +3 \\ \hline \end{array}$$

How much in all? Write the numbers.

4.

_____ ¢

$+$ _____ ¢

_____

¢

Add.

1. 4 + 3 = ____   6 + 0 = ____   3 + 2 = ____

2. 4 + 4 = ____   5 + 4 = ____   3 + 7 = ____

3.
```
   4        1        8        3        4        2
  +5       +7       +2       +7       +4       +5
```

4.
```
   1        6        2        9        9        6
  +9       +3       +6       +0       +1       +4
```

5.
```
   4        2        3        1        3        3
   1        6        1        8        4        3
  +5       +2       +2       +1       +2       +2
```

How much in all? Write the numbers.

6.     7.

```
   ____ ¢                              ____ ¢

 + ____ ¢                            + ____ ¢
 _____                            _____
      ¢                                   ¢
```

EXTRA PRACTICE

CHAPTER 4

FOR USE AFTER CHECKPOINT 1

Subtract.

1. $4 - 2 =$ ___ $6 - 3 =$ ___ $2 - 1 =$ ___

2. $5 - 2 =$ ___ $4 - 3 =$ ___ $2 - 2 =$ ___

3. $3 - 2 =$ ___ $6 - 3 =$ ___ $3 - 1 =$ ___

4. $7 - 4 =$ ___ $4 - 1 =$ ___ $5 - 3 =$ ___

FOR USE AFTER CHECKPOINT 2

Subtract.

1.
$$\begin{array}{r} 4 \\ -4 \\ \hline \end{array} \qquad \begin{array}{r} 6 \\ -1 \\ \hline \end{array} \qquad \begin{array}{r} 5 \\ -3 \\ \hline \end{array} \qquad \begin{array}{r} 4 \\ -1 \\ \hline \end{array} \qquad \begin{array}{r} 7 \\ -2 \\ \hline \end{array} \qquad \begin{array}{r} 5 \\ -0 \\ \hline \end{array}$$

2.
$$\begin{array}{r} 6 \\ -5 \\ \hline \end{array} \qquad \begin{array}{r} 7 \\ -0 \\ \hline \end{array} \qquad \begin{array}{r} 3 \\ -3 \\ \hline \end{array} \qquad \begin{array}{r} 6 \\ -2 \\ \hline \end{array} \qquad \begin{array}{r} 4 \\ -0 \\ \hline \end{array} \qquad \begin{array}{r} 7 \\ -4 \\ \hline \end{array}$$

Write + or − in the ☐.
Then add or subtract.

3.

How many are left?

$7 \; \boxed{} \; 2 =$ ___

Subtract.

1. $3 - 2 =$ _____ $5 - 4 =$ _____ $7 - 4 =$ _____

2. $4 - 1 =$ _____ $1 - 0 =$ _____ $6 - 6 =$ _____

3. $6 - 0 =$ _____ $5 - 1 =$ _____ $7 - 2 =$ _____

4.
$$\begin{array}{cccccc} 3 & 5 & 6 & 7 & 7 & 3 \\ -1 & -3 & -3 & -0 & -1 & -2 \\ \hline \end{array}$$

5.
$$\begin{array}{cccccc} 6 & 5 & 2 & 6 & 3 & 1 \\ -4 & -5 & -0 & -1 & -3 & -0 \\ \hline \end{array}$$

6.
$$\begin{array}{cccccc} 4 & 6 & 5 & 3 & 2 & 4 \\ -2 & -5 & -2 & -0 & -1 & -3 \\ \hline \end{array}$$

Write + or − in the ☐.
Then add or subtract.

7.

How many in all?

5 ☐ $3 =$ _____

EXTRA PRACTICE   CHAPTER 5

FOR USE AFTER CHECKPOINT 1

Subtract.

1.
$$\begin{array}{r} 9 \\ -7 \\ \hline \end{array} \qquad \begin{array}{r} 9 \\ -4 \\ \hline \end{array} \qquad \begin{array}{r} 8 \\ -8 \\ \hline \end{array} \qquad \begin{array}{r} 9 \\ -6 \\ \hline \end{array} \qquad \begin{array}{r} 7 \\ -4 \\ \hline \end{array} \qquad \begin{array}{r} 9 \\ -3 \\ \hline \end{array}$$

2.
$$\begin{array}{r} 9 \\ -0 \\ \hline \end{array} \qquad \begin{array}{r} 8 \\ -5 \\ \hline \end{array} \qquad \begin{array}{r} 9 \\ -2 \\ \hline \end{array} \qquad \begin{array}{r} 8 \\ -4 \\ \hline \end{array} \qquad \begin{array}{r} 7 \\ -7 \\ \hline \end{array} \qquad \begin{array}{r} 6 \\ -0 \\ \hline \end{array}$$

FOR USE AFTER CHECKPOINT 2

Subtract.

1.
$$\begin{array}{r} 10 \\ -\ 4 \\ \hline \end{array} \qquad \begin{array}{r} 9 \\ -1 \\ \hline \end{array} \qquad \begin{array}{r} 10 \\ -\ 0 \\ \hline \end{array} \qquad \begin{array}{r} 6 \\ -1 \\ \hline \end{array} \qquad \begin{array}{r} 10 \\ -\ 3 \\ \hline \end{array} \qquad \begin{array}{r} 10 \\ -\ 6 \\ \hline \end{array}$$

2.
$$\begin{array}{r} 8 \\ -4 \\ \hline \end{array} \qquad \begin{array}{r} 9 \\ -6 \\ \hline \end{array} \qquad \begin{array}{r} 10 \\ -\ 9 \\ \hline \end{array} \qquad \begin{array}{r} 8 \\ -2 \\ \hline \end{array} \qquad \begin{array}{r} 10 \\ -\ 5 \\ \hline \end{array} \qquad \begin{array}{r} 10 \\ -\ 7 \\ \hline \end{array}$$

Write + or − in the ☐.
Then add or subtract.

3. Mary has **8¢**.
   She spends **2¢**.

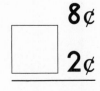

$$\begin{array}{r} 8¢ \\ 2¢ \\ \hline ¢ \end{array}$$

4. Ron has **6¢**.
   He saves **4¢**.

$$\begin{array}{r} 6¢ \\ 4¢ \\ \hline ¢ \end{array}$$

Subtract.

1. $\begin{array}{r} 9 \\ -3 \\ \hline \end{array}$ $\begin{array}{r} 10 \\ -7 \\ \hline \end{array}$ $\begin{array}{r} 9 \\ -9 \\ \hline \end{array}$ $\begin{array}{r} 8 \\ -0 \\ \hline \end{array}$ $\begin{array}{r} 10 \\ -1 \\ \hline \end{array}$ $\begin{array}{r} 7 \\ -5 \\ \hline \end{array}$

2. $\begin{array}{r} 7 \\ -2 \\ \hline \end{array}$ $\begin{array}{r} 8 \\ -3 \\ \hline \end{array}$ $\begin{array}{r} 9 \\ -4 \\ \hline \end{array}$ $\begin{array}{r} 10 \\ -8 \\ \hline \end{array}$ $\begin{array}{r} 10 \\ -0 \\ \hline \end{array}$ $\begin{array}{r} 8 \\ -6 \\ \hline \end{array}$

3. $\begin{array}{r} 8 \\ -5 \\ \hline \end{array}$ $\begin{array}{r} 9 \\ -5 \\ \hline \end{array}$ $\begin{array}{r} 10 \\ -4 \\ \hline \end{array}$ $\begin{array}{r} 8 \\ -7 \\ \hline \end{array}$ $\begin{array}{r} 9 \\ -6 \\ \hline \end{array}$ $\begin{array}{r} 10 \\ -6 \\ \hline \end{array}$

4. $\begin{array}{r} 9 \\ -3 \\ \hline \end{array}$ $\begin{array}{r} 10 \\ -3 \\ \hline \end{array}$ $\begin{array}{r} 10 \\ -9 \\ \hline \end{array}$ $\begin{array}{r} 9 \\ -7 \\ \hline \end{array}$ $\begin{array}{r} 10 \\ -5 \\ \hline \end{array}$ $\begin{array}{r} 10 \\ -2 \\ \hline \end{array}$

Ring the correct example.

 5.

$$7 + 2$$

$$7 - 2$$

$$5 + 2$$

6.

$$5 - 3$$

$$8 - 3$$

$$5 + 3$$

Chapter 5 Extra Practice

EXTRA PRACTICE CHAPTER 6

Write the number.

1.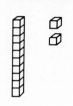

____ ten ____ ones

____

2.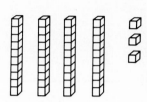

____ tens ____ ones

____

3.

32	33		35	

4.

78	79			82

Write the number.

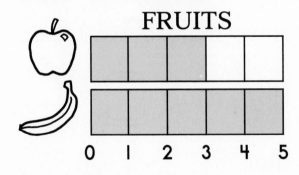

FRUITS

0 1 2 3 4 5

1. 🍎 ____

2. 🍌 ____

Ring the third car.

3.

Ring the number that is greater.

4. **29**   5. **74**   6. **71**   7. **43**

   36   **68**   **83**   **42**

Write the number.

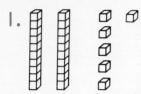   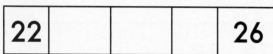   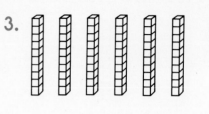

____tens ____ones   _____   _____

Write the missing numbers.

4.

22				26

5.

63				67

Write the number.

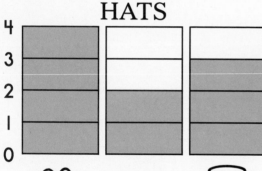

6. How many 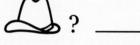 ? ____

7. How many 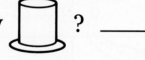 ? ____

8. How many ? ____

Ring the number that is greater.

9. **44 41**   **25 30**   **86 79**

Ring the number that is less.

10. **16 19**   **37 40**   **93 57**

Ring the fourth letter.   11. A   B   C   D   E

Count by twos.   12. **2, 4,** ____, ____, ____

     Chapter 6 Extra Practice

EXTRA PRACTICE

CHAPTER 7

FOR USE AFTER CHECKPOINT 1

Count by fives.

1.

5	10				

Write the amount.

2. _____ ¢

3. _____ ¢

FOR USE AFTER CHECKPOINT 2

Write the amount.

1. _____ ¢

2. _____ ¢

3. _____ ¢

4. _____ ¢

Continue the number pattern.

5. **8, 10, 12,** _____, _____, _____, _____

6. **27, 37, 47,** _____, _____, _____, _____

Count by fives.

1. 5, 10, _____, _____

2. 35, 40, _____, _____

Write the amount.

3.

_____ ¢

4.

_____ ¢

5.

_____ ¢

6.

_____ ¢

7.

_____ ¢

8.

_____ ¢

Continue the number pattern.

9. 24, 26, 28, _____, _____, _____, 36

10. 2, 5, 5, 2, 5, 5, 2, _____, _____, _____

11. 45, 50, 55, _____, _____, _____

EXTRA PRACTICE CHAPTER 8

FOR USE AFTER CHECKPOINT 1

What time is it?

_____ o'clock   _____ : _____   _____ o'clock

FOR USE AFTER CHECKPOINT 2

Solve.

1. Carlos went to play baseball at **1:00**.
   He played for **3** hours.
   What time did he stop playing?   _____ o'clock

Ring the fourth month of the year.

2.   March   April   May

Write the time.

TIMES

	recess	lunch
Bill's class	10:00	12:00
Cathy's class	10:30	1:00

3. When does Bill's class
   have recess?   _____ : _____

4. When does Cathy's class
   have lunch?   _____ : _____

What time is it?

1.

_____ o'clock   _____ o'clock   _____ :_____

Solve.

2. Anne started reading at **7:00**.
   She read for **2** hours.
   What time did she finish?   _____ o'clock

Ring the day that comes just after.

3. Friday | Sunday   Thursday   Saturday

Ring the eighth month of the year.

4. July   August   September

Solve.

THINGS WE COLLECTED

	Kim	Robert
shells	7	9
rocks	8	6

5. Who collected **7** shells? _____

6. Who collected **6** rocks? _____

EXTRA PRACTICE CHAPTER 9

Add.

1.

4	3	2	5	3	8
+7	+6	+9	+6	+7	+3

2.

5	9	6	6	9	5
+5	+2	+4	+5	+3	+7

Draw as many more as needed.
Then write the answer.

1. Dina needs 10 jars. She has 5 jars.
   How many more does she need?

   ____ jars

Subtract.

2.

12	12	11	12	11	12
− 6	− 4	− 4	− 7	− 2	− 3

Solve.

3. Bob has 7 blue ribbons.

   He wins 5 more.

   How many does he
   have now?   blue ribbons

Add.

1.
$$\begin{array}{r} 7 \\ +3 \\ \hline \end{array}$$
$$\begin{array}{r} 5 \\ +5 \\ \hline \end{array}$$
$$\begin{array}{r} 7 \\ +5 \\ \hline \end{array}$$
$$\begin{array}{r} 3 \\ +8 \\ \hline \end{array}$$
$$\begin{array}{r} 3 \\ +9 \\ \hline \end{array}$$
$$\begin{array}{r} 2 \\ +9 \\ \hline \end{array}$$

Subtract.

2.
$$\begin{array}{r} 11 \\ -3 \\ \hline \end{array}$$
$$\begin{array}{r} 11 \\ -7 \\ \hline \end{array}$$
$$\begin{array}{r} 12 \\ -5 \\ \hline \end{array}$$
$$\begin{array}{r} 10 \\ -7 \\ \hline \end{array}$$
$$\begin{array}{r} 11 \\ -6 \\ \hline \end{array}$$
$$\begin{array}{r} 11 \\ -8 \\ \hline \end{array}$$

Draw as many more as needed.
Then write the answer.

3. Bob needs 10 stamps. He has 6 stamps.
How many more does he need?

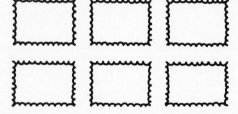

_____ stamps

Solve.

4. Joan has 12 eggs. She uses 7.
How many are left?

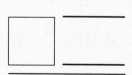

eggs

EXTRA PRACTICE CHAPTER 10

How long is it?

1.

_____ centimeters

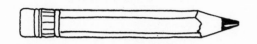

_____ centimeters

Ring the one that holds less than a liter.

2.

Write the number of kilograms.

3.

_____ kilograms

How long is it?

1.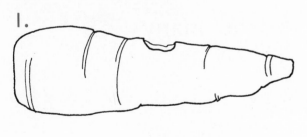

_____ inches

Color how many can be filled.

2.

Write the number of pounds.

3.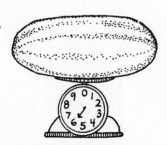

_____ pounds

How long?

1.

_____ centimeters

2.

_____ inches

How much?

3.

_____ kilograms

4.

_____ pounds

Write the number.

SHOES

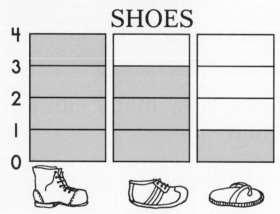

5. How many  ? _____

6. How many ? _____

7. How many ? _____

Ring the one that holds
more than a liter.

8.

Color the number you
can fill.

9.

EXTRA PRACTICE   CHAPTER 11

FOR USE AFTER CHECKPOINT 1

Add.

1.
30	20	32	50	12	40
+10	+40	+64	+20	+82	+25

FOR USE AFTER CHECKPOINT 2

Subtract.

1.
80	57	86	79	68	29
−10	−22	−12	− 5	−15	− 3

Add or subtract.

2.
95¢	54¢	38¢	44¢	85¢
−24¢	+33¢	−26¢	+21¢	−41¢
¢	¢	¢	¢	¢

Write the numbers. Then add or subtract.

3. Bill wants to buy a car and a boat. How much are both?

4. Pat has **43¢**. She earned **35¢** more. How much does she have now?

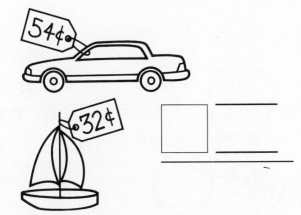
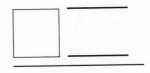

Add.

1.
70	17	43	51	44	26
+20	+12	+46	+14	+ 4	+23

Subtract.

2.
80	98	76	67	99	82
−70	−72	−55	− 6	−19	−41

Add or subtract.

3.
35¢	48¢	77¢	74¢	97¢
+14¢	−26¢	+20¢	−31¢	−21¢

Write the numbers.
Then add or subtract.

4. Brian has **69¢**.
He spends **47¢**.
How much does
he have left?

5. Ginny wants to buy
an apple and
an orange.
How much are both?

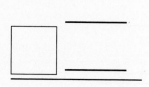

EXTRA PRACTICE CHAPTER 12

Color the shapes.

1. cube

   cylinder

   cone

   sphere

2. triangle

   circle

   rectangle

   square

Write the number.

SHAPES

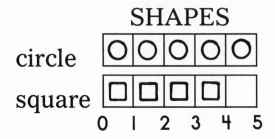

circle

square

0 1 2 3 4 5

3. How many circles? ____

4. How many squares? ____

Ring the shape.

1.

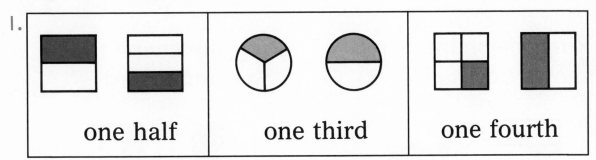

| one half | one third | one fourth |

Solve.

2. Tom has **6** more marbles than Bill.
   Bill has **4** marbles.
   How many marbles
   does Tom have?   ____ marbles

1. Ring the circle.
   ✓ the triangle.
   X the square.

2. Ring the sphere.
   ✓ the cube.
   X the cone.

Write the number.

SHAPES

triangle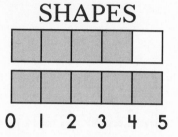

rectangle

0 1 2 3 4 5

3. How many triangles? ____

4. How many rectangles? ____

Write the number of equal parts.

5.

____   ____   ____   ____

Ring the shape that shows one half.

Ring the shape that shows one third.

6.

7.

Solve.

8. John has an apple and an orange.
   His favorite is not the orange.
   What is his favorite? _____

Chapter 12 Extra Practice

EXTRA PRACTICE CHAPTER 13

Add or subtract.

1.
$$9 + 5 \quad\quad 7 + 6 \quad\quad 8 + 7 \quad\quad 4 + 9 \quad\quad 6 + 8 \quad\quad 9 + 6$$

2.
$$14 - 8 \quad\quad 13 - 9 \quad\quad 15 - 9 \quad\quad 13 - 6 \quad\quad 14 - 8 \quad\quad 12 - 7$$

Solve.

3. Michael bought **3** red, **6** blue, and **5** yellow cars.
   How many did he have in all? _____ cars

Subtract.

1.
$$14 - 9 \quad\quad 17 - 9 \quad\quad 16 - 8 \quad\quad 13 - 6 \quad\quad 16 - 9 \quad\quad 17 - 8$$

2.
$$15 - 6 \quad\quad 18 - 9 \quad\quad 16 - 7 \quad\quad 15 - 7 \quad\quad 14 - 6 \quad\quad 18 - 9$$

Write the numbers.
Then add or subtract.

3. Carlos has **17¢**.

   He buys a toy for **9¢**.

   How much does he have now?

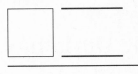

Add or subtract.

1.
$$\begin{array}{r} 6 \\ +9 \\ \hline \end{array}$$
$$\begin{array}{r} 9 \\ +4 \\ \hline \end{array}$$
$$\begin{array}{r} 7 \\ +7 \\ \hline \end{array}$$
$$\begin{array}{r} 8 \\ +6 \\ \hline \end{array}$$
$$\begin{array}{r} 5 \\ +9 \\ \hline \end{array}$$
$$\begin{array}{r} 8 \\ +4 \\ \hline \end{array}$$

2.
$$\begin{array}{r} 8 \\ +7 \\ \hline \end{array}$$
$$\begin{array}{r} 6 \\ +6 \\ \hline \end{array}$$
$$\begin{array}{r} 8 \\ +9 \\ \hline \end{array}$$
$$\begin{array}{r} 7 \\ +8 \\ \hline \end{array}$$
$$\begin{array}{r} 5 \\ +8 \\ \hline \end{array}$$
$$\begin{array}{r} 8 \\ +8 \\ \hline \end{array}$$

3.
$$\begin{array}{r} 9 \\ +9 \\ \hline \end{array}$$
$$\begin{array}{r} 7 \\ +9 \\ \hline \end{array}$$
$$\begin{array}{r} 6 \\ +8 \\ \hline \end{array}$$
$$\begin{array}{r} 14 \\ -8 \\ \hline \end{array}$$
$$\begin{array}{r} 13 \\ -9 \\ \hline \end{array}$$
$$\begin{array}{r} 15 \\ -9 \\ \hline \end{array}$$

4.
$$\begin{array}{r} 13 \\ -8 \\ \hline \end{array}$$
$$\begin{array}{r} 18 \\ -9 \\ \hline \end{array}$$
$$\begin{array}{r} 16 \\ -8 \\ \hline \end{array}$$
$$\begin{array}{r} 14 \\ -9 \\ \hline \end{array}$$
$$\begin{array}{r} 17 \\ -8 \\ \hline \end{array}$$
$$\begin{array}{r} 16 \\ -7 \\ \hline \end{array}$$

5.
$$\begin{array}{r} 15 \\ -7 \\ \hline \end{array}$$
$$\begin{array}{r} 13 \\ -4 \\ \hline \end{array}$$
$$\begin{array}{r} 14 \\ -5 \\ \hline \end{array}$$
$$\begin{array}{r} 15 \\ -6 \\ \hline \end{array}$$
$$\begin{array}{r} 16 \\ -9 \\ \hline \end{array}$$
$$\begin{array}{r} 17 \\ -9 \\ \hline \end{array}$$

Solve.

6. Jamie has **6** red, **5** yellow, and **3** blue
   balloons. How many balloons does he have?

   _____ balloons

7. Doris has **18**¢.
   She spends **9**¢.
   How much does she have left?   _____ ¢

USING YOUR CALCULATOR

answer

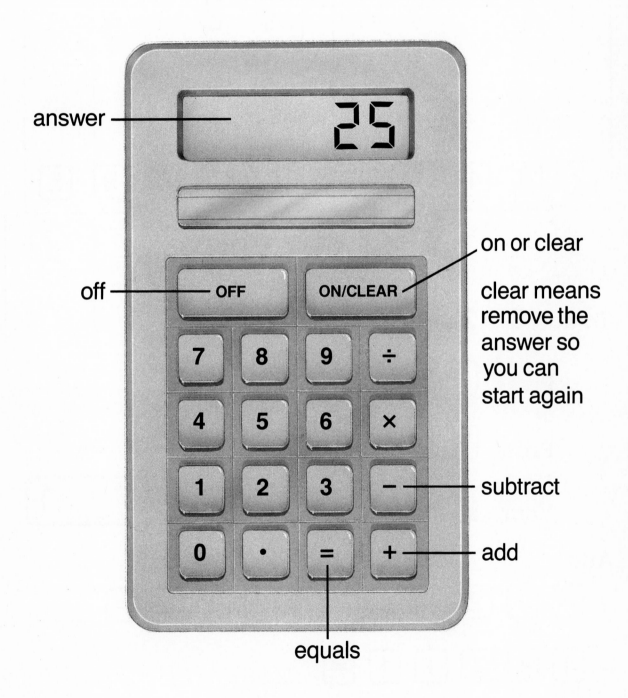

off

on or clear

clear means remove the answer so you can start again

OFF

ON/CLEAR

7	8	9	÷
4	5	6	×
1	2	3	−
0	·	=	+

subtract

add

equals

CALCULATOR ACTIVITIES

CHAPTER 1

Match.

1.

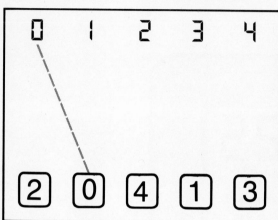

2.

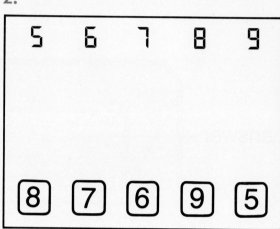

CHAPTER 2

To add **5** + **2** on a calculator you do this.

Press $\boxed{C}$.

Press $\boxed{5}$ $\boxed{+}$ $\boxed{2}$ $\boxed{=}$

Your calculator will show ⇨ | 7 |

Add.

1.  $\boxed{4}$ $\boxed{+}$ $\boxed{2}$ $\boxed{=}$ ___   2. $\boxed{2}$ $\boxed{+}$ $\boxed{5}$ $\boxed{=}$ ___

3. $\boxed{4}$ $\boxed{+}$ $\boxed{1}$ $\boxed{+}$ $\boxed{1}$ $\boxed{=}$ ___

4. $\boxed{2}$ $\boxed{+}$ $\boxed{1}$ $\boxed{+}$ $\boxed{3}$ $\boxed{=}$ ___

CALCULATOR ACTIVITIES

CHAPTER 3

Write the number to complete the number sentence.
Use your calculator to help check your answers.

1. ⬚ + ⬚ + ⬚ = 9

2. ⬚ + ⬚ + ⬚ = 8

3. ⬚ + ⬚ + ⬚ = 10

CHAPTER 4

$$4 + 2 = 6 \Rightarrow 6 - 2 = 4$$

$4 \; + \; 2 \; = \; 6 \; - \; 2 \; = \; 4$

Add and subtract on your calculator.

1. $5 \; + \; 4 \; =$ ___ $- \; 4 \; =$ ___

2. $3 \; + \; 5 \; =$ ___ $- \; 5 \; =$ ___

CALCULATOR ACTIVITIES

CHAPTER 5

How many ② can we subtract from **4**?

④ ⊖ ② ⊜ | 2 | ⊖ ② ⊜ | 0 |

We can subtract **2** ② .

1 How many ② can you subtract from **10**? ____

2 How many ③ can you subtract from **9**? ____

CHAPTER 6

Count by **10** on your calculator.

1 Press ⒸC .

Press ① ⓪ ⇨ ¦0

Press ⊕ ① ⓪ ⊜ ⇨ 20

Press ⊕ ① ⓪ ⊜ ⇨ 30

What number comes next? **10, 20, 30, 40,** ____

2 Press ⒸC .

Press ④ ⇨ 4

Press ⊕ ① ⓪ ⊜ ⇨ ¦4

What number comes next? **4, 14, 24,** ____, ____,

Calculator Activities

CALCULATOR ACTIVITIES

CHAPTER 7

Your calculator writes money without the ¢ sign.

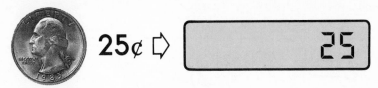

25¢ ⇨ | 25 |

Use your calculator to find the amount.

1.

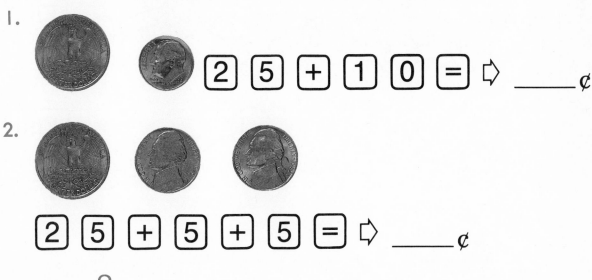

2 5 + 1 0 = ⇨ _____¢

2.

2 5 + 5 + 5 = ⇨ _____¢

CHAPTER 8

Find how long the trip takes. Use your calculator.

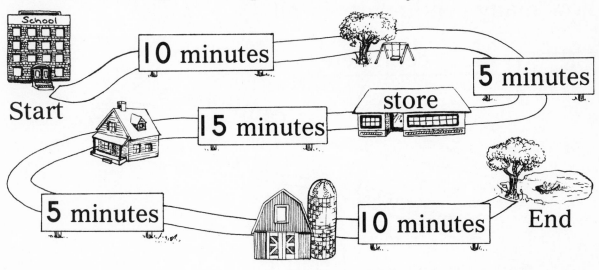

School

10 minutes

5 minutes

store

Start

15 minutes

5 minutes

10 minutes

End

_____ minutes

CHAPTER 9

Use your calculator to add or subtract.

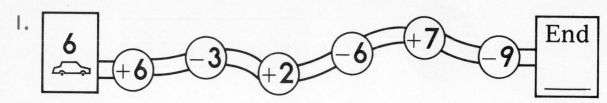

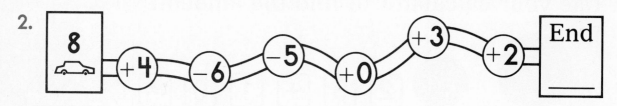

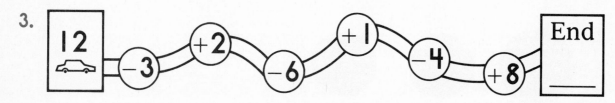

CHAPTER 10

Measure to find how long.
Then use your calculator to find
how many centimeters in all.

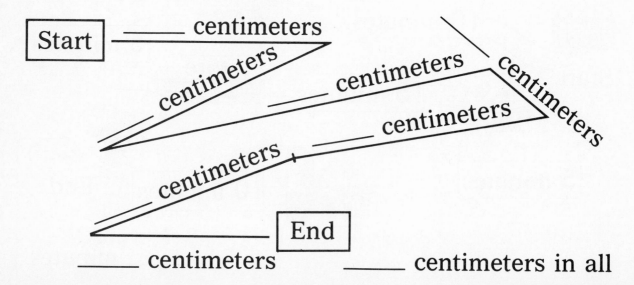

CALCULATOR ACTIVITIES

CHAPTER **11**

Which way does the car go?
Color the path.

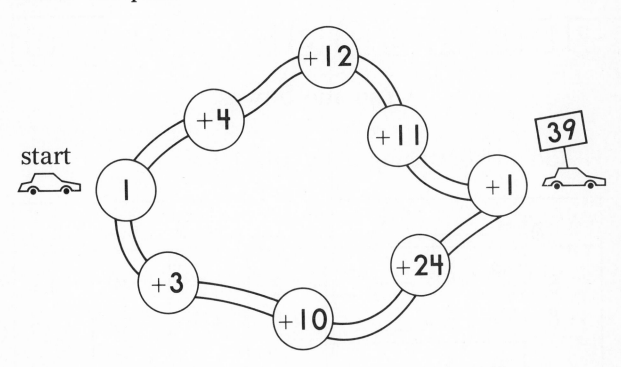

CHAPTER **12**

Find the missing number under the ⭐.

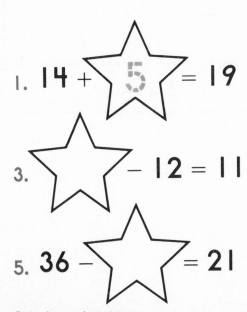

1. $14 + \boxed{5} = 19$

2. $3 + \bigstar = 28$

3. $\bigstar - 12 = 11$

4. $\bigstar + 10 = 35$

5. $36 - \bigstar = 21$

6. $23 + \bigstar = 36$

CALCULATOR ACTIVITIES

CHAPTER 13

Can you find the sum 10 by adding twos?
Your calculator can help.

2 + 2 + 2 + 2 + 2 + ⇨ 10

You add **5** twos.

1. Add without using your calculator.

$6 + 3 =$ ___	$5 + 4 =$ ___		$8 + 1 =$ ___		
6 +8	$9 + 8 =$ ___ $7 + 5 =$ ___ $4 + 3 =$ ___	8 +8	7 +4	5 +5	11 − 4
7 +6	9 +4	15 − 8	$5 + 8 =$ ___ $15 - 6 =$ ___ $14 - 9 =$ ___	10 − 3	6 +5
$16 - 9 =$ ___	$18 - 9 =$ ___		$7 + 8 =$ ___		

2. Use your calculator to find the sums
   that can be made by adding twos.
   Color those boxes red.

3. What is the message? ____

Calculator Activities

CHAPTER **1**   PROBLEM SOLVING ACTIVITIES

Cut out pictures from a magazine.
Paste them on this page.
Show **I** dog, **2** children, and **3** trees.

Tell a story about your page to a partner.

Use counters to show different ways to make **7**. Here is one way.

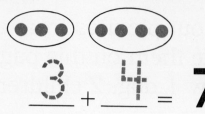

$$\underline{3} + \underline{4} = \textbf{7}$$

Draw counters to show your work.
Write the number sentence.

1.

$$\underline{} + \underline{} = 7$$

2.

$$\underline{} + \underline{} = 7$$

3.

$$\underline{} + \underline{} = 7$$

4.

$$\underline{} + \underline{} = 7$$

CHAPTER 3   PROBLEM SOLVING ACTIVITIES

Use punchout pennies
Show how to make the sum.
Draw pennies in the boxes to show your work.
Write the number sentence.

1.

____ ¢   +   ____ ¢   =   **3** ¢

2.

____ ¢   +   ____ ¢   =   **5** ¢

3.

____ ¢   +   ____ ¢   =   **2** ¢

4. How many pennies do you have
    for the bank? Tell a partner
    how you found the answer. Did
    your partner use a different way?   _____ ¢

Mike catches 10 fish at the fair.
Draw an X on each fish that he catches.

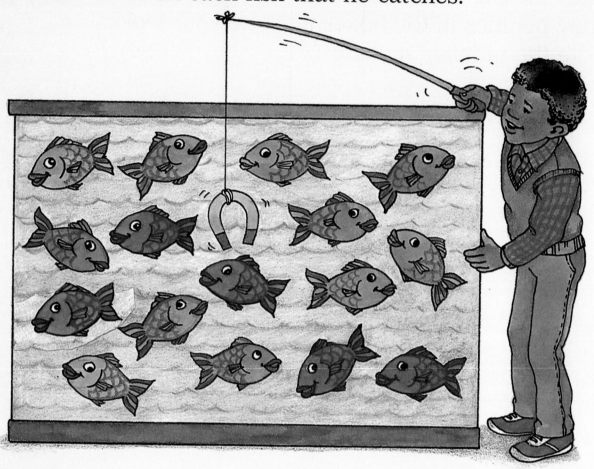

Complete.

1. Mike catches ____ .

   There are ____  left. $7 - \underline{\hspace{1cm}} = \underline{\hspace{1cm}}$

2. Mike catches ____ .

   There are ____ left. $\underline{\hspace{1cm}} - \underline{\hspace{1cm}} = \underline{\hspace{1cm}}$

3. Mike catches ____ .

   There are ____ left. $\underline{\hspace{1cm}} - \underline{\hspace{1cm}} = \underline{\hspace{1cm}}$

CHAPTER 5   PROBLEM SOLVING ACTIVITIES

Your partner writes the subtraction sentence to show your story.

Work with a partner. Take turns.
Use the picture to tell a subtraction story.

___ − ___ = ___   ___ − ___ = ___

Share your subtraction sentences with another group. What do you notice?

Play this number game with a partner.
Make **2** sets of cards like this:

| 0 | 1 | 2 | 3 | 4 | 5 | 6 | 7 | 8 | 9 |

Mix the cards in a pile.
Each of you takes **5** cards.
Think of a number clue like this one:

I am thinking of a number. It has 3 tens and 8 ones.

Tell your partner your clue.
Can your partner use his or her
cards to show the number?
If yes, your partner scores I point.
Each of you takes a turn.

Mix the cards again.
Take **5** new cards.
See who can score 10 points first!

CHAPTER 7   PROBLEM SOLVING ACTIVITIES

This is the money that you can spend.
Use punchout coins.

Cut out the pictures below.
What would you like to buy?
Paste the pictures in the box.

Do you have any money left over? _____

How much?   _____

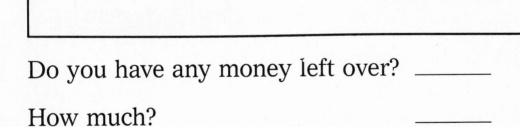

Write the time.

MY DAY

I get up at _____:_____.

I go to school at _____:_____.

I eat lunch at _____:_____.

I come home at _____:_____.

I eat dinner at _____:_____.

I go to bed at _____:_____.

Now work with a partner.
Compare your days.
Ring the times that are the same.

CHAPTER 9   PROBLEM SOLVING ACTIVITIES

Write number sentences to show the
sum or difference.
Draw balloons to show your number sentence.

$$5 + 6 = 11$$ $$10 - 5 = 5$$

1.

2.

$$\_\_ + \_\_ = 10$$ $$\_\_ - \_\_ = 7$$

Now draw pictures for a partner.
Let your partner write the number sentence.

3.

4.

$$\_\_ - \_\_ = \_\_$$ $$\_\_ + \_\_ = \_\_$$

Cut out the unit stick at the bottom of the page.
Find these objects in your classroom.
Measure them with the unit stick.

1.    _____ units

2.    _____ units

3.    _____ units

4.    _____ units

5.    _____ units

6. Share your work with a partner.
   Are your answers the same?

CHAPTER **11**   PROBLEM SOLVING ACTIVITIES

Use these circles to make spinners.
You need a pencil and paper clip.

Take turns with a partner.
Spin each spinner once.
Write the numbers you spin.
Add the two numbers.
Use this chart to find your score:

sum	0–20	21–40	41–60	61–80	81–100
points	1	2	3	4	5

See who scores **20** points first!
Now use one spinner for both spins.
Which spinner will you use? Why? Try it.

Color inside the rectangle blue.
Color inside the circle yellow.
Color inside the triangle red.

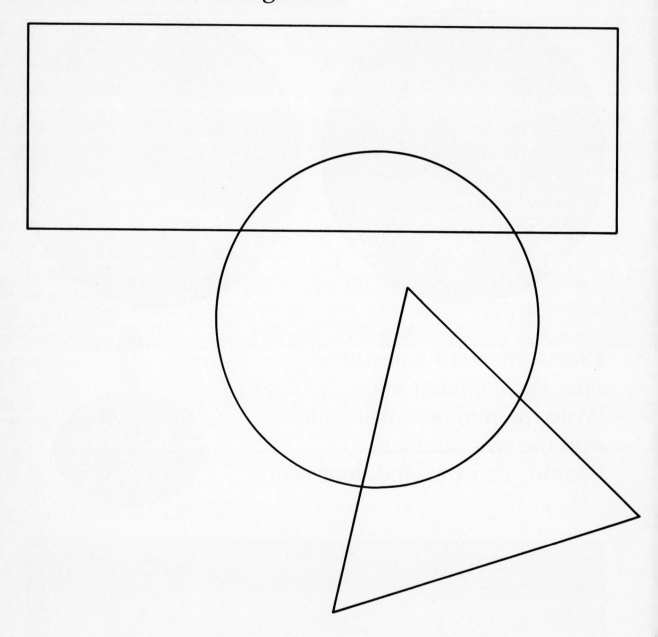

Talk with a partner. What happens
to the colors of the shapes?
Try this with other colors on a sheet of paper.

CHAPTER 13   PROBLEM SOLVING ACTIVITIES

Use the clues to write number sentences.

1. I am an addition fact. One of my numbers is 6. What number sentence could I be?

_____

_____

_____

2. I am a subtraction fact. My answer is more than 5. What number sentence could I be?

_____

_____

_____

3. I am a subtraction fact. My first number is 15. What number sentence could I be?

_____

_____

_____

4. I am an addition fact. My sum is less than 17. What number sentence could I be?

_____

_____

Now work with a partner.
Make up some clues of your own.
Your partner writes the number sentences. Take turns.

_____   _____

_____   _____

PICTURE GLOSSARY

centimeter

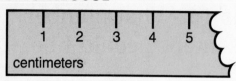

circle

cone

cube

cup

cylinder

difference

$$10 - 6 = 4$$

⇧
difference

dime

graph

FRUITS

0 1 2 3 4

greater than

15 is greater than 12.

inch

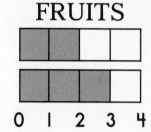

kilogram

less than

37 is less than 63.

NAME _____

liter

quart

nickel

quarter

one fourth

rectangle

one half

sphere

one third

square

penny

sum

$$2 + 7 = 9$$
⇧
sum

pint

pound

triangle

GAMES AND ACTIVITIES

MAKE THE MOST NUMBERS

0	1	2	3	4	5	6	7	8	9	10	11	12

Play this game alone or with friends. You will need 2 number cubes (1–6) and some paper and a pencil. Each player should copy the game form above.

Take turns rolling the 2 cubes. On each turn, add or subtract the numbers and make an X through the sum or difference on your game form. Play for 12 turns. The player with the most X's wins.

HOW LONG IS IT?

Do this activity with a partner. You will need an inch or centimeter ruler. Collect 10 objects that have different lengths, such as a pencil, a straw, a paper clip, a stick, a book, and an umbrella. Estimate how long you think each object is. Then measure each object. See how close your estimate is.

SHAPE HUNT

Work with a partner. You can do this activity almost anywhere. Choose a shape: circle, square, triangle, rectangle, sphere, cylinder, cone, or cube. Make a list of objects that are this shape.

CONTACT 1

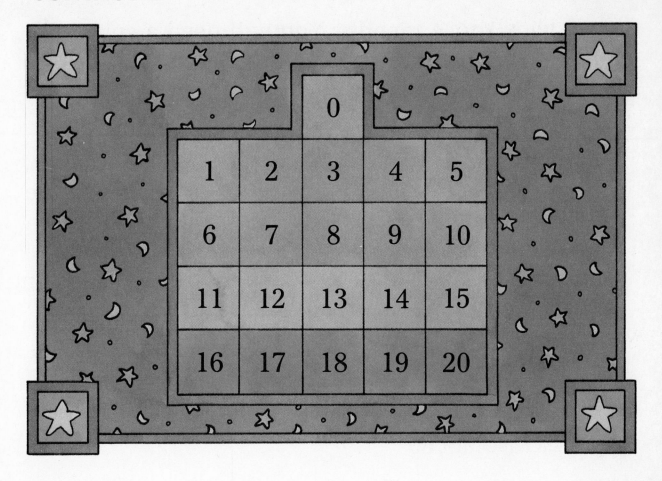

Play with a friend. You will need a spinner (1–10) and some different markers for each of you.

Take turns spinning 2 numbers. Add or subtract the numbers. Put one of your markers on the box with the sum or difference. You get a point for every box that has a marker and is touching your box on the side or corner.

Play until you have each had 5 turns. Then add your points. The player with more points wins.

You can play this game alone. See how many points you can make in 10 turns.

MAKING CHANGE

Play with 1 to 3 friends. You will need a spinner (0–9) and some play money (3 quarters, 5 dimes, 5 nickels, and 10 pennies each).

Take turns spinning the spinner twice to make an amount of money. The first number is the number of tens and the second is the number of ones in the amount. All players then use their play money to try to show the amount 3 different ways. Check each other's ways and then give each person 1 point for each different way to show the amount.

Play for 5 rounds. The player with the most points is the winner.

MISSING NUMBERS

Choose a partner. Take turns counting a string of 5 numbers but skipping one number. You might count: 3 4 5 7 8. Your partner must tell you what number you skipped (6). You may also count backwards and skip a number.

DESCRIBING WORDS

Do this activity with a partner. Take turns saying a word from your math book. Your partner must tell at least 3 words that describe your word or that go with it. If you said "clock," your partner might say, "hour, time, and alarm."

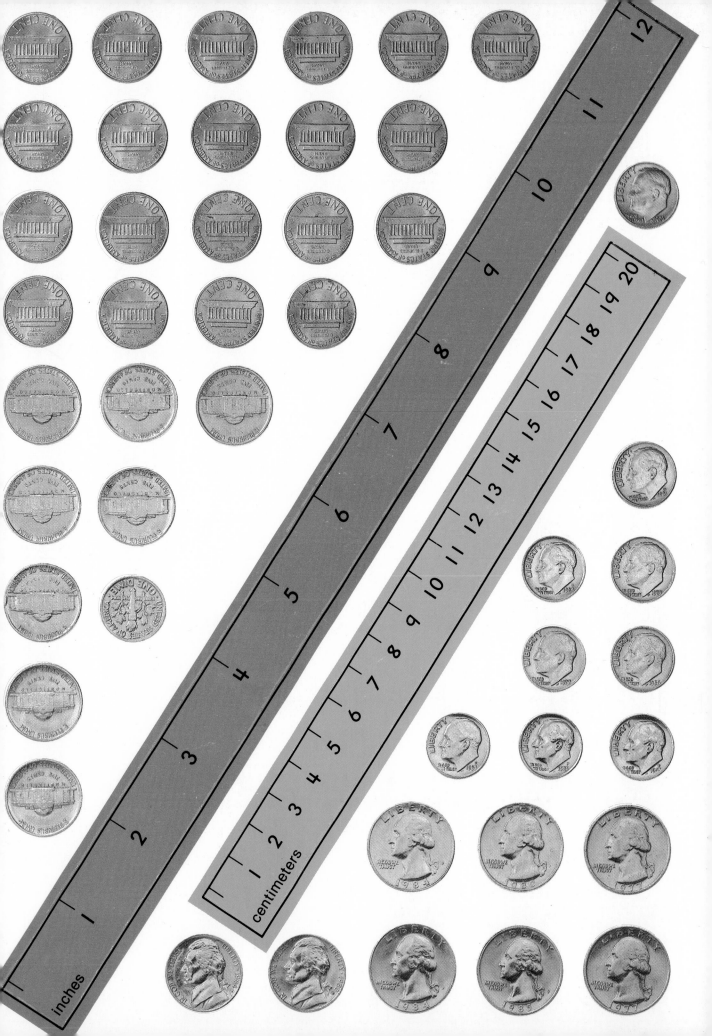

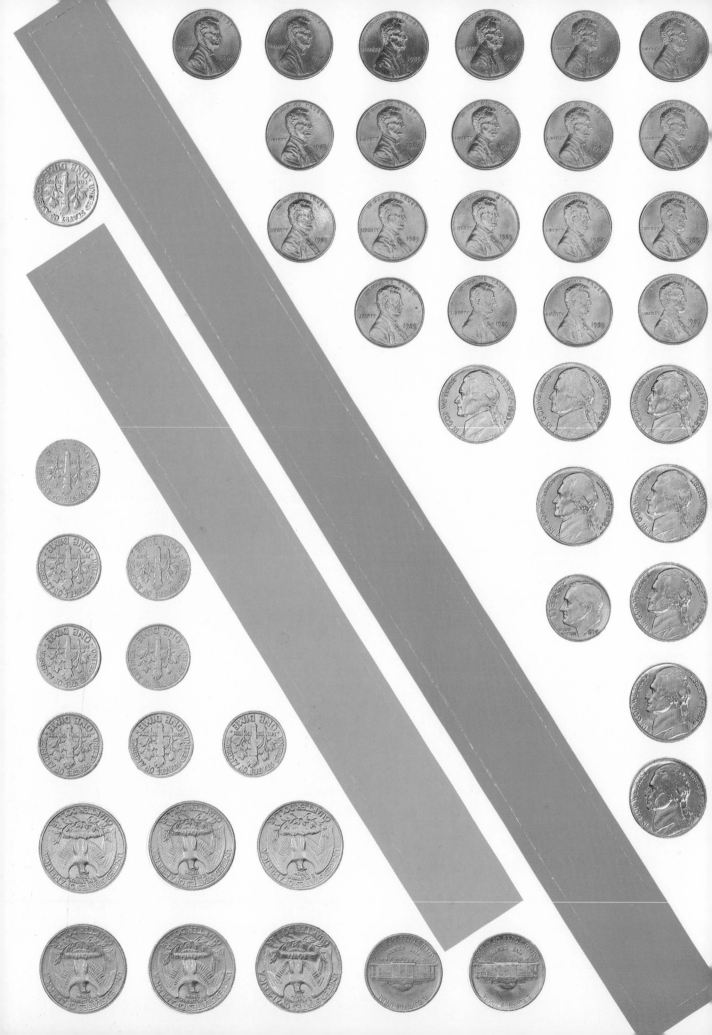

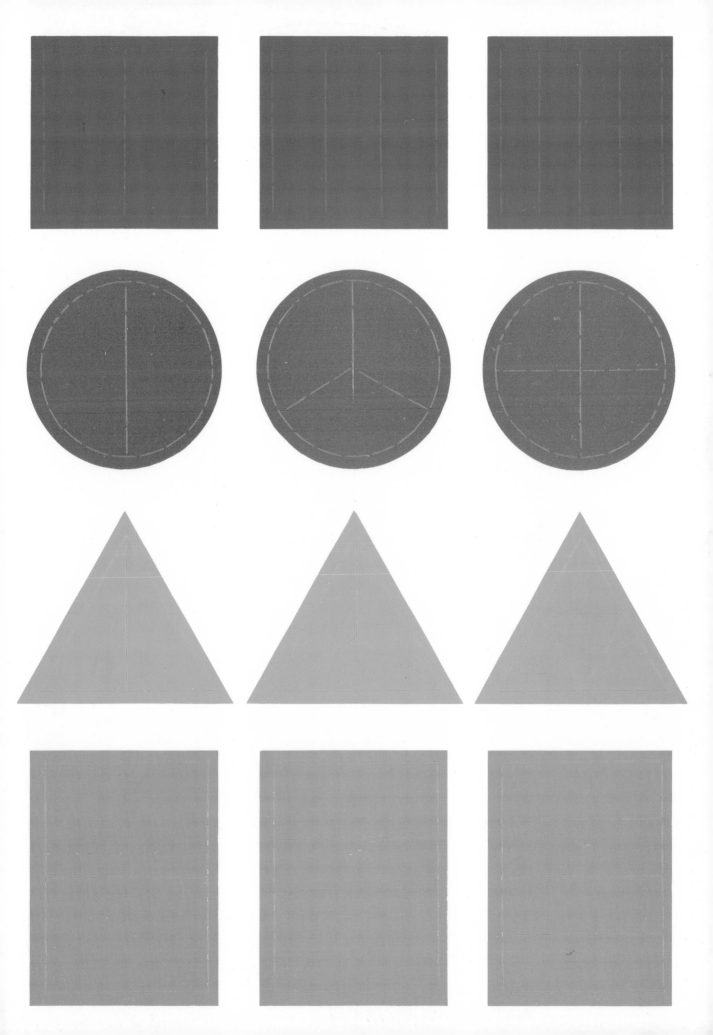

$\frac{1}{4}$ $\frac{1}{4}$ $\frac{1}{4}$ $\frac{1}{4}$ $\frac{1}{3}$ $\frac{1}{3}$ $\frac{1}{3}$ $\frac{1}{2}$ $\frac{1}{2}$

$\frac{1}{4}$ $\frac{1}{4}$ $\frac{1}{3}$ $\frac{1}{3}$ $\frac{1}{2}$ $\frac{1}{2}$

$\frac{1}{4}$ $\frac{1}{4}$ $\frac{1}{3}$

$\frac{1}{4}$ $\frac{1}{3}$ $\frac{1}{3}$

$\frac{1}{4}$ $\frac{1}{2}$ $\frac{1}{2}$

$\frac{1}{4}$ $\frac{1}{4}$ $\frac{1}{3}$

$\frac{1}{4}$ $\frac{1}{3}$

$\frac{1}{4}$ $\frac{1}{3}$ $\frac{1}{2}$

$\frac{1}{4}$

$\frac{1}{4}$ $\frac{1}{3}$

$\frac{1}{4}$ $\frac{1}{3}$ $\frac{1}{2}$

ones

tens

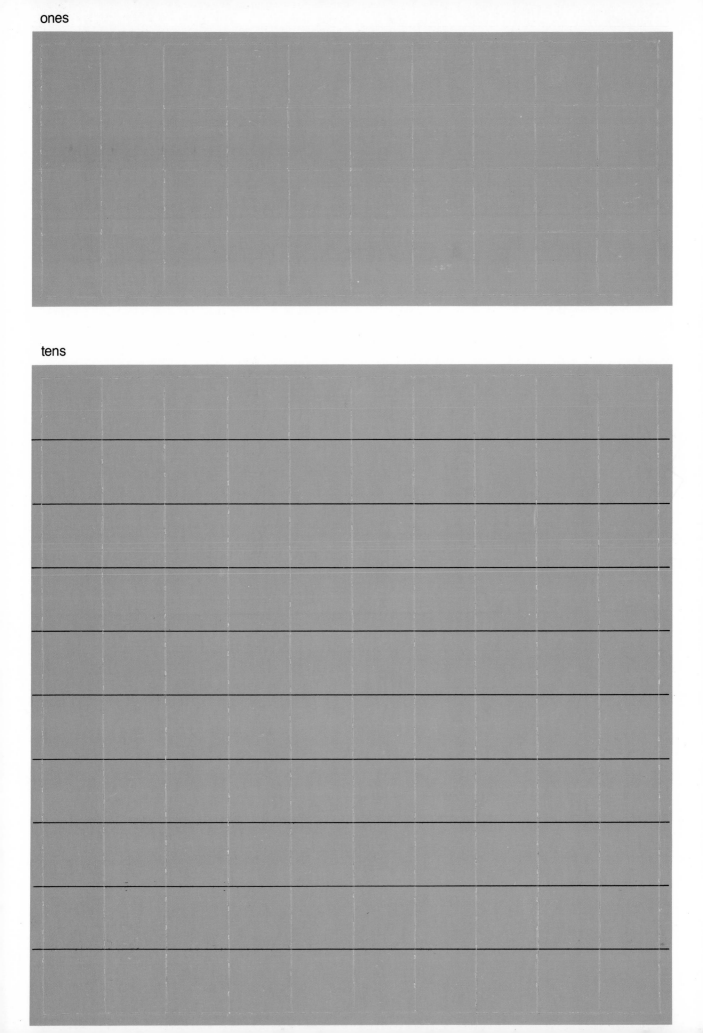